UNSTOPPABLE
WOMAN

UNSTOPPABLE
WOMAN

The Forgotten Story of 'Galloping Granny'
Mavis Hutchison
First Woman to Run Across America

David & Gillene Laney

Foreword by Professor Tim Noakes
Author of the "Lore of Running"

Endorsements

"I see in Mavis Hutchison some of what I see in myself: Someone who had a dream and wouldn't let it go. Fulfilling her dream, however, took courage and tenacity to a new frontier. And that's what allowed her to make world history at an age when people plan retirement. Her story is well worth reading. It's inspiring. Anyone struggling to get somewhere will learn from it. Like myself, Mavis applied the principles that govern success. We were not born with silver spoons; we had to work for it."

– Golf icon & Grand Slammer, Gary Player.

"Everyone knew who you were talking about if you simply said 'Mavis', or the 'Galloping Granny'. It was because she did the most extraordinary things...And she still continues to run. A few months ago I chatted to Mavis...She looked fit and well and was as bright as a button. I realized then that she had inspired me to be a lifetime runner. I may never run across the USA, but I want to be a lifetime galloping Grandpa.

"A biography is long overdue."

– Comrades Marathon great Bruce Fordyce.

"In the history of women's running some names will be remembered forever – Roberta Gibb for being the first woman to run the Boston Marathon; Joan Benoit-Samuelson, winner of the first Olympic Marathon for women; Grete Waitz whose dominance of the New York City Marathon in the seventies and eighties brought the marathon to the attention of women around the world; Anne Trason for her peerless dominance of ultramarathon running in the eighties and nineties.

But before all of them was an almost forgotten South African, a pathfinder, who led the world in establishing that women can run like any man..."

– Professor Tim Noakes, author of the "Lore of Running."

The long road and long thoughts

Synopsis

It took 3000 miles and six million steps for a South African grandmother to become the first woman ever to run across America. She made history and fulfilled a dream.

The crowning moment of her success, however, did not come easy. In fact, she rose to the pinnacle from the depths of timidity and underachievement. By her own admission she had *"no guts and no backbone"*.

Her rise from a 'whispering hope with no hope at all' to that triumphant finish proves once more that success is available to all who are willing to pay the price and will accept that 'there are no limits other than those we impose on ourselves'.

Dubbed one of the most amazing woman athletes the world has known (you could lose track of the number of astonishing feats accomplished both before and after the trans-America epic), Mavis started her athletics career at age 37, when many athletes think of retiring. And at 87 she is still running competitively.

To her, age is but a state of mind: *"You're only old when you stop growing."*

Any account of the multi-award winning, world record setting veteran would be incomplete without underlining her role as a national and international trail blazer for women distance runners. In a world where the 'old boys network' of sport only grudgingly accepted women running even short distances, and literally threw women off the road who dared sneak into marathons, she would not accept her 'proper place'.

Although South African officials never succeeded in throwing Mavis off the road, she did spend many years as an unofficial 'ghost runner'. Other women soon followed her example, inspired by her pluck and passion.

Looking back on close to 50 years in the spotlight, she has one overriding goal: to stay fit til her dying day, a day she wants to approach running. Maybe it has something to do with what competitive athletics does for her: *"When I compete, I am always an athlete and not just an inconvenient old lady."*

(Wikirun – www.wikirun.com/List_of_runs_across_America – still lists Mavis as holder of the women's record for her 1978 trans-America run.)

About the authors

Gillene Laney (neé Sneyd) is a retired journalist from South Africa who took up residence in America's Rocky Mountains in 2008. She shares her life with husband and coauthor Dr David Laney, currently resident astronomer at a mountaintop observatory.

Her career spans many years, during which she wrote for some of South Africa's leading newspapers and magazines, and edited corporate publications in the fields of finance and education.

David – after graduating with a Ph.D. in physics and astronomy – spent the bulk of his career as a senior research scientist and media liaison officer for the South African Astronomical Observatory in Cape Town.

They have no children, but find joy in their marriage and in personal interests: traveling, books, music and the arts.

Dedication

Unstoppable Woman! is dedicated to the Hutchison and Vaughan family, and to all those who want to be all they can be – whatever the odds.

Acknowledgments

- to Providence – for bringing together authors and subject;
- to Cathy Bisshoff and Cedric Wampach – for facilitating the contact;
- to Geoff Spires and author Jean Young – for their excellent input;
- to Nick Heerschap – for a fair share of slog;
- to Mavis Hutchison – for sharing her story, including the painful parts;
- to Allan Hutchison – for helping Mavis write up some of her important races;
- to photographers/publishers – for use of archived images the authors couldn't trace.

To the authors

"If I could have written my own story, this is the book I would like to have written."

— Mavis Hutchison

Foreword

The choice of who is the greatest South African male ultramarathon runner of all time is between four runners – Arthur Newton, Wally Hayward, Jackie Mekler and Bruce Fordyce. All are such exceptional runners and human beings that any attempt at designating a "winner" is churlish. Each is an immortal in the history of South African running.

But if we are to consider the greatest female South African ultramarathon runner of all time, there is only one candidate – Mavis Hutchison – the subject of this timely biography. Here we learn why there is no other choice. And why in some ways Mavis Hutchison's achievement exceeds those of the four male immortals.

For like Arthur Newton, Mavis was the original lonely pioneer. Like Newton she undertook a training regime that was ahead of its time for women. And like Arthur Newton, she dreamed a future that none before her had imagined.

For when Mavis began training regularly in 1961, women had since the 1928 Olympics been considered "too weak" to run more than 200m in competition. Yet in 1963 Mavis established a new world record of 9 hours and 36 minutes for a 50 mile (80km) walking race. A few months later she entered and completed her first standard 42km marathon running race, finishing in 3hours and 50 minutes. Few are those who know that her performance on that day is one of the landmark achievements in the history of women's running.

For the first record of a woman completing a marathon is that of Stamatis Rovithi who seems to have gatecrashed the male-only 1896 Athens Olympic Games Marathon. Then in 1918 Marie-Louis Ledru completed the Tour de Paris Marathon in 5 hours and 40 minutes. Eight years later Violet Piercy ran a marathon in London, establishing the woman's best time of 3 hours and 40 minutes. And then for 37 years, nothing anywhere in the world.

So when Mavis completed her first marathon race in 1963 she was only the fourth[1] woman in history to have run the marathon distance. Her time was the second fastest on record. Her performance predated by a few months the entrance of American women into marathon running when Merry Lepper completed the Western Hemisphere Marathon in California in 3 hours and 37 minutes.

Today history tends to remember the next two American runners, Roberta Gibbs and Katherine Switzer who completed the Boston Marathon in 1966 and 1967 respectively, as the iconic female runners who overturned the false idea that women were too weak to run marathons. **But the truth is that Mavis Hutchison predated their performances and is the true modern original.**

Then like Arthur Newton, Mavis ran across continental America, not like Newton as part of an official running race – a race that became known as the "Bunion Derby" or officially the 1928 Transcontinental Race – but by herself. And unlike Newton, who did not complete the distance because he developed a severe Achilles tendinosis, Mavis, in 1978, completed the distance from Los Angeles to New York in an astonishing 69 days. In so doing she was 4 days faster that fellow South African Don Shepherd who in 1964 completed an unsupported transcontinental crossing in 73 days. But perhaps the true measure of her performance is that she was only 4 days slower than the 1969 performance of English middle distance runner and former European champion, Bruce Tulloh.

Like Wally Hayward who in 1953, at age 44, set world running records at 100 miles and total distance run in 24 hours before winning his final Comrades Marathon the following year, Mavis, in 1971, at age 47, also set world records at 25, 50, 75 and 100 miles and was the first woman ever to complete a 24 hours running race. And like Hayward she never stopped running, continuing to compete in the World Master's Games and running 800m in an astonishing 5 minutes and a few seconds in her mid eighties.

Like Jackie Mekler, Mavis overcame significant domestic challenges, any one of which would have turned a lesser human to misery and self-pity. Instead, like Mekler, who discovered running in his early teens when he lost his family, Mavis used her hardship to discover herself: *"I was fighting the demons of my past and subconsciously I seemed to sense that if I could persist I would overcome them and the achievement would mean a new start for me"*. And through her persistence she learned a key truth: *"That was when I recognized the power of the mind and realized that what we become is what we choose to become"*.

And like Bruce Fordyce, Mavis became a much-beloved national icon, transcending social and racial divisions in a divided country, earning the endearing and instantly recognizable nickname "The Galloping Granny". Like Fordyce, through her personal example and tireless enthusiasm she has spent her life selflessly promoting the value of physical activity for optimum bodily and mental health.

And like all these men, Mavis did not ever quit – she has continuously explored new boundaries, unprepared ever to slow down; to accept being anything less than her very best.

In the history of women's running some names will be remembered forever – Roberta Gibb for being the first woman to run the Boston Marathon; Joan Benoit-Samuelson the winner of the first Olympic Marathon for women; Grete Waitz whose dominance of the New York City Marathon in the seventies and eighties brought the marathon to the attention of women around the world; Anne Trason for her peerless dominance of ultramarathon running in the eighties and nineties.

But before all of them was an almost forgotten South African, a pathfinder, who led the world in establishing that women can run like any man – perhaps at a slightly slower pace, but with no other observable difference.

The value of this book is that it records for posterity the special role that Mavis Hutchison played in the global evolution of long distance running for women.

And the path she followed to become what it was she chose to become.

—Professor Timothy Noakes OMS, MD, DSc, PhD (hc)
Discovery Health Professor of Exercise and Sports Science
University of Cape Town and Sports Science Institute of South Africa
(Boundary Road, Newlands, 7700.)

---

[1]*As noted in chapter 5, the 1896 Olympic marathon was only 40 km, and Violet Piercy apparently had herself timed over a course near London over which a marathon had been run some months earlier. (authors)*

Introduction

Unstoppable Woman is a biography that almost wasn't.

When we first met Mavis Hutchison, we weren't looking for a project. Even after listening to her sharing parts of her story with a small group gathered in the home of friends one evening, there was no thought of getting involved. It was an intriguing story, but that was it.

However, by the time we left that night, a seed was sown and Gillene agreed to read an informal, unpublished retelling of some of the outstanding events of Mavis' running career, compiled by her son Allan from an extensive set of notes she had previously sent to all her children. This later proved to be an invaluable resource.

Dave followed course and subsequently we both felt that we were dealing with an ultra running legend, whose all but forgotten story begged telling – in a comprehensive, coherent biography, which surprisingly nobody had yet undertaken to write.

Innumerable newspaper clippings, other media bits and pieces, as well as Mavis' original notes and files, also made their way into the Laney's collection of Mavis memorabilia – all portraying a woman who not only did remarkable things, but did them in the face of trials so severe that it was hard for the mind to wrap itself around them.

Hers was an indeed a very compelling story – one we both thought people would want to read and that Gillene now felt needed to be written since Mavis herself had been unable to.

"It's not easy for me to write. I sometimes find it hard to put my feelings into words. When I read what I have written…it isn't what I want, but this is a problem I'm sure I'll overcome."

She was right and a formal commitment was made, but with only one half of the writing duo.

Numerous and very probing interviews followed, serving as a kind of road map through a life dense with story material, and adding insight into the mind of a tenacious woman who rose to legendary success from the position of all-time loser.

The sessions were lengthy but throughout, 87-year old Mavis remained upbeat, showing such a zest for living that it was contagious.

By the time all the pertinent facts and figures of her life were safely gathered in and transported to the Laney home in America, another realization set in: the task at hand called for a cooperative writing effort. At last, Dave was fully in the equation.

Putting together *Unstoppable Woman* proved to be a monumental undertaking that impacted our lives immensely. Personal agendas and work obligations had to be juggled, and disagreements about how to deal with certain parts of the manuscript had to be resolved. But if there was a higher purpose in the mix, we figured it would all be worth it.

And it was. In fact, looking at the whole thing retrospectively, it seems clear that Providence was at work.

To us Mavis is truly an inspiration, an inspiration amplified by the fact that this extraordinary little woman never allowed her fame to suck her into that suffocating self-absorption sometimes so apparent with celebrities.

We hope that every reader will not only find her life as inspiring as we do, but will be able to say: ***If Mavis can, so can I!***

—The Authors

CONTENTS

Chapter 1: NOT OUT TO PASTURE

"I'm not over the hill yet, for the hill looms in front of me....It's my challenge – that hill and the one after that and the one after that, till the race is run."

Looks can be very deceiving. Just looking at Mavis Madge Hutchison will never reveal the true story behind those bright green eyes, now set in a deeply lined face, framed by snow white hair.

Everything about her and the set of circumstances she was born into could be described as pretty average, but when she starts to speak it's clear you are not dealing with 'average'. In fact, as she unfolds to you the facts of her life, the softly spoken 87-year old athlete leaves an indelible impression.

You begin to understand the reason for the accumulation of an impressive list of accolades and awards earned over some 20 years of ultrarunning in the spotlight. You know she speaks with the voice of authority when she equates marathon running with "*conquering one's instincts of surrender.*"

You grasp why the media followed her every step, why she became South Africa's 'First Lady' of road running, why she was referred to as a 'national treasure', a 'modern-day Joan of Arc', and why she was firmly captured in the annals of sporting history.

You come to know why she rose to international athletic prominence despite her very late start at age 37, without a coach and without any other prior accomplishments; why she deserved to be called a pioneer.

In an era when distance running worldwide was male dominated and controlled, she blazed a trail toward official recognition of women distance runners, not only in South Africa but also in the US and in the UK, winning hearts by her gritty endurance even when she had to compete as a 'ghost runner' without any official recognition.

She first caught the eyes of the wider world in 1978 as the first woman to run across America. She was then a 53-year old grandmother. Two years later she did it again when she ran north to south through the UK, breaking a world record that had stood for 20 years. Before and after achieving international recognition she set other world records, astonishing the public with mind-boggling feats of endurance.

Mavis had become a household name and a truly bright star in the athletics firmament.

And the more you engage with this grand old dame of the ultrarun, the more convinced you become that she possesses far more than just athletics prowess. She has some real wisdom to dispense – to anyone who cares to listen.

And listen countless thousands did, as the Press eagerly published her comments in volumes of newsprint – comments all steeped in real life lessons learned in the demanding world of marathon running which became her schoolmaster.

That's where she came face to face with her own limitations. Through sweat, tears and sheer agony she overcame them and earned the right to her public voice – as she earned the title 'queen of endurance'.

"In my running I knew I was also learning life lessons – here a little, there a little. In fact, everything to do with personal development and growth I learned while running. But if anyone would have told me that running would take on the profile it did so I could learn and teach those lessons, I would have laughed in their faces."

Be that as it may, running was in her blood and became a way of life, a natural progression since she ran 'for the love of it' and not just for the sense of achievement.

"It also became a path to self-discovery. I believe that for many people self-discovery is the greatest challenge, because it comes when you are pushed to and sometimes past your extremities.

"There's some scary stuff there that just has to be learned the hard way. Making demands will get you nowhere. You only achieve things when you are prepared to do things – hard things."

After she ran through the US and the UK she realized this with deepened conviction. In America she came up against what seemed to be her limits. In the UK the concept of 'no limits' was etched into her very soul.

"If you're prepared to sacrifice and to pay the price, there really are no limits. You have to let go of self-imposed limitations at all costs."

Self-limitation is still one of her pet subjects. She says she thinks much like Donald Trump who said in his book, The Art of the Deal: "If I'm going to be thinking anyway, I might as well think big!" And the record shows she thought big. But not only did she think big, she did big, empowered by first acquiring the ability to stay the course.

"Running has done more for me than just moving from A to B. It has taught me that there is more to life than just dreaming and thinking big...I have learned endurance, perseverance and most important of all, self-discipline."

Those were the things that always set her apart and helped her overcome seemingly insurmountable obstacles. The naysayers were obstacles too. *"When you want to reach for the stars they'll be there. You might even land up being your own worst naysayer."*

Success, happiness, aging and health were, and still are, also favorite topics – not to toot her own horn but to help others. Throughout her running career she was always keen on sharing what she had learned with audiences wherever she found them. And now in her sunset years she still loves to share.

About happiness she says: *"It is the result of honest effort, doing a little extra; working towards something worthwhile – the natural outcome of a lot of correct actions, like* doing *something for someone and* seeing *the positive results. There's nothing passive about it. You can't wait for happy things to happen."*

Success seekers also took note as she explained concepts from her personal experiences.

"As I became successful as an athlete it led to other successes, because more opportunities opened up. Success breeds success. I thoroughly enjoyed the chance to share my successes in talks and in coaching, along with the principles behind them. I learned that helping others to become successful was very much part of my own success."

It was always clear from Mavis' example and her public narrative that she understood that success was hard work. It was about sticking to tasks till they stuck to her. Giving up was never an option. *"There are far more starters than finishers, and I want to be among the finishers"*.

On aging and health, she attributes her longevity and well being in some degree at least to genetics, but to a much greater degree to life style: nutrition and exercise, emotional and spiritual health, and a personal connection with God.

"Back to genetics, I was once asked whether I thought sportsmen and women were born or made. My answer remains the same. They are born in the sense that if they work it right and work it hard, they will always have the edge over the ones who do the same and aren't genetically favored. How favored I am, is anyone's guess."

'The greatest granny of them all' is probably genetically blessed. That might account for why she is still at it, albeit at a slower pace: *"I now have to do 100% more for 50 % less."* But she still displays the spirit of an athlete with legs to match – legs that explain why that part of her anatomy was so noticed by the media when she was younger.

She still trains several days a week at the sports field of a nearby school, and still competes. She is clearly not out to pasture. And she's still in the news. As recently as August 2010, the magazine *Modern Athlete* proclaimed, "She Is Still…the Galloping Granny!"

But to this day Mavis is not overly fond of that longstanding nickname. "*I kicked hard against 'Galloping Granny' since I don't gallop, never have! But later on I made my peace, even adding the description to a business card.*"

The sprightly granny, who still does not gallop, but rather strides, even feels a spurt of youth every now and again. "*When I trained with a young coach recently to prepare for a Masters event, he showed me a few tricks and helped me better my times. I was quite taken by the results and I felt like I was 20 again!*"

That reminded her that when she competes she is first and foremost an athlete – not some inconvenient old lady. "*That's a good feeling.*"

But reality is reality. She is a senior, but one who is clearly made of stern stuff, who paid her dues in full and now can happily reminisce about those glory days. She remembers them with a sense of accomplishment. "*What is nice about the present, though, is that I can now run for the sheer fun of it.*

"*Of course, if I keep on running I'll sooner or later run out of people my age to run against!*", a comment made with that characteristic Mavis sense of humor. But whether or not she has anyone to compete against, she still has one goal and that is to stay fit and to leave this life running.

There's every chance she will do exactly that. Observing the unmistakable Hutchison stride, as she recently prepared for upcoming track competition, was very convincing. The legs, lean and long, did not belong to a 20-year old, but they did belong to a champion – a champion that became the apple of the Press's eye.

She was often described in glowing terms: A 'wisp of a woman with the heart of a lion', a 'true champion with true grit', the 'most remarkable long-distance woman athlete in the world', the 'greatest woman in athletic history', the 'unstoppable woman', 'tough as steel' with 'enough guts for 10 men'.

And it went on and on: 'Sportswoman for all seasons', a 'running phenomenon' setting a 'new standard in distance running', a 'wonder woman' who 'took a continent in her stride' and 'astonished the world,' a 'marathon wonder', a 'long-distance marvel', a 'running machine' – 'stunning, intrepid, amazing, magnificent....legendary.'

The late Wally Hayward, one of the world's best male distance runners, can have the last word from the past: "...one of the most fantastic women in the world", to which her biographers add: "Another 'Iron Lady' with an iron will, every bit as powerful in her own right as the woman with whom the phrase originated."

Some final observations: Mavis is remarkably modest, totally unassuming, refreshingly void of airs and graces, a gracious lady in whom not a vestige of pretense is detectable when she speaks about her remarkable life. She's just grateful for the stairs in her Fish Hoek apartment that help to keep her fit.

Even at the height of her prominence, when she was a standard fixture on the sports pages, fame never went to her head.

Maybe her faith, and her public acknowledgment that God's hand was manifested in her achievements, kept her grounded. Maybe that's why she ran her way into so many hearts.

"I enjoyed the recognition my running brought me, but I never was motivated by fans. Besides, I haven't the confidence or personality for fame."

It's a pity many of the younger generation have forgotten 'Aunty Mavis', who once gripped the imaginations of her countrymen. But there are many who do remember, especially since articles and profiles still appear in the media.

Her son Jess left this image of Mavis in her prime:

> *A wisp of a woman with silver-grey hair,*
> *Trotted in with the morning and the cool blowing air.*
> *I asked her some questions which she pondered a while,*
> *Eyes turning to laughter then warmed to a smile.*
> *She spoke of her travels in the words on her mind,*
> *Of a world going crazy being led by the blind.*
> *Words spoken so softly, with bright shining eyes,*
> *Words seeming so simple with meaning so wise.*
> *She asked for some water, then went on her way,*
> *On to the next town, and into the day.*
> *Her footsteps like music went tripping along,*
> *Soothing the warm day with her gentle foot song.*

Chapter 2: A SHAKY START FOR A WHISPERING HOPE

"...I was very shy and withdrawn with absolutely no confidence at all...I had no personality and was a timid frightened individual...a coward..."

Mavis Hutchison's arrival at the pinnacle, where she remained until her very last long runs in the eighties, was a journey that started humbly and hesitantly. It was filled with heartbreak and struggle, with crippling timidity and incapacitating ill health. She describes herself as someone who had *"no guts, no go, no backbone,"* always *"whimpering and nervous"* – a real *"whispering hope"* in desperate fear of failure.

"My first memory of wanting to succeed was my teenage aspirations to become a champion athlete. This desire stemmed from my belief that being a winner was what mattered most in life. Notwithstanding this belief, I was too scared to try to win in case I failed."

And so victory, not just as an athlete, but seemingly in all aspects of her life, eluded her for many years.

Ironically, guidance toward success, at least in athletics, was readily available right at home.

"My father had been one of the top middle distance runners in the country, a tenacious provincial rugby player and someone I admired because he was so outgoing and generous and so forgiving. And he certainly was willing to coach me, along with other teenagers he was training at the Convent I attended in Kimberley.

"Although I started out full of enthusiasm it seemed to me that I got nowhere fast. I mistakenly thought that if I did not have instant success I would never succeed. Consequently, I found plausible reasons to give up. My father was probably disappointed that I never sustained the effort to succeed, but he never showed it and he never forced me to continue training."

She recommenced a few times, but it always ended the same - in failure. The only running she participated in was the annual Sunday School races in which she excelled.

She was to become 37 before she tried something more adventurous - and then only after many personal trials.

SHAKING HER CONFIDENCE

By the time Mavis and her identical twin sister Doreen were born on November 24, 1924, Mavis had already drawn somewhat of a short straw in terms of future athletic performance. She refers to one of her legs as always having been a bit "*slow*", although she was infinitely better off than Doreen whose damaged hip at birth forced her to limp through life.

From an early age she also suffered from debilitating headaches, and at twelve her nervous system developed an autoimmune response to rheumatic fever infection, bringing on bouts of Sydenham's chorea, commonly known as St Vitus' Dance (SVD), a horrible condition attacking the nervous system, resulting in a loss of muscle control as well as mental disturbances. It's most common in girls between the ages of 10 and 16.

She endured three very unpleasant nervous breakdowns, each requiring three months of convalescing, and accompanied by the uncontrollable physical spasms associated with SVD. In an era before antibiotics, her doctors could do little but try to keep her comfortable as she recovered.

Her first breakdown came at the age of twelve, the second when she was fourteen and the third at age sixteen.

During each of these occasions she required hospitalization and was unable to walk or talk, or even use a finger to point. "*I had to relearn these skills. These experiences left me feeling very fragile - physically, spiritually and emotionally.*"

She clearly remembers the precursor to the second breakdown. One of her hands started to shake uncontrollably, prohibiting her from holding on to any object for long. Full-blown SVD set in shortly afterward as a result of trauma caused by a dog charging her, and she was back in hospital. To this day she is scared to death of anything canine.

Referring to this particular episode in her life, she still has a vivid memory of how the nurses used to laugh at 'that mad woman in the private ward'. "*I guess I acted a bit mad. I recall throwing a bottle of Oros (orange* soda) and some pastry at the nurses, and then collapsing . Hospital staff sent for my mother who stayed the night with me."

Just before her third hospitalization she found herself on the floor at home one day, deliberately placed there to prevent her from falling out of bed since by then her muscle control had already deteriorated quite significantly.

Somehow her spastic body motions got her head hooked round the leg of a dressing table. To save her life she couldn't dislodge herself. "*My mother came into the room just in time to prevent me from choking myself to death.*"

Again she was rushed off to hospital where her father, in the army at the time, visited her, having been sent for urgently since the worst was expected. "*His nearness seemed to have had a very soothing effect that set in motion my third 3-month recovery. I would not wish what I had endured on my worst enemy. How fortunate I am not to have suffered any after effects. I eventually learned to control my nerves.*"

Needless to say her schooling suffered, which may help to account for the fact that she did not graduate from high school, something she regrets intensely to this day. Mavis herself is not sure of all of the dynamics at work at the time.

She put it this way: "*At this point of my life the full reason for quitting is a bit fuzzy. Maybe it was the old fear thing of the past where I was easily overcome by what I perceived to be difficult.*" And maybe three brushes with mental instability, having to relearn the most basic skills of life over and over again, had shaken her confidence in herself at a very deep level.

LIGHTER MOMENTS

But there was an upside to the down side. She and her twin used to get up to all kinds of mischief, the brunt of which was sometimes suffered by their younger sister, Ivy. When Ivy (a spinster and retired nurse living in Johannesburg)) was a baby they would remove her from her stroller and get in themselves. They were about three years old at the time. One day they did it again and put the baby in a tub with a bunch of washing in the back garden where she was later rescued from suffocation by the maid. Maybe not their brightest moment, Mavis concedes, but immense fun for them.

"*Thinking of Ivy, I'm sure Doreen and I neglected her. She was always the 5th wheel on the wagon. I only realized it later in life and I tried to compensate by being extra nice and helpful. Now I feel very close to her and will remove heaven and earth for her."* Just recently Mavis flew to Johannesburg to take care of Ivy after an operation.

"I'm also reminded that Ivy became the one who race walked with me for about two to three years. In fact, I think she was the better athlete. Athletics just didn't appeal to her that much."

The two little sisters (who were later joined by a younger brother, George, who also lives in Cape Town), found it equally amusing to play on the fact that they looked identical.

They took great pleasure in causing confusion. When they did something wrong, Doreen would say, "Me's Mavis" and Mavis would say, "Me's Doreen." Fortunately, their mother wasn't fooled so easily. (Ma Kitty died in 1996 at age 96.)

Their school teachers were given a hard time too. They were always changing places and would answer to each others names. *"I would also copy Doreen's homework and she would copy mine, depending on who didn't do homework.*

"After I had already left school one of the nuns came into the shop where I worked one day and in conversation told me she was never fooled by our tricks and identity games."

Once a boyfriend was the object of the sisters' escapades. *"He came to the house to pick up Doreen and we decided to trick him by having me receive him as though I was Doreen. After a short while I excused myself, pretending I was going to quickly get ready to leave with him. I was scarcely gone when my sister walked in. The boyfriend said he had never seen someone dress so fast. He never caught on."*

Their lookalike behaviors even extended to their teeth sometimes, and when one had a missing tooth they saw to it that the other one lost hers. *"We did it ourselves! We were about 6 years old."*

During World War 2 the twins had a great time with young soldiers, despite the initial damper of their father being called up to serve in North Africa - a situation which was luckily reversed when he was pulled off the ship he had already boarded because of his age. He was then posted elsewhere in South Africa.

The soldiers occupied the Air Force camp in Kimberley and had tea served to them by the girls. Because they were never on duty together the men never knew there were two of them. Dressing exactly alike ensured that the wool remained pulled over their eyes. All very entertaining to the tricksters.

Tea duty was all part of Mavis' post school war work, which she proudly executed. She also put in long shifts at the government Mint in her home town. She did tool room duty, working on a lathe making tools for the manufacture of weaponry - all under supervision of skilled artisans. She actually wanted to join the army, but her father refused to give his consent, maintaining she wasn't strong enough.

In Shadow

George Vaughan was probably right, but there may have gone an opportunity for Mavis to become more independent. And she so needed to do things on her own. As much as she had fun with Doreen, her personal development was being stifled by someone who was naturally more dominant and assertive. In retrospect Mavis admits that to a significant extent she was cowering in her twin sister's shadow.

"I loved her dearly, and we were close and relied on each other, but it was very easy just to let her take the lead, including making all the approaches to our parents about things we wanted to do. She was like my protector. I felt incapable of doing anything by myself, always very frightened I'd make a mistake and that I would be rejected. To complete the picture I was even claustrophobic and feared heights. Doreen helped me to compensate. I can see that wasn't a good thing.

"And I don't think dressing exactly alike helped matters either. We only stopped that after we left school. Ultimately, I felt I had no personality and was just this timid, frightened, extremely insecure and really cowardly individual."

But she hastens to add: *"I don't think for a moment my sister set out to cause my insecurities, and I certainly can't hold her accountable for the struggle I had learning how to stand up for my self.*

"Nevertheless, it took a long time to overcome the worst of my insecurities. It was only after leaving high school that I even started to become more of my own person, although it was always a person very attached to Doreen - right to her death in November 2010.

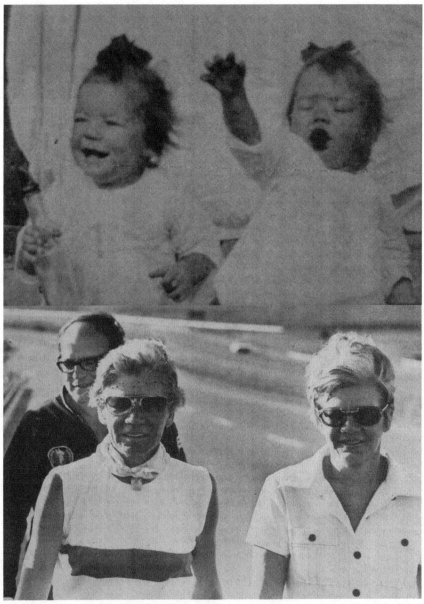

Top: Mavis (probably left, although even Mavis isn't sure) and Doreen as babies.
Bottom: Mavis (left) and Doreen in 1973.

"*But I finally did make progress, learning to stand up for myself more and more. I remember a particular incident at work where some colleagues, who were known to make fun of me, were quite startled when I told them off. 'Wow, the little whispering hope is getting it together', would best describe their reaction.*"

Moving from reactive self defense to the success of later years was, however, an entirely different matter. It would take a long time and much personal growth before her rather nebulous concept of success sharpened into a pattern of achievement.

"*I do remember a vague feeling somewhere along the line, though, that I wanted to be successful at something, quite aside from my teenage athletics aspiration.*"

How to pursue it would only gradually unfold and the progress curve wasn't always as steady as she would have liked. Years after the 'whispering hope' incident, when her running career was moving ahead and she realized she would need more public speaking skills, she was once more up against her old fears – this time the fear of addressing an audience.

When she finally did pluck up the courage to do a Dale Carnegie course in effective speaking and human relations, and to join Toastmistresses, her anxieties almost got the better of her.

"*When I arrived at the registration venue* (for the Dale Carnegie course), *I very nearly didn't go through with it. I was beginning to leave and then was called back. I felt cornered and so I stayed and that was a very good move. I was helped a lot though my knees still knocked at my 1st speaking opportunity.*

"*Afterward it became easier and, miraculously almost, I got to cope with three talks a day. I can't say that all of the shyness left me, but I have learned to mask it, and importantly, I have overcome the impulse to run.*

"*What I found helpful, then and now, is visualizing the accomplishment of the goal. I see myself confidently speaking with knowledge and understanding.*"

That must have helped do the trick since she has spoken successfully to many audiences – some of them large – many times. As she put it: "*I learned to stand up and speak up, and to know when to shut up.*"

SYMBIOTIC RELATIONSHIP

But for many years, as Mavis emerged from her twin's shadow, there remained a rather uncanny side to their relationship.

"When one of us felt pain, the other one also felt it. On my long runs through the US and the UK, Doreen suffered pain in her right leg at exactly the time I experienced pain in that leg."

When Doreen's daughter, Marion, was born in Johannesburg, Mavis shared her labor pains very far away in Kimberley - 12 hours of it. Unmarried at the time and very uninformed about the facts of life, she didn't know what was happening to her.

"When we checked later, we found that my pains started at precisely the time her birth pains commenced and stopped when she was done."

Sometimes there was an imbalance in the symbiosis that may have mirrored there uneven relationship as children, for Doreen didn't feel Mavis' labor pains - only an urgency to see her.

When Doreen sailed to South America, Mavis again responded symbiotically and shared her twin's sea sickness.

"Even when she took laxatives I had the runs too! I had to tell her to stop. Later we stopped sharing these kinds of things with each other in the hope they would just go away".

And eventually they did, although not for many years.

MARRIAGE MISERY AND THE 'REFINER'S FIRE'

Mavis' relationship with her sister remained close and loving, but her first close relationship outside the family was a total disaster.

Her marriage to Gerald Charles Powell brought a measure of misery she could not have imagined. It was a 'refiner's fire', scorching and unrelenting, heaping more coals on the fire of her fears and her feelings of inferiority. To say that she was traumatized would not be an over statement.

Mavis married Powell in September 1946 and started on what she refers to as *"the most strenuous and difficult period of my life."* Not only was her new companion a very heavy drinker who never knew when to stop, making promises he never kept, but he was also to prove his gross ineptness as a father, leaving his young and inexperienced wife to cope with the trauma that came with her first babies.

In May 1947, 22-year old Mavis gave birth two months prematurely to twin boys. One twin lived only 24 hours, and she was only told of his death on the day he was buried. When her mother said, "One is gone," Mavis remembers going ice cold and that there was silence for a few minutes.

"It didn't seem to register at first. I asked which one. They wouldn't say. I knew instantly it was the baby born last. I remember going into a state of severe shock."

The shock lasted for days, and worried about her fragile mental/emotional condition, hospital staff kept her from seeing the surviving child. *"I was only allowed to see him when he was 10 days old, and even then they would not let me see him alone."*

There were reasons for that. When Mavis first saw her baby she fainted at the shock of his appearance: Jess was severely disfigured with a very bad harelip and a cleft palate.

As she desperately struggled to cope, her only support was Doreen because the bottle remained her husband's closest companion. Her sister was on constant 'Gerald duty' to prevent the man from showing up at the hospital drunk.

During those dark days the refiner's fire burnt hot and her heart ached for the son she would never raise. To this day she misses him. Jess missed him too. *"He and his brother Allan, not born very long afterward, were great friends, but Jess always missed his twin. He didn't say anything, but I sensed it."*

When little Jess was finally discharged and Mavis had to administer his three hourly feed with the help of a pipette to accommodate his impediment, more struggles were hers to deal with. In fact, she became frantic when the infant pushed the pipette right up the opening on his lip. She was sure great pain was being inflicted on her poor baby.

After hours of crying, feeling quite helpless in the face of her new challenge, she was rescued by a very timely house call from the doctor, who explained how things really worked. She finally understood that her boy was in fact not hurting himself, and after a couple of days she had the feeding task under control.

Meanwhile, Gerald was drinking himself into a stupor, putting away on average one bottle of brandy daily. This resulted in behavior that was fast turning Mavis into a complete nervous wreck. *"What sanity remained I owed to my baby.*

"When he left for work in the mornings I would plead with him to come straight home at the end of the day. And then the whole day I would sit and worry about whether or not he would be sober when he got home. I used to sit at the bedroom window night after night waiting for him to return. Every time I heard a police car or an ambulance I would go quite cold until it passed. Then when he eventually arrived I would be so exhausted and relieved to see him that I would just put him to bed."

In the mornings she got him up, got him fed and on his way - ostensibly to work. One day would turn out much like the previous one, the stale smell of liquor always clinging to the man she still hoped would change.

The next episode in the Gerald saga that added significantly to the limited length of the Powell marriage, revolved around Jess' first corrective surgery, for which the few months old child had to be taken to Johannesburg.

Mavis wasn't doing very well at that point, and her husband's insistence on going along only aggravated things. Fortunately, her parents joined them on the trip up country, knowing Gerald couldn't be relied on. They were all to stay with family in the big city.

The first night in their hosts' home Gerald got so intoxicated that he figured relieving himself in bed was as good as anywhere else. *"I was so ashamed and embarrassed. Only because of the baby was I able to live through his disgraceful behavior."*

What followed is best cut short.

Baby Jess went in for his operation (during which he developed pneumonia, just to add to his mother's burdens) and his parents sat in the waiting room. Gerald announced about 10 minutes into the waiting exercise that he was going to buy some matches. This was just after 10 am. At about 4 pm Mavis' parents arrived, and two hours later the man of the moment - blind drunk with his arm around the neck of the hospital's matron and using the same 'relief technique' as before with a bewildered Mavis running after him bedpan in hand, trying frantically to prevent a mess in the ward. And what a mess it was.

Afterward he nonchalantly climbed onto a vacant bed in Jess' hospital room and promptly fell asleep – indecently exposed. There he remained until he slept off his intoxication. Mavis, naturally, got him covered up as soon as she could, switching off the light in the room so no one would see him in his embarrassing condition. But that only partly addressed her predicament since

Mavis' pleas that a group of doctors who came to see how Jess was doing, be barred from entering, fell on deaf ears.

"I died a thousand deaths when they walked into that hospital room, even though they ignored the person on the bed and attended to their patient. When Gerald finally came to, my parents took him away and I remained behind with our son. From then on my father took charge of the situation and never let Gerald out of his sight, which was a blessing to me."

After the young patient had his stitches removed he returned home with his family, but for Mavis life was not going to return to normal, not that 'normal' ever applied to her circumstances. A few months later she came down with scarlet fever and became deathly ill.

Upon her refusal to go to hospital to be isolated there, the doctor consented for her to stay home - but only if Jess would be removed. Grandma Vaughan then took over care of the little boy.

During this desperate time Gerald once again glittered in absentia, refusing to go to work and locking himself in a spare bedroom with his old liquid standby. But that didn't prohibit him from doing more damage, felt keenly by Mavis when he barred a neighbor from their home under threat of death if she didn't stop seeing Mavis.

She was a nurse who attended to Mavis' daily needs. Gerald threatened to shoot her with a shotgun if she ever set foot in the house again. He then barricaded himself in his room and drank himself into oblivion.

When Mrs Vaughan got wind of the appalling circumstances of her daughter, she alleviated her misery without delay by taking her home with her. And after Mavis' recovery she was ready to end what had proved to be nothing short of a disastrous marriage. But unfortunately she allowed herself to be swayed from her decision to leave Gerald. Softhearted, she just couldn't resist the pleading of some of his family to take him back.

A wealthy brother stepped in and set the couple up in his grandmother's country home. This was a three-month respite during which Gerald went on the wagon. But true to form he fell off with a thundering crash after a mere month back in town and in his old job as a car salesman.

An 'Old Woman' at 24

The unfortunate turn of events proved to be a double whammy: Mavis had fallen pregnant again during the blissful normality that followed her husband's short-lived sobriety. Allan was about to make his entry into a world where the 'bottle' still ruled supreme.

"Night after night he would pass out in the driveway where I would leave him until dark so the neighbors wouldn't see me dragging him into the house. By this time I was a total wreck and my attitude very negative. I was just a bundle of nerves and had blackouts and fainting spells at least three to four times a day. The doctor warned me to not go anywhere alone. I was worn out mentally and physically, and at age 24 felt like an old woman."

But no matter how she felt, she couldn't abdicate her parental duties, and so when Jess was 18 months old she trekked back up to Johannesburg for his second corrective surgery – this time to another hospital as Mavis could not face the staff of the previous facility.

Adding to her challenge was a long train journey to an unfamiliar place with no one but her pregnant self to take care of things. Gerald couldn't be relied on, which was proved one more time when he reneged on an arrangement to meet his wife and child at the train station to give them much needed money for the trip. He drew the money all right, he just never arrived with it, or much of it - not until his father-in-law dragged him out of a pub, high as a kite, full of drinkers' remorse and bemoaning Jess' pending surgery.

"I was in a state of panic since all I had on me was a train ticket. My father rescued the day when he went in search of Gerald, trying all the local drinking spots. Apart from being drunk he was minus quite a lot of money. But I took what I could."

In Johannesburg Jess' operation went well enough – a lip repair, fixing his cleft palate and a tongue tie. And he recovered fairly quickly from the pneumonia that set in again after surgery.

But when mother and child eventually got home, home wasn't a fun place to be. Gerald was in a bad way. He had lost his job and just pretended to go to work, leaving on a Monday and returning at the end of the week with no earnings and under the pretext of working in the country.

"I had to accept charity from my parents and my in-laws and that wasn't easy. That was the only way Jess and I had food. After a few weeks of 'working in the country' Gerald started bringing home the most unsavory types. I felt my home was becoming a pigsty, and although already seven months pregnant I knew I had to get out."

But even her hardships did not remove the tendency to be easily swayed and so after moving back to her parents' home and working in her mother's dress shop, she couldn't resist bringing Gerald to their home when she found out he was very ill with the DT's.

"Of course I couldn't keep this a secret. I was so naïve and when my dad found out and told him to leave, I thought him very cruel."

Gerald disappeared well before the birth of Allan on May 14, 1949, an event that must not have interested him much since he remained out of touch. Mavis' family eventually tracked him down and *"made him come to the church for the christening"* of his three-month-old son. *"After that I never saw him again and never received any maintenance."*

But she had Allan and what a blessing he was. *"He was a beautiful baby and so good that I thought he must have known how little time I had to give him. I used to take him to work with me and leave him in his stroller at the back of my mother's shop. He used to sleep most of the day, waking only to be fed. My parents' house help looked after him."*

Meanwhile, Jess' had just turned two and his third surgery was due, as was another lesson for his worn-out mom: how to deal with unsympathetic people in the form of a particularly blunt charge nurse who told her off in no uncertain terms when she dared to pick Jess up and comfort him after the operation.

"I knew I was disobeying orders, but I just couldn't resist. When he started to cry, it alerted the nurse and she told me exactly what she thought of me. After all that, I was permitted only to peep into Jess' room through a crack in the door."

IS HE OUR FATHER?

All in all Mavis was ready for a break. And it came - two years after leaving Gerald when her divorce from him had become official. A very trying time in her life had ended, but not until the man who brought so much misery inflicted one last blow: taking their very young, impressionable boys on a pub crawl. And that sadly was the only memory her sons retained of their father. He became the man 'who took them from pub to pub in a taxi'.

It all stemmed from Gerald asking Mavis after their separation to allow the boys to spend a day with his mother. He collected them in a taxi, which was a real novelty for them. But contrary to the arrangement, he completely bypassed his mother's home. They only reached their grandmother's house late that night, tired and hungry, not having had any food all day. The only thing they got to do was sit in the car while dad imbibed.

A bit baffled by the whole experience, they later asked their mother whether the man who took them to all the bars was really their father.

With pubs and drinking finally behind her, she was more ready than ever for a new life, but single parenting with no maintenance money for her kids (in spite of a court order) proved to be no rose garden either.

She could of course have dodged the 'single' issue since there was an offer of marriage shortly after the divorce. But what crashed that idea pretty quickly was that Mavis' children (Allan then two and Jess four) were not welcome in the proposed new arrangement. *"When I was asked to send away my boys, I knew this was not the solution to my problems."*

A FRESH START

A still very timid and nervy Mavis, severely weakened after all the drama with Gerald, and pressured by her child rearing duties, realized that if she did not make a definite attempt to change things about her circumstances and about herself (a very upbeat attitude was hard to come by after what she had gone through), she would be 'choking her children'.

"I really tried to act like a responsible adult and to do something positive." So she sought a fresh start in Johannesburg where she found a job in sales, leaning on her little bit of experience as a saleslady in Kimberley. First she worked for an art dealer and later for record companies, having found suitable accommodation in a sub-economic housing tract in South Hills. She was set up for the time being - especially as she had one *"very precious blessing."*

"My old nanny, who had been with my family for 25 years, came along to look after the boys. She was very good to them and they loved her." Even so, she often wondered what would become of her and her children.

Chapter 3: JOURNEY TO HOPE
Lessons in a new family

"I always want to be with my own family, and the Lord has shown me that I can..."
(a favorite children's song)

A STROKE OF GOOD FORTUNE

When Ernest John Hutchison came into Mavis' life it was as if the heavens were smiling on her. He was a great stabilizing influence, always supporting her, and the one person she could completely rely on as she first became established as an athlete.

This stroke of good fortune entered Mavis' fledgeling household a few years after her arrival in Johannesburg. She and Ernie met and married on June 10, 1955. He was a miner, a quiet man, quite a bit older than her, but exactly the man she needed. Their short courtship became a lasting union that ended only when he died in June 1991.

Mavis and Ernie at their wedding reception, 1955.

At the outset they decided theirs was going to be a real family with no 'halves, steps or yours and mine.' His two children, Ronald and Pam, would simply receive two new brothers, while Mavis' boys acquired a new brother and sister. To prove the point Ernie legally adopted Jess and Allan when they were 12 and 14 respectively. *"Our kids were brought up as real brothers and sisters and there has always been a strong bond between them."*

Four years later Gayle was added to the new family unit, followed by Beverley in 1961. This completed the Hutchison collection of six children, who all turned out to be 'ambitious, sound thinking people', members of a 'sound family with no hang-ups, due to their attitudes'.

"All the children showed the greatest respect for both Ernie and me, and for that we were grateful."

The father of the combined flock led the way, *"and they were only too eager to be guided by him. In the words of our children, 'We chose our parents very wisely'."*

TRAGEDY STRIKES AGAIN

But family life would have more challenges. In June 1969, some eight years after Mavis got started in athletics, young Beverley was hit by a truck while crossing a road after an afternoon at the movies with sister Gayle and two friends. She bled profusely and remained unconscious for two weeks.

A neurosurgeon said her skull was fractured and a splinter was piercing her brain. He would have to operate immediately. For agonizing hours Ernie and Mavis sat in the corridors of the hospital with their son Allan. When Beverley was finally wheeled back into the ward, her whole body was shaking like a leaf.

"I was very worried and asked the sister why. She replied that someone with a brain injury has to be kept cold to avoid brain fever."

Mavis was too distraught to do anything but spend most of her time at the hospital, worrying not only about Beverley's recovery, but also about Gayle who saw the accident close-up. She was in a state of severe shock, suffering nightmares.

When Beverley regained consciousness she was blind, but thankfully that was a short-lived complication. Sadly, though, after her discharge from hospital she could no longer cope with school. She was in third grade and all things of a scholastic and emotional nature became challenging.

"She just used to sit and play at the back of the class. But she also became

very highly strung. At times she could be very mature, or again she might throw a tantrum like a three-year-old."

After another round of surgery some months later, during which a plastic plate was inserted into her brain to close the fracture, Beverley was placed in a school where the emphasis was practical skills, and she steadily improved over time. But she always remained of special concern to Mavis and Ernie, for her needs became much greater after the accident.

"As we tried to work with her we became aware that Gayle felt neglected. When we realized how she felt, we tried to compensate. Probably not enough or soon enough."

To this day Mavis worries about possibly having neglected both her youngest children as result of her sports career. That's why she felt moved recently to apologize if they felt that this was indeed the case. She remembers only too well that Beverley was just a baby when she got serious with athletics.

"Fortunately, Ernie's Mom lived with us and she was a great help with the kids and the household generally. She also supported me as an athlete, but however one would judge my choices, the past is the past ." Mavis' mother also helped out with the kids during some of the longer runs, so any perceived neglect was probably pretty minimal.

LESSONS LEARNED, LESSONS TAUGHT

In reality, the welfare of all her children was always very close to Mavis' heart and she wanted to ensure they were properly taught. She emphasized the value of formal education, as well as the acquisition of life skills with activities such as scouting. She wanted them, in fact, never to stop learning. The drive for their education no doubt stemmed from her own floundering beginning and leaving school prematurely.

"I took pride in the fact that some of them obtained college degrees and that they handled their lives pretty well. I'm especially thankful that alcohol abuse never became an issue in either Allan's or Jess' lives. Being the biological offspring of an alcoholic father did worry me at one stage."

She also ensured that her children saw the value of being there for one another as a family, and that they understood the need for respecting their elders. According to Mavis the latter was especially instilled into them by Ernie. He must have gotten the idea across solidly since they always treated their mother with the greatest respect, *"as something quite special, a courtesy they extended to all women"*, says Mavis.

Lessons to the children were also about the truth that all work and no play makes Jack a dull boy: *"I wanted them to know that no matter how hard one had to work, you were entitled to enjoyment."*

And she taught them to see things through, a lesson she painfully learned as a runner. It came along with her urging that developing their talents was important: *"As I was developing a talent, I tried to encourage them to recognize theirs and to pursue their gifts actively and not give up. I'd like to think I did have an influence on them in this regard.*

"Gayle had a talent for computers and discovered it after a few jobs rejections. Today she is successful at her chosen field. Allan became a teacher and later a psychologist, using his gift for counseling first in South Africa with students, and later in Australia.

"Jess was an extra miler, probably working extra hard to compensate for his impediment. His professional success only came after failing an important exam three times and after I encouraged him to go back a fourth time, which was when he passed. Spurred on, he subsequently completed a B.Com degree part-time and went on to good employment. He also became an excellent athlete and published the booklet, 'The loneliness of the long distance runner.'"

"But whatever I tried to teach them, they were always strong individuals, including Jess who was determined not to let his physical disadvantage get the better of him. I remember how thrilled I was with his performance as MC during a parents day at the conclusion of his grade 7 year.

"But strong individuals speak their minds as Gayle did on occasion: 'Mom, you have no dress sense, no common sense and you can't cook - but you smell great!'"

Recalling her efforts to teach her children revived memories of her parents' efforts to teach her. Advice that stands out came from both her mom and dad.

"My father always emphasized, 'It's so nice to be nice, so be nice'. And 'enough is enough', (maybe referring to my tolerance of abuse by others), 'listen more than you talk', 'stand up for yourself' (which took me a long time), 'it's not all hard work', and 'take time to smell the roses'. He was also fond of saying, 'Give me my roses now; don't wait till I'm gone.'

"My mom was a very private person, but some things did rub off and what rubbed off on me most was about going the extra mile, working hard, being not just a starter but a finisher, and being there for one another.

Mavis with her mother after finishing her difficult UK run in 1980.
Picture from an article by Trevor Samson .

Exercising her limited sewing talent doing tapestry.
—Picture from a late 70s interview with The Star.

"I did, however, not inherit her cooking or sewing talent. I was given a sewing machine some 15 years ago and it became my prize white elephant, the nicest ornament in the house! But although my home making skills never became my strong point, I did actually manage to acquire some other skills which brought me great pleasure, like making 'prick and sew' greeting cards – the closest thing to sewing I can manage!

"Tapestry (during my early running years), crocheting dresses, skirts and tablecloths (learned from my grandmother), were likewise things I managed to develop some skill at. These days fabric painting takes my fancy. I'm even hoping to finally use the 'white elephant', given me by my daughter Beverley."

A LEG OF BEEF?

Her general lack of domesticity, which incorporates her lesser endowment of culinary flair, might have something to do with an intensely embarrassing moment as a young bride.

"When I first got married I made roasts every day, served with roast potatoes. That's one of the few things I did manage to absorb from my mom. One day I planned to have friends over with a little deviation in the menu, only to discover that something very important did not sink in during kitchen time at home – something that embarrasses me even now.

"On this particular day I went to the butcher and asked - believe it or not - for a leg of beef, which resulted in a very unhappy man who explained it couldn't be done. Was it not maybe a leg of lamb I wanted. A phone call to my mother revealed the extent of my ignorance."

Then there was the 'steak' incident.

"During my second marriage my hopelessness in the kitchen was still very present. One day I opened the fridge and saw some lovely 'steaks'. My mother-in-law must have put them there for one of our dinners, I concluded. I promptly removed them and enthusiastically prepared them for the family. A winner, I thought. And that felt good since winning in the kitchen wasn't always the case. When it was discovered I had fed them Granny Hutch's very special cat meat, carefully put aside for her highly prized feline, Gayle was very vocal: 'Yes mom, you did feed us cat food!'

"Other than that there were no negative comments after the meal, or ill effects for that matter. That was a relief since the kids would often say one of

two things about my cooking: When the food was good, it was a 'success night' and when it wasn't, it was a 'failure night'."

Apart from very freely commenting on things culinary, they would also make it known when mom was just an embarrassment. "*I was permitted to be involved with their scouting and athletics, but with academics the message was: 'Mom, stay out!' It took me a while to learn that most teenagers are desperately embarrassed by their parents.*

"*But no matter what embarrassment I may have caused, I rejoiced in my kids' successes. Whether they succeeded because of me or in spite of me, is an open question.*"

LOSING A CHAMPION

"For me it's the long road and the long lonely miles."
(Jess Hutchison)

One of her children's achievements that she particularly savored was Jess' completion of the taxing 54-mile Comrades Marathon in 1965. Both she and Jess ran this particular race. He was 18 and the first junior across the finish line, winning the Lyle Lightbody Trophy.

"*It was a proud moment. I always felt very connected to him. Maybe it was because he was the twin that survived and had such a hard time as a baby and young child. It was a close relationship from both sides, not that the other kids were not also very important to me.*"

Thinking about Jess at this point in her life is a tender thing, and talking about him clearly tugged at her heartstrings because what she was about to reveal she had never before shared publicly.

We picked up Jess' story when he was 42 years old, and by all accounts a successful accountant working for British Petroleum in Cape Town. He was seemingly happily married (since 1972) to his high school sweetheart, Lyn, and they had two wonderful children, David and Susan. Both were bright and capable – David would later become a bank consultant in England, while Susan would hold a managerial position in Cape Town. All seemed well.

Christmas of 1988 came and went, and then dawned the first working day after the holidays. "At the very start of that day things were a bit odd. I saw Jess that morning since I had been checking on him regularly, knowing he was suffering some from depression.

Mavis and Jess, in one of the Rand Daily Mail 50 km walks.

"The whole family, in fact, was worried about him, and his brother Allan had come up from Durban especially to visit and counsel with him over the Christmas season. He did feel a little better immediately afterward, I remember, but whatever was troubling him wasn't completely resolved.

Jess also had a pending ear operation to investigate a growth (cholesteatoma) in his left middle ear, to see how close it had come to his brain. (Apart from the risk of worsening hearing, a cholesteatoma can eat away the thin bone covering that separates the top of the ear from the brain. It can also eat into the small bones of the middle ear, causing deafness and vertigo. Surgical removal normally cures the problem.)

Maybe all that added to his low mood, even though the op was designed to help him preserve his hearing and health.

"All the time, though, I could sense something wasn't right about him. After Allan left, his mood had sunk again. He told his brother things that made it clear he wasn't coping well, however much he might have tried to pretend to others. I didn't know how to help him. I was constantly worrying about him. And what really left me at a loss was that he was preparing to start a new business.

"That morning when I checked to see if he was okay, I didn't even go back home. I felt to stay with my daughter-in-law for the entire day. When Lyn checked with BP to see whether Jess was at work, only to learn he wasn't, their reply that he was likely out with a client, did not put me at ease. So we decided to go to his office. We waited and waited, but he never returned."

Later on the police located Jess' car near a railway station where he was found decapitated after being hit by a train. Understandably, the news of his gruesome death put his mother and wife into a state of total shock.

"Identifying my son's body was the most painful thing I have ever had to do, and although both Lyn and I suspected things had gone horribly wrong for him, even before the police arrived to tell us so, it was still an unspeakably horrible experience.

"Afterward I used my running as a means of relief. I would go out on the road and just cry all the way." Grieving in this manner lasted for almost two months.

To now speak about the greatest tragedy of her life to a relative stranger gathering information for her biography, was definitely not something she had planned on. It just happened, and was probably cathartic as she was able to use our conversation to address some of her innermost feelings, carefully tucked away after fruitlessly analyzing the reason for her son's suicide.

"For the first time I feel more at peace, more content, especially after a decision to pray about this unresolved heartache. I also made a point of visiting the site of his memorial plaque, and that helped too."

She will always treasure the poem Jess wrote for her, titled 'Mavis', with its unforgettable image of *"A wisp of a woman with silver-grey hair..."*

Shortly after losing Jess, Mavis discovered that Ernie's life was also about to end. He had been diagnosed with lung cancer. *"Strangely enough, Ernie's illness helped to take my mind off Jess.*

"Ernie felt sure he'd get well, but I didn't share his optimism, even though he stopped smoking. It was too late and he suffered a lot of pain."

After being at home for a period, he was hospitalized and subsequently moved between home and hospice. *"I did my best for him at home where he was for the bulk of the time. He died in June 1991, about 1 ½ years after Jess."*

Chapter 4: RUNNING AFTER THE BOYS
Learning to Succeed – One Step at a Time

Some folks are taking their bows out,
I'm taking my bow in -
Getting ready, ready steady,
I'm about to begin.
(From a song by Gillene Laney)

HAPPY FURRY BOOT DAY!

Although Ernie was always her single greatest support, her boys were really the ones who got Mavis into athletics. By 1960, Jess and Allan were involved in running and the new fad of race walking, and Mavis and Ernie naturally watched them train and compete.

For Mavis the key date was July 23, 1960. She and Ernie drove out to see Jess and a niece pass by in a Junior Big Walk, sponsored by the Rand Daily Mail newspaper. As Mavis looked on in motherly pride, she could see Jess hadn't quite been properly equipped for the race. His ill-chosen old pair of shoes had quit on him even before the halfway mark, and he was walking in his socks with his feet in a bad state.

His mother wasn't going to let him try to finish the race that way. It was warm for a winter's day, but Mavis was wearing a pair of fur-lined boots which she promptly gave Jess to wear.

He was probably embarrassed by his odd new footgear, but his feet hurt enough that he accepted the offer and finished the race in his mom's furry boots. It wasn't Jess's finest moment, but at least 14-year old niece Marion won in her age group with a bicycle to show for it.

But the event made it's deepest impact on Mavis. *"My interest and devotion to the sport started on that warm July day."*

THE BOYS, THE GOLF COURSE, AND THE FIRST RACE

Her sons continued to pull her toward greater involvement in athletics. As she watched Jess and Allan run, she not only realized she needed some form of exercise, but the long-lost desire to be a good athlete rose up again.

"Although I was very unsure and nervous at the time, I started training with the boys by running around the local golf course every afternoon."

The two young men were preparing for competition as members of the Johannesburg Harriers Athletics club, one of the oldest and best known in the country.

"Ernie was there too as we liked doing things together as a family. Later, as I got into the athletics thing, both he and I participated. Ernie didn't become a champion, but both boys became good athletes."

Besides 'running after the boys' as they trained, Mavis began to dream of participating in competitive race walks, if she could pluck up enough courage. After a visit to Durban in December 1961, she started going out for a four-miler with her sister Ivy after supper each night. Although at this stage everybody thought it was a huge joke, Mavis and Ivy entered for an 8-mile walk.

Mavis wore her very first athletics outfit, and it remains a clear and somewhat embarrassing memory. She was too shy to wear the customary running shorts, so she had her mom sew her a little white tennis dress which she wore with a pair of black tekkies (tennis shoes), *"so I didn't have to clean them all the time."*

It wasn't a great decision. There was a strong wind blowing and the *"white tennis dress was most irritating as the wind kept blowing it up and I found the dress brushing against my arm, which was most uncomfortable. I must have looked quite a sight."*

That wasn't a day Mavis (or Ivy) set records or won medals, but such things probably weren't foremost in her mind at the time. One of the reasons these very popular race walks attracted Mavis was that if she entered a competition among a huge crowd, nobody would notice her.

That would change as her love of the sport grew, but in the beginning it was largely the idea of improving her poor health that seemed attractive. *"I took the challenge of training with the boys because at 37 I wanted to be healthier and fitter. With six children, a husband and a home to run I realized I had to improve my health and toughen up, or else life would become increasingly miserable."*

After about a year of training, her poor circulation began to improve, the chilblains she suffered every winter disappeared, and the black-outs she regularly endured ceased. Headaches, which used to be her constant companion, were getting fewer and fewer. Gone as well were hay fever, bronchitis and pleurisy.

But she did not just feel physically stimulated. *"I was also spiritually lifted,"* she adds. There was a new self-discipline and self-control and a new enjoyment. Things were changing for Mavis of Moffat View, who was developing an entirely new view of herself.

THE BOYS RUN (AND WALK) ON

But at this stage it was definitely still Jess who was the family's leading race walker, receiving provincial colors for representing his province both as a junior and senior.

"He won many titles at the peak of his career, setting up many records and I was proud to compete with him in a number of race walks - in my own category of course..."

The tradition of competing with her sons continued even in later years, when Mavis finished ahead of 61 men in the Comrades Marathon, but far behind Jess, who won the junior trophy. She also competed against Allan on the occasion of the 24-hour run in which she set a new world record for women.

Meanwhile, by 1962 Mavis' training, running around the City Deep golf course with her boys, had made her pretty fit – she thought.

IF AT FIRST YOU DON'T SUCCEED...

"Sport has enriched every aspect of my life. I feel like a bird set free from a cage."

In the early sixties, the Rand Daily Mail, a morning paper in Johannesburg at the time, held a series of 'Big Walks' from the Rand Daily Mail Head Office to the Brakpan City Hall and back, a distance of 80 kilometers or 50 miles. These walks generated overwhelming interest with thousands of participants, mostly novices, accepting the challenge. The result was a race walking boom throughout the country, and Mavis thought it was time to get serious.

"After some sustained training I decided I was ready for a challenge and made my first attempt at the 'Big Walk' in 1962. It was a disaster! After 35 kilometers I had had enough. The following year I tried again. This time it was different. I was better prepared, knew what to expect and completed the distance in 9 hours some minutes, which was a new women's record for the event. It sure felt good. I then knew what success felt like, although I never expected to set a record. All I wanted to do was finish."

One press report gives an entertaining cameo: "Men were following the woman with the striking figure who was walking through the heavy rain. She was sopping wet but not even her husband offered her a lift. Mavis Hutchison was heading for the woman's record...They told her in the end that she had broken it, but she couldn't believe it. 'It was so easy,' she said, and called for a check on the times. There was no doubt however: 9 hours 35 minutes. Yet the previous year she gave up after only 16 miles."

That's about 22 kilometers. Clearly Mavis' later memory of her drop-out point differed from what appeared in this report.

After that bit of success it was not long before Mavis was recognized as one of the top race-walkers in the country.

But she was still wearing that little white tennis dress and the black tennis shoes.

Early Recognition

Along with the great victory in the 1963 RDM Big Walk came recognition as the 'Most Progressive Woman Walker'. She got her club colors with the Johannesburg Harriers, and was hailed in the press as one of the leading woman walkers in her province. She was on her way, and went from strength to strength, covered in the papers as she progressed.

In a press piece written three days after her record-breaking Big Walk, Mavis got her first chance to share success tips with other women:

"Walk with a goal. Go in for competitive walking. It doesn't matter if you don't do more than a quarter of a mile. A mile at first -- it gets easier and easier. Soon you will be saying like me, "I never thought I had it in me."

Your step will become springy, your figure toned up and you'll have a sense of achievement and you'll enjoy yourself."

A 1964 article, published 8 days before Mavis' RDM Big Walk victory that year, contained a challenge from a well known Rhodesian (Zimbabwean) walker, Mrs. Laura Maud Precious "who would like a contest against Mavis Hutchison". This was to take place during an envisioned return by the challenger to Johannesburg at a later date, since Mrs. Precious heard about the RDM 50-miler while she was on vacation. She was even happy just to do an inter-town walk with Mavis, who was quoted as saying that whenever Mrs. Precious was ready she was willing.

But more precious to Mavis was the deep pride her father George took in her achievements as she began to reach her potential.

JOIN THE CLUB

Mavis was also involved with other aspects of race walking and was often used as a time keeper, recorder, fundraiser and organizer by the athletics club she belonged to. She came to realize just how important these clubs were in the development of a sports career, and over the years belonged to a good few of them: Johannesburg Harriers, Germiston Callies, Fish Hoek Athletics Club, Collegian Harriers (Newlands), Highway Athletics Club in Durban and the Sasolburg Athletics Club. Right now she belongs to no particular club, but her athletics needs are different at this stage of her life.

"*I gained greatly from belonging to them as I went along. I met fantastic people who would go the extra mile. In particular, I received a lot of encouragement from Johannesburg Harriers members who egged me on toward my first dream race, the Comrades Marathon, and from the Germiston Callies club. People went out of their way to assist me, helping my career in different ways at different stages.*"

With the encouragement of club members, she began to think about running as well as race walking, especially over long distances.

Mavis on her way to her third victory in the Rand Daily Mail Big Walk. The distance had changed from 50 miles to 50 km.

Chapter 5: MARATHON WOMAN
Catching the Bus

"When I started running I was unsure, insecure. I did not have any goals and I was sure I would never achieve anything in my lifetime."

By the time this picture was taken, she'd gained more confidence.
She appears here training near a horse track, sometime in the sixties.

THROUGH SAND AND SAWDUST – LEARNING THE HARD WAY

At the time Mavis was establishing herself as a noted race walker over fairly long distances in the early 60s, it was only natural for her to take the idea of *running* longer distances more and more seriously.

But it was a member of her Johannesburg Harriers athletic club whose suggestion got her to try the idea. Allan Ferguson, captain of the men's cross country team at the club, knew that 'a few of the girls in the Transvaal' wanted to give his sport a try, and asked her if she'd ever thought of running cross country. It sounded like an exciting new challenge, but she wasn't certain whether she had any ability at running. After all, she'd never tried competitive running and wasn't sure her build was right for it.

But challenges were becoming hard for Mavis to resist – and how hard could it be? In a 1981 article for *Health Counter News*, she put it this way: "*It was my turn to try my hand at cross-country. Everybody can run. When the bus comes and you see you're going to miss it, you run.*"

So she began running. Figuring that she needed more strength, she "*started training at a course of sand and sawdust used for training horses at City Deep. A few of us trained together, but we chose this site to strengthen our legs.*"

Her first competitive run was on a four-mile course around Zoo Lake in central Johannesburg, a much safer venue then than now. This was actually a radical step at the time, when the longest races for women were only 880 yards, and the women in the race "*were all pretty excited about the whole thing.*"

Mavis was particularly excited because South Africa's half-mile champion, Anne McKenzie, was in the race. After all that running through sawdust, she remembers "*…thinking how I was going to show her a thing or two. I really thought I could outdo her. What ignorance on my part.*"

In this barrier-breaking first cross-country race for women in South Africa, Mavis lined up once again in her white tennis dress and black tennis shoes, and did everything wrong. She started out almost sprinting, and "*came in at the back of the field somewhere.*"

"*As a comparative novice I knew nothing about pacing, either as a solo runner or running with others. So all I wanted to do was to get ahead of Anne right from the start and stay ahead. My reward? I used up all my energy at the beginning, had nothing left for the finish and had to bow to Anne's superiority.*"

THE ROPES AND FRED

But Mavis didn't let this disaster stop her. She learned from it, kept running, and continued to seek advice from experienced runners at her club, along with emulating her heroes. *"One individual in particular became a real role model to me – the late Fred Morrison, a wonderful athlete and president of the Germiston Callies. I admired other athletes like 1952 Olympic high jumper Ester Brandt, who was described as the only 'passenger' on the team but became the only one to return with a gold medal; the Dutch sprinter Fanny Bankers-Koen, my own father who was such a good sportsman; and Gary Player, a golfer still known for his integrity and perseverance. But Fred stood out for what he did to help me improve as a runner in a hands-on way. He basically taught me the ropes.*

"He was always encouraging me and telling me that I could do better and why don't I try this or that, steering me in the right way. His suggestions on road races were always very helpful and I specifically remember him saying: 'The more time on the road, training, the less time in the race.'

"He helped me set my sights as I got more into road running at a time when long distances for women were considered unwise and unsafe. 800 meters was about the limit (set by the IAAF) and there I was wanting to be a marathoner."

BEYOND THE CROWD

As an undiscouraged Mavis kept on running as well as walking, she no longer wanted just to be one of an anonymous crowd on the road. Running was something she really enjoyed, even though *"running on a track is a very individualistic type of competition, with the spectators on the grandstand, the officials inside the track and the runners on the track."*

And she learned as she ran.

After that day at Zoo Lake, in competitive races Mavis tried to stick behind the lead till she was ready to make her move. *"In a mass start it is easy to go faster than you think you're going."*

Anne McKenzie's lesson came in handy even when there were no other runners. *"I got the pacing lesson down well and when it came to my really long runs later, I was able to work out pretty exactly where I needed to be at a particular point in the race."*

Another lesson along the way that paid great dividends for her was the up-and-down-hill technique: *"I soon learned the value of shortening my stride up a hill and lengthening it down hill. So doing I saved my knees – one part of the 'running outfit' all athletes need - like oxygen."*

THE 1963 JOHANNESBURG MARATHON

Mavis began trying longer distances, despite those who considered it 'unwise and unsafe'. In the same year as her record-setting 50-mile Big Walk, she ran in a standard marathon (26miles/42.2 km) in Johannesburg, the only woman among about 75 men. The officials were not especially enthused but allowed her to run 'unofficially', perhaps because a woman who could race walk 80 km in record time was unlikely to embarrass them by collapsing.

The race began and ended that year at the Jeppe Quondam Club, originally founded in 1907 as a sports club for the 'old boys' of Johannesburg's famous Jeppe High School. The race was run on a fairly flat course through roads and streets in the surrounding built-up area, and runners had to complete the 21.1 km loop twice.

Mavis got lots of encouragement from the other athletes (usually as they passed her) and their seconds, and from bystanders along the route. She ran the distance easily, feeling good and feeling fit. After she finished in 3 hours 50 minutes, the press told her that she was the first woman in history to complete a standard marathon, and there was extensive publicity for what was thought to be an unprecedented achievement.

She was certainly the only South African woman running marathons at the time, and it would be another 11 years before a woman would run in a Johannesburg marathon again. So little known were the achievements of the very few women who had tried this distance before that neither Mavis nor any athlete she knew – nor the press – had ever heard of them. None is *generally* recognized as having participated in an organized marathon race.

So even though Mavis had to run unofficially in 1963, she may have some claim to being the first woman in history to be allowed to participate in an official marathon race at all.

THE ERO OF CLOSED DOORS

Race walking, as a reborn fad, was much more open to women than distance running, where the longest Olympic event for women was only 800m. Even that was a novelty restored only in 1960, more than three decades after the newly instituted 800m Olympic run for women (1928) had ended in what press reports from Amsterdam claimed was disaster.

John Tunis of the New York Post, for example, wrote that "Below us on the cinder path were 11 wretched women, 5 of whom dropped out before the finish, while 5 collapsed after reaching the tape." A more spectacularly fact-free report would be hard to find, since there were only 9 women in the race, all finished, and only one fell at the finish line. But since Tunis and others reported what many thought *should* have happened, their purely fictional accounts of the 1928 women's 800m were widely believed.

Papers opined that the 'terrible exhaustion' of running such distances would 'desex' women and damage their reproductive capacity. Britain's Daily Mail reportedly 'affirmed that women who raced longer than 200m would age prematurely'.[1]

So horrified were the Olympic committee by the news from Holland that for 32 years, no Olympic women's race over 200 meters was permitted, This was an improvement over the first 32 years of the modern Olympics, when women were excluded altogether, and over the ancient Olympics, when women risked execution if they sneaked in even as spectators, but it shows the enormous difficulty in winning acceptance even of the concept of female athletics.

Women *had* run long distances – but their achievements were regarded as unwise, unsafe ventures into freakish territory – much as mathematics had been in the nineteenth century, when a prominent British academic warned that such heavy thinking might injure the delicate female brain and divert energy from the reproductive system, threatening fertility and general well-being! It took a long time for people to realize that this was a dog that never barked.

Mavis didn't know it, but the first woman believed to have run a (not-quite-standard) marathon may have done so in 1896, the year when the Olympic Games were restored. According to historian Karl Lennartz, a woman named Melpomene is said to have run the 40-km course about a month before the official race, completing it in four and a half hours after about three weeks training. This time includes a 10-minute pause near the halfway point to suck a few oranges.

According to one press report, she was "a woman of the people with marked features, of a tough and lively temperament." Her application to participate in the actual Olympic marathon was turned down[2], so she missed a race which only 10 of the 17 male entrants finished, with the third man across the finish line then being disqualified for covering part of the distance in a carriage.

Newspaper reports at the time state that a woman named Stamata Revithi then ran the course the day after the men, although Olympic marathon historian Charles Lovett claims she warmed up out of sight, then ran alongside the course, eventually passing exhausted men who had dropped out. According to Lovett, she was then denied entry to the stadium and had to complete the race by running around the outside.[3] She told a reporter she was only that slow because she stopped to sightsee and visit shops along the way!

Other women marathoners were very few and far between. Marie-Louise Ledru (1918, 5 hours 40 minutes, Paris) and Violet Piercy (October 1926, 3:40:22, near London) are the only ones on record.[4] Only Violet Piercy ran over a course that was the standard distance of 42.195 km.

Mavis appears to have been the first woman in 37 years to attempt a marathon, but the crack in the dike was very soon to widen. A few months after Mavis' marathon run, Lyn Carman and Merry Lepper hid along the sidelines at the start of the 1963 Western Hemisphere Marathon in California, then joined the men after the start. One race official tried to remove them from the course, only to have Carman shout "I have the right to use the public streets for running!" Merry Lepper finished in 3:37:07, displacing Mavis from 2nd fastest to 3rd fastest woman over the standard marathon distance[5].

Roberta Gibbs would likewise hide behind a bush before jumping into the Boston Marathon and setting a new record of 3:21:25 in 1966, while in 1967 teammates from Syracuse body-blocked a race official who tried to remove Kathrine Switzer from the race, and Roberta Gibbs was "forced off the course just steps from the finish line".[6]

Women would not be allowed to compete in an Olympic marathon until 1984, but other competitions opened much sooner. The New York Marathon opened a women's division in 1971; the Boston Marathon did the same a year later, the same year that Mavis ran another marathon in the tiny neighboring country of Swaziland.

[1]*"Eleven Wretched Women"* by Roger Robinson (Running Times, May 2012) gives a detailed account of events at the 800m women's race at the 1928 Amsterdam Olympics, based on available film, and of the bizarrely distorted reporting of what happened.

[2]*"Two Women Ran the Marathon in 1896"*, by historian Karl Lennartz (http://www.la84foundation.org/SportsLibrary/JOH/JOHv2n1/JOHv2n1h.pdf), gives evidence to support his theory that a woman named Melpomene ran the marathon course on about March 8, 1896, and failed in her application to run in the official Olympic marathon itself. According to Lennartz, Stamata Revithi then ran the marathon course a day after the official event, finishing in about five and a half hours on April 11, 1896.

[3]*Olympic Marathon* by Charles Lovett states that 'Melpomene' ran the Olympic marathon with the men, while Stamata Revithi had run the same course a month earlier. The Greek historian Athanasios Tarasouleas believes that the same woman ran both days (The ISOH Journal1: (3), p. 11-12, 1994, and Olympic Review 26 (17): 53-55, 1997). He gives a delightful account taken from a contemporary newspaper: *"...on Saturday, 30 March 1896 at 8:00 am, Stamata Revithi was ready to run the Marathon alone. Before setting off, she recorded the time at which she started and this document was signed by the school master, the mayor and the magistrate of Marathon. She began in Marathon at 8:00 in the morning and "having run the entire route at a brisk pace" she arrived, perspiring and covered in dust, at 1:30 pm, at the 'old shacks' (a location close to the present Evangelismos Hospital). There she met some officers, and asked them to sign the record, attesting to her time of arrival in Athens. 'Why did you run all that way and tire yourself?' they asked.*

'So that the king might award a position to my child. I am now going straight to Timoléon Philimon (the secretary general of the Greek Olympic Committee) to let him know how long it took me to run from Marathon, and tell him that whoever wishes may come to compete with me.'

'Were you running quickly?'

'You should have seen me! I stopped at various shops on the way. If I had run straight, I would have finished in three hours at the most. Now I'm going directly to Timoléon Philimon.' Having said that, she took up her shoes, which were falling apart, and barefoot she started on the way to Athens."

With that she vanishes into the mists of history. No record exists of her after that day.

[4]*The Association of Road Racing Statisticians credits Marie-Louise Ledru with fin-ishing the Tour de Paris marathon on Sept. 29, 1918, giving a time of 5:40 over 42.29km, nearly 2 and half hours more than the winning time for the Tour de Paris that year. The International Association of Athletics Federations, described as the international governing body for athletics, recognizes Violet Piercy of England as the first woman to run a standard marathon, giving a time of 3:40:22 achieved on Octo-ber 3, 1926. Some have claimed that she participated in the Polytechnic Marathon, but this was run on May 18, so it seems likely that she ran over the same course (which in 1926 ended at Stamford Bridge in the London suburbs), but more than four months after the actual race.*

[5]*The 1963 Western Hemisphere marathon is said to have been run over a 'short' course.*

[6]Olympic Marathon, *by Charlie Lovett.*

Chapter 6: GOING THE DISTANCE
"…What We Become Is What We Choose to Become"

———•◦•———

*"Just as Mount Kilimanjaro stands out above the
mountaintops of Africa, there is a milestone which stands
out in my life. That peak is the Comrades Marathon.
To any South African distance runner the 'Comrades' is
special; it is sacred. It is considered to be one of the most
difficult, most classic marathons in the world."*

THE SPORTSWRITER AND THE BROTHERHOOD

By 1964, Mavis had demonstrated that her capabilities went far beyond the 800m distance that was the longest the International Amateur Athletics Federation would sanction for women.[1] The prejudices of what she calls the 'Brotherhood' would not limit her any more than she could help. But what should be the next hill to climb?

It was a suggestion from sportswriter Sam Mirwis that captured her imagination, opening "another chapter in a remarkable human story."[2] At a cross country meet where Mavis was competing, he told her that he thought she could run the Comrades Marathon.

Despite the name, it was far more challenging than the standard marathon she'd run the year before., and the demands on her endurance would be of a different order of magnitude than cross country. In her own words: *"It is a run of approximately 86 torturous hilly kilometers between Pieter-maritzburg and Durban run in alternate directions annually."* Only two women had ever run in the Comrades, the last being Geraldine Watson[3] in 1933, more than three decades earlier.

Not surprisingly, being told she'd never make it only egged Mavis on. *"At first I was undecided about attempting to run the Comrades until being une-quivocally informed by my male contemporaries that the physical challenge was too severe for women; it was a race for men, tough men. Having already learned that physical challenges can be overcome by strengthening one's spirit, their taunts served to convince me that this was a challenge I had to confront."*

According to Flavia Pascoe in a 1976 Fair Lady article ('The Unstoppable Woman'): *"She'd been vacillating about entering, but when someone said: 'It's a man's race – you could never do it' she stopped hedging. She could do it and took great pleasure in proving it."*

Knowing only too well that for decades only men had participated, she next wrote to the organizers of the race (Collegian Harriers athletic club in Pietermaritzburg) for permission to run. It didn't hurt her cause that her own club supported her: *"The secretary of the club to which I belonged at the time (Johannesburg Harriers), Dave Sanson, wrote to the organizing club supporting my application, suggesting that I 'had what it takes' to complete the race. The official reply was that 'women were not allowed to participate officially in the Comrades Marathon', but that if I wished to line up unofficially they would not stop me."*

This may seem a bit absurd, but it was far ahead of the attitude in England, where Mavis' enquiries about participating in races were to be answered even years later by declarations that she not only would not be allowed to participate officially, but would be required to start an hour after everybody else – just to make sure nobody confused her with a real participant! Not surprisingly, she declined the 'offer'.

The Comrades officials, on the other hand, promised to give her all the assistance that they could on the road. Not surprisingly, she 'thanked them for their offer of help'.

TRAINING IN THE DARK

Now it was time to prepare, and it helped that both her husband and her son Jess would be training with her for the same race. There were nine months to go, but she was already excited: *"This was going to be the highlight of my athletic career, to be able to compete in a Comrades Marathon. The thrill of just thinking about being a participant was palpable and I found it difficult at first to contain my excitement."*

Preparing was no joke. Somehow she juggled family life, work and training as she managed the house and the cooking for her husband and six children, continued her work as an order clerk with a record company, and ran hours every day. Her husband's shift work schedule as a mine worker complicated things further, since (at the time) Mavis didn't like training alone. She and Ernest must have run mostly in the dark, since their usual sessions began at either 5 in the morning or 8 at night.

Now came the first real test over a longer distance than she'd run before. *"As was standard practice for most distance runners who were preparing to run the Comrades Marathon and who lived on the Highveld, I competed in the Pieter Korkie Marathon in 1965. The 'Korkie' is run from the Fountains in Pretoria to Callies home ground in Germiston, a distance of about 56 kilometers. It is held annually in memory of Pieter Korkie, a notable athlete who was killed in the late 1940s on the road while training."* Only men were allowed to compete, so Mavis had to run unofficially. Perhaps even that was good practice.

Bruce Fordyce referred to the Korkie as the 'slow poison', a dull, slightly uphill run through brown winter veld and smoky industrial zones, and he repeated the conventional runners' wisdom that a good time in the Korkie usually meant a decent performance in the Comrades. But we learn why in later runs Mavis took a navigator along...

"On that day, the irony was that, although I had run the distance, I failed to complete the run, as I ended up at the wrong finishing point. When I arrived at what I thought to be the clubhouse at which the race was meant to finish, there were no race officials. I thought I had been snubbed so I just went home. The next day Pam Norquay, Secretary of Germiston Callies, phoned to find out what had happened as they waited for me until dark. It was then that I discovered the venue originally advertised as the finish had been changed from the clubhouse at Delville to Herman Immelman (now Germiston) Stadium. I finished at the wrong venue."

But the star of 'Who Moved My Finish Line?' was uncrushable, and kept on running with her husband through the dark to get ready for the main event. She'd proved she could finish the 'Korkie' in reasonable time after all, and would run it three times more in preparation for later Comrades races . Navigation remained a weak point, however. *"1970 was another disaster. Alan Ferguson...informed them he had passed me on the freeway. I was on the wrong road. I have no idea where I would have ended had the officials not collected me, driven back to the start, measured the distance I had run, then dropped me off. From there all went well."* But at least in her later Korkies she always ended in the right place.

THE BUZZ AND THE FEAR

She felt she was ready. *"As Comrades race-day approached I felt that I had prepared well for the challenge. I was doubly excited because my husband Ernest and my eldest son Jess were official entries in the race."*

Pre-race events added to the excitement, as Mavis got to attend a 'special evening' where local athletes could meet Bernard Gomersall, the ultrarunner from the UK who'd won the London-to-Brighton race (the unofficial 'world championship' for distance runners at the time).

"Jackie Mekler (who had won the Comrades previously and was one of the favorites for that year's race), Wally Hayward (one of the all-time great Comrades runners), Tommy Malone and many others were at the social to welcome Bernard to South Africa. I could hardly contain the flow of adrenalin as I rubbed shoulders with such esteemed runners. To add to the excitement we looked at filmed recordings of previous Comrades runs, which conjured feelings of reliving history."

And then she was in Pietermaritzburg for the start of the race itself. In a pre-race meeting at the Imperial Hotel, *"I was awe-struck by the number of Comrades blazers I saw, worn proudly by those who had previously completed the grueling run. It dawned on me how exclusive this 'club' was and I could only dream that one day I would also be accepted as a member, notwithstanding my gender. I was mighty nervous – it was an intense nervousness that I would experience many more times in the years that lay ahead."*

In a recent interview for the South African TV program 'Kwela', Mavis admitted she is still a very nervous person, but has learned to control it. But in 1965, control was a bit more tentative.

"It rained the night before the race. This worried me, and as I could not sleep from nervousness, I passed the time praying for the rain to stop before morning. Emotionally I felt as though I had run three or four Comrades marathons that night. How would I cope if it continued to rain? Would I be able to stay the distance? Had I trained enough for such a tough assignment?"

In an earlier retelling of her story, Mavis says simply that she ran about three or four Comrades that night. Her doubts become more understandable in light of the fact that women in this postwar era were so poorly accepted as capable of distance running that (as mentioned in the last chapter) Roberta Gibbs was forced off the course just before completing the

1967 Boston Marathon, while teammates of K.V. Switzer had to fend off a race official with body blocks so she could finish in the same race.

Sunday evening had brought a welcome 'mothering break' from worries about herself. *"I was able to be partially distracted as I attended to my son Jess who had traveled from Cape Town, where he had competed in the Arthur Grey Memorial 50 kilometer walk the day before. Immediately after the walk he and Willie De Beer, a fellow athlete, drove the 1900 km to Pietermaritzburg nonstop to be in time for the race. They arrived at about 6 pm on the Sunday evening, very tired and hungry. At least this helped me temporarily get my attention off my own nervousness."*

WEATHER OR NOT

It was race day, Monday morning. Mavis was up early, and after a light breakfast the three Hutchisons jogged to the City Hall for the start. Thousands would run in later Comrades races, but Mavis was seriously impressed by the nearly four hundred who lined up in 1965.

She wasn't as impressed by the weather. Initially it was just cloudy, but *"unfortunately it began to rain softly just before the race started. I tried to convince myself that the rain would not last long; in any event it would give the runners a cool start to the day."*

At six o'clock sharp as the City Hall clock began to strike, Max Trimborn, in what had become the traditional prelude to the starter's gun, sounded the crowing of a cock. The gun echoed, and the hundreds of runners left the city hall in Pietermaritzburg on their way to Durban.

"What a thrill – the only woman to line up with nearly 400 men. Instantaneously the doubts started to niggle. Would I reach the destination before the maximum allowable time of eleven hours?"

The weather didn't help her anxiety much: *"Horror of all horrors, it rained the whole day without a break. In addition, instead of the temperature rising as the day unfolded, it dropped, seeming to get colder and colder. I began the race wearing a tracksuit top, which I had intended to discard as the day got warmer. In the beginning it protected me from the cold, but as I got progressively wetter, the top became increasingly heavy with the water it soaked up. I felt my dreams freezing over as the temperature decreased sharply on the 2000-foot high hilltops between Inchanga and Kloof. I now knew what it meant to be 'bitterly cold'."*

Mavis wasn't exaggerating. One journalist wrote that the appalling weather had tested the popularity of the Comrades as never before, while Morris Alexander described the weather conditions in 1965 as the worst in the history of the race. "This 40th occasion of the running of the Comrades saw the rain still streaming down when the last of the 281 finishers dragged his wet and weary body toward Durban's D.L.I. Drill Hall in the late afternoon."

Desperate runners were willing to try anything as they battled their way over the hills: "*I was reminded of the origins of this great race as I saw the struggling 'army' of weary runners searching for any kind of apparel that could keep them warm. Some were running in layers of jerseys and wind cheaters. Some even wore multiple mackintoshes and track suits, while several drew long woolen stockings over their arms to keep them warm. Another indelible memory!*"

In theory, the Hutchisons could ask for ask for assistance from brother-in-law Reg Wilkins, but Jess rapidly drew so far ahead that he "*had to make do with whatever roadside assistance he could get along the way. He finished more than two hours ahead of me and managed to scrounge a blanket in which to wrap himself until Reg arrived with his tracksuit. The shame was that no family member was there to see him finish as the first junior, no mean feat considering his schedule of the previous two days.*"

Ernie Fades Out

Meanwhile, Mavis was struggling toward Drummond, very worried and frozen to the bone. Ernest was a bit ahead of her, but walking more than she liked to see. She felt she was in real trouble too.

"*Just before Drummond I caught up with Ernest. He was really in a bad way; the cold and rain were just too much for him. He signaled his intention to withdraw and this left me very ambivalent. Should I continue or would the cold and the wet inevitably get the better of me as well? I remembered that the struggle was more a spiritual than a physical one, so I decided to press on.*"

"*I had not seen my second for over an hour and I badly needed a rubdown. My muscles felt like they were seizing up and I urgently wanted to get rid of all the wet and heavy extra clothing. The anger that was welling up inside of me because of the scarcity of my second seemed to provide the energy I needed to keep going. Luckily there was a further delay before I saw him, because had he arrived at that moment he would have got a blast from me, and I might have lost both my source of energy and my second. At last I reached Drummond. The sense of relief left me feeling that somehow I would make it to the end. Shortly after this Reg showed up with Ernest in the car. Ernest was so cold he could hardly talk."*

She reached another crisis point at Hillcrest when the day was at its coldest. Once again she was strongly considering giving up, but somehow plodded on hoping to become the third woman in history to (unofficially) finish the race. She had serious misgivings when she reflected that although she was battling against the elements and herself, much as every man in the race was, her efforts would not be officially recognized. If she finished she would not receive a Comrades medal, which all the finishers within the time limit received, nor would she be permitted to wear the cherished blazer. These thoughts soon passed, but once again the temporary anger saw her through the bad patch.

"After what seemed to be an eternity I finally caught a glimpse of the sky-scrapers of Durban in the distance. It was like a new day dawning. I was maintaining a steady pace and during these latter stages of the race I had started to pass a number of runners. Even without the extreme weather, very few people expected me to finish and so when I entered the finishing ground at a little after four o'clock on that miserable Monday afternoon, it was to the astonishment of the race organizers, the media and my club mates. After enduring those extreme conditions for 10 hours and 7 minutes I would never say 'never' again."

DISCOVERING HIDDEN STRENGTH

It was a moment of far more than physical triumph, and it was far more than just anger that had seen her through the exhaustion, and the *"extreme cold, rain and a howling wind for most of the course. There were plenty of people encouraging me, but a thousand times I just wanted to give up. I began to realize that to become a good athlete, the challenge was not merely a physical one but a more spiritual one."*

That spiritual challenge was also rooted in a very deep need, a need that meant that far too much was at stake for her to admit defeat. Her early life as a spineless failure haunted her: *"I was fighting the demons of my past and subconsciously I seemed to sense that if I could persist I would overcome them and the achievement would mean a new start for me. That was when I first recognized the power of the mind and realized that what we become is what we choose to become...*"

What this meant in her life only became completely clear with time. A fellow participant put it this way: "In retrospect that first Comrades was not merely a milestone but was the turning point of her life. You see, until then her running had been a purely physical thing. The Comrades demanded something more than just that. Since then running has become almost a way of life. In the course of that first Comrades she discovered for herself the meaning of 'mind over matter'. To complete that run her mind had to enforce its will over the body. When she got to the end of that torture trail, and looked back, she could recognize a thousand places where she just wanted to give in and yet a thousand places where she just kept on. She now knew the meaning of discipline and perseverance. From the Comrades a new chapter was begun."

Not surprisingly, Mavis called her own account of this first Comrades: *Discovering Hidden Strength.*

The next year she completed the Comrades again, and went on to finish six more times, in 1971, 1973, 1976, 1977, 1980 and 1981.

THE DIGNITY OF WOMAN

Toward the end of race day in 1965 she made a memorable appearance. A fellow participant in the race recorded: "That evening after the Comrades the hotels of Durban were filled with hundreds of normally healthy-looking men, worse for the wear as they hobbled, limped and groaned their way about the hotel. A group of us had gathered in the foyer of our hotel just before supper and it was painfully obvious we had just completed the toughest marathon in the world. Mavis was the only woman to have run that year and we were all speculating on how poor Mavis must be feeling. You can well imagine our amazement when Mavis walked out of the lift looking her elegant best (described by Mavis as "*a 'smart dress' and high black-and-white heels*") and without any signs of distress.

When asked how she could wear such high heels after that grueling race, she replied, 'I am a woman, and as such have a certain dignity to maintain.'" Mavis commented later that she was determined not to let the men know she was suffering.

By finishing with a touch of style, she hadn't let down her 'side' or any of the 'wonderful' people along the road, who had cheered her all the way. More payback for skeptics came the next day.

"At breakfast the next day Eddie Pritchard, one of my club mates, came to our table to commiserate with me, thinking that I had given up. 'Mavis, don't be too upset. It was not possible for any woman to withstand the severe conditions. I am sure you will be able to try again.' What a good feeling it was to be able to see his reaction when I told him I had in fact finished, and in a credible time considering the weather."

It seems that almost all the runners and many of their seconds were very stiff and sore the next day, but there was one exception. Bernard Gomersall from the rainy land of England had found the weather ideal, and won the race in record time with South Africa's Jackie Mekler second.

The one thing Gomersall feared was heat, and there hadn't been much of that.

But Mavis' mind had moved beyond the weather to her own situation. She decided not to complain about her unofficial status, and ran another three Comrades before attitudes changed. Medals for those four runs would arrive years later.

"I would like to believe that those early efforts pioneered the acceptance of women's road running in South Africa. I was not expecting women to be given any special concessions or privileges – all I wanted was to have my efforts recorded and recognized. Women runners experience the same hardships as men, so my feeling was: why deny us the small reward of an official finish in the country's premier road race?"

DEEPER RECESSES OF THE MIND

Mavis' first Comrades still holds a very special place in her memory.

"It confirmed what I had begun to learn during the 50-mile walks, that to succeed in achieving one's goals does not merely require a physical response. Running my first Comrades demanded something more of me than that. On reflection I can now see that on that day the seed was planted for real growth in my life. In the process of running that 86 km I stumbled into the deeper recesses of the mind."

"I could recognize a thousand places where I just wanted to give in, and yet a thousand times I kept going. That was the first time my mind was able

to force its will over my body. The experience introduced a new dimension into my life."

She had become aware that forces deep in the mind and spirit are the key to opening doors to fulfillment.

For years after her first Comrades, as she tested her limits over and over again, Mavis continued to think about what she had learned about endurance and success against the odds. As she continued to develop her deep love for athletics, running longer and longer distances, she further developed an exhilarating sense of physical well-being which had eluded her for most of her early years, gaining a sense of how wonderful an instrument the body is, especially when it is finely tuned.

With the physical in place and the mind in control, she could now steer her life to some purpose.

"It seemed as if up until then I had gone through life rather aimlessly, like a piece of driftwood being dashed to and fro on the ocean of life. In overcoming that first great challenge, I had to find the self-discipline which is required to succeed and which, as a consequence, leads to self-belief. Running introduced a definite purpose in my life. It was to become the vehicle through which I would make the most of my talents."

What was so special about running?

"The beauty of running is that it is so uncomplicated. It needs no elaborate facilities, nor does it have complex rules, nor is one dependent on others to be able to run. You run to suit yourself. You need only run as far and as fast as you are individually capable. All you need is a comfortable pair of running shoes; it is as simple as that."

The experience also taught her about the folly of pride:

"Running is a great leveler. When we are reduced to running gear and to sweating it out on the open road there is not much to distinguish you from your fellow man or woman. There is no facade, and there are no material trappings to hide behind. It does not really matter whether you are a doctor or dustman, university professor or meter reader. On the open road we are all reduced to one common denominator – HUMAN BEINGS."

And those human beings reached out to each other.

"Although distance athletes are generally portrayed as 'the lonely breed', I have found the more outstanding feature to be companionship. There is a very strong feeling of comradeship (which, after all, is what the 'Comrades' is all *about) among road runners. There certainly is a definite bond, a down-to-earth sort of fellowship among these marathon and ultramarathon runners."*

MADAM YOU MAY PASS

However, there were always those who had a tougher time with comradeship across the gender line than others. At least one man in the 1965 Comrades was absolutely 'determined not to be beaten by a woman. She caught up with this 'little chap' about halfway.

"Every Comrades is a story of its own, and every runner has a story to tell, comedy as well as tragedy...each time I caught up with this 'gentleman', he would grit his teeth and accelerate away from me saying, "No woman is going to beat me," or "Oh no, not you again." The struggle was painfully obvious. This cat-and-mouse game continued for many kilometers until eventually he could hold off the challenge no more. Finally he stopped, turned to me and said, "I give in Madam. You may pass."

He was on the wrong side of Comrades history in any event. Frances Hayward had finished ahead of two of the 29 men who ran in 1923, and Geraldine Watson ahead of 15 of the 56 men who completed the race a decade later.

Comrades memories still linger with Mavis, of those who tried to help, those who might have been inspired, those who did things almost guaranteed to make them fail...

"I often wonder about a young boy who gave me his beret to wear during one of my runs. He was at the finish to applaud me in and collect his beret; I wonder if he has been inspired to run the Comrades? I also have wonderful memories of the considerate man who gave me his rain coat toward the end of that first race. Then there was the man who gave me some magic potion near the end of a race. After one mouthful I realized I would be in serious trouble if I had another; finishing on a high in this instance would have had a different connotation. At the start of one race there were some seconds in a lorry looking after a team of runners who were giving them some kind of wine from a big glass vat. You could smell the wine a mile away. They were very rowdy and jolly but I wonder if they ever finished?"

And there was the memory of Geraldine Watson, the formidable woman who'd finished the Comrades in 1931 and 1933, and who appeared along the course in 1965 to cheer that year's runners (including Mavis), just as she'd done for many years. 'Lots of encouragement' from Geraldine Watson helped Mavis over the hills through the rain and cold.

Left: Mavis in her 1st Comrades. Right: Mavis and fellow marathoner Lettie van Zyl training together for a later Comrades run. Picture on right by Frank Black, The Star.

FINISHERS WANTED

That's what made the difference in her first Comrades. Neither the training nor the race were especially 'jolly' – but she finished. Walking or running, she *would* keep going, defying the demons of her past through torrential rain, howling winds and cold until she reached the finish. She'd learned the satisfaction of living by Thomas Monson's often-quoted slogan: 'Finishers Wanted", although it would be many years before she heard his name.

Mavis would never again be the only woman to run the Comrades. Inspired by her example, two women joined her at the starting line the next year.

Six years and several Comrades later, they let her order an official Comrades blazer. Ten years after Mavis' pioneering Comrades run, women were finally allowed to enter officially -- but only half of them. In a curious turn of the rules, only two of the four women in the Comrades that year were allowed to be 'official'. Fittingly, one of them was Mavis.

---

[1] *The 800m run for women was only added to the Olympics in 1960, and the 1500m in 1972.*

[2] *Quoted from writer Nathan Broido.*

[3] *Geraldine Watson ran the Comrades in 1931 and 1933. Apparently feeling a need for a greater challenge, she entered a 100-mile road race in Durban, South Africa in 1934, finishing in less than 23 hours. According to Andy Milroy's 'History of the 24hr race', "Geraldine Watson was a very tough individual who would set off on very long walks – 200 miles was quite an ordinary sort of distance for her – with only a small automatic pistol for protection." Her 100-mile record stood for 37 years until Mavis ran the distance slightly faster in 1971. As far as we know, however, Mavis never carried a gun.*

Chapter 7: MOVING MOUNTAINS
Belcher's Goat Scramble

———————•┅●┅•———————

"This race is tough! Never again. It's the toughest obstacle in the whole world". (Wally Hayward, record-setter in the 100-mile race, the 24-hour race, the Comrades ultramarathon and others)

Mavis, who knew Wally Hayward, wasn't put off by his reaction to the notorious Harrismith Mountain Race. Five months after she proved that the Comrades wasn't just a race for 'men, tough men', 40-year-old Mavis was ready to pit her strength and stamina against Harrismith's towering Platteberg, a 7800-foot mesa in the NE corner of South Africa's 'Orange Free State'.

A newspaper article put it this way: "For the first time in its long history, a woman is to tackle South Africa's most punishing race – the 10½ mile Harrismith mountain race on Saturday." However, after her Comrades triumph the media were wise to her abilities. "Mrs. Hutchinson is expected to finish the race comfortably."

But not because it was easy. The race began in 1904, while a Major A.E. Belcher was visiting the town of Harrismith where he'd been stationed during the Anglo-Boer War. Not liking Belcher's repeated references to the Platteberg as 'that small hill of yours", a local resident bet that Belcher couldn't get to the top in less than an hour.

Belcher won the bet by 8 minutes, and the race has been run every October since then, with a special Belcher trophy for the first runner who reaches the top of the mountain. The following (from a South African guide to the race) gives an idea: "You run the first 3 km from town, and from there it's a grueling climb up the slopes of the Platteberg. Stock up well at the first watering point, for it is a tough climb to…the base of One-Man pass.…you come to the knee jerking, quadriceps ripping downhill run…Your legs will take a beating…" Streams, huge gullies, barbed wire fences, snow storms and cloudbursts are all part of the fun.

A record 87 of South Africa's best runners entered the race in 1965, and snow was falling on top of the mountain at the start. Mavis started a bit briskly – at first. "*I went out too fast and soon realized what I was doing and settled down.*" Her experience with Anne McKenzie had paid off again.

"*Once I got to the foot of the Platteberg I found it was so steep I had to go up on all fours grabbing support where I found a hold.*" If she needed to be a mountain goat, so be it. An enterprising photographer asked her to smile for a picture as she reached the top, but "*I was so frozen I could feel the ice crack on my lips as I tried to smile.*"

After three miles of running along the top of the mountain, it was time for the descent, where Mavis had to run sideways to prevent going head over heels through the dense bush and trees. In her notes, she describes it as a downward plunge through streams, deep gullies and mountain passes, with lots of loose stones which made things more difficult. Climbing over a barbed wire fence gave her a gash in her leg that was still bleeding badly as she crossed the finish line.

New records had been set in all stages of the race, but three men finished after her, and her time of 95 minutes would still be considered respectable today, matching the winning times for women in 1999, 2001 and 2005.

CHALLENGING ALL RUGBY PLAYERS

So impressed was her coach/mentor Fred Morrison that he issued a challenge the following year to South Africa's rugby players, saying that he would only consider the players fit if they could run with Mavis for 80 minutes. Mavis was a bit embarrassed. "This was Fred's doing, not mine. I never agreed to it and was surprised when the press asked me about it." The rugby players never did respond.

Running along the top of the Platteberg

1966: MAY THE BEST WOMAN WIN...

Apparently unable to resist the punishment, Mavis ran at Harrismith again the next year – but this time there was another woman in the race, Mrs. A. De Wit from Harrismith. She was younger and looked very fit, not to mention rather formidable compared to 'wisp of a woman' Mavis. Harrismith residents were sure their local heroine had the edge.

And at the start of the race Mrs. De Wit raced ahead – much too fast. She was already slowing down as Mavis passed her just before the climb up the mountain, and Mavis stayed ahead for the rest of the race. Despite her poor pacing, Mavis' rival did finish – although so exhausted that she collapsed and needed attention from the first aid team. Mavis comments, "I know what she felt like – I've been there." And she had.

Mrs. De Wit didn't have the advantage of Mavis' painful lesson in pacing at the hands of the great Anne McKenzie. On that day at Zoo Lake two years before, it was Mavis who raced ahead only to drag far behind at the finish, exhausted.

1971: THE DOUBLE PIRATE

Mavis and her clubmates were pleased at this victory, but it was to be another five years before she once more appeared in Harrismith – this time as a 'pirate runner'.

In 1970, Sergeant Dennis Read (age 47) had collapsed and died at the end of the Mountain Race. Despite the fact that no less than 14 women had competed successfully, beating many of the men, the Free State Amateur Athletic Association banned all female runners, and all male runners under 17 or over 40. Even those meeting the age and gender requirements were to have a medical certificate of fitness.

The organizers of the race were far from pleased, especially since the number of entries dropped drastically, and defied the Athletic Association by inviting Mavis, along with male runners outside the age limits. A town council member, Arthur Kennedy, told a newspaper reporter, "Please tell Mavis we simply adore her and that she must run in the race...We will give her a wonderful welcome." Mavis felt she 'was not very fit', possibly because she had run a 24-hour ultramarathon only two months before, but she came.

Twenty-four other 'pirate runners' were there too, including Fred Morrison, Mavis' friend and mentor, and president of her running club.

Sixty-six years old, he was definitely not welcomed by the Free State Athletic Association official sent to make sure that the new rules were kept. His attempt to keep the 'illegal' runners from starting ended in farce when Fred Morrison pointed out: "This is a public road and you cannot stop us from running on it."

All 25 'illegal' runners finished, and the 'wonderful welcome' was very evident. A newspaper report said Mavis was the 'biggest attraction in the field of 137, and received the warmest ovation when she crossed the finishing line." Despite her supposed lack of fitness, she had no trouble finishing and said afterwards, "I enjoyed it immensely and had no ill effects. I intend running again next year." That never happened, but Mavis had enjoyed her outing as a 'double pirate' (both over 40 and female).

Arthur Kennedy gets the last word: "We were delighted that Mrs. Hutchison ran. She is a great favorite here and will always receive a big welcome."

DESERT PRINCESS

Mavis' next invitation was to another challenging race, 50 miles over dubious roads through the desert hills and mountains of South Africa's Great Karoo. This was a new race, first held the same October as Mavis' pirate excursion to Harrismith. Twenty men had started that year, though only 14 finished.

Not long after that inaugural Karoo Marathon, noted Sunday Express sports writer Sam Mirwis wrote about the invitation under the headline: "Karoo Welcomes A Princess." Mavis received her invitation to the next year's race through the Express from one of the organizers (also a keen distance runner) whom she beat in the 1971 Comrades. "Please tell Mrs Hutchison that her presence here next year will be appreciated by everyone in the Karoo and we shall welcome her as a princess." She was assured there would be at least one other lady in the race, as well as some leading South African distance runners. According to Mirwis: "The people of the Karoo can expect to see the slim, greying Mrs. Hutchison in action next year".[1]

Whatever may have happened in 1972, newspaper articles make it clear that she completed the race in 1974, and was once more the first woman to manage it. The first stretch of 17 miles wasn't too bad. This followed the National Road from the 100-year-old town of Laingsburg over mild hills to the pretty tourist village of Matjiesfontein.

But when she turned off the main road, things started to change. By this time it had become 'extremely hot', and the road to the remote town of Sutherland was in shockingly bad condition, leading over energy-sapping mountains and hills for 12 miles.

The last stretch, 21 hilly miles of gravel and stones in extreme heat, was even more exhausting. 9 hours and 17 minutes after the start, she arrived in Laingsburg amid great applause, ahead of 11 of the 49 men in the race, but she wasn't the only hero of the day. Running 47th was her friend, the 72-year-old blind runner Ian Jardine. The race wasn't without its moments of beauty, but Ian Jardine was the one competitor that day who couldn't see the abundant late spring flowers.

---

[1] *There's no record indicating that Mavis ran the 1972 Karoo Marathon. What definitely did happen in 1972 is that Mavis entered the Swaziland Marathon, run over tar and gravel through the green hills and mountains of this tiny landlocked African kingdom. This may have been a standard marathon – Mavis thinks it was – but information about the race is hard to come by as it's no longer run. Entering the race that year were some 30 or so men and one black woman – Swaziland was a black African kingdom where 'apartheid' wasn't a feature. Mavis' coach Fred Morrison was there, and told Mavis that "If you let her beat you, I'm not speaking with you again." He needn't have worried. Like Mrs. De Wit, the woman started too fast and was 'totally finished' by the end of the race. Mavis beat her easily.*

Chapter 8: LET THE LASSIES RUN
'Women Racing in Mud'

———•·•·•———

"Never in South Africa's athletic history has a tour been carried through under more difficult circumstances, and never has a South African athletic team received so little credit for performing so well against international competition." (I.H. Mark, tour organizer)

A UNIQUELY SOCIAL SPORT

Mavis was by no means a champion at everything she tried – her outstanding contribution to women's cross-country running had little to do with setting records, but much to do with her enthusiasm, mentoring, organization and leadership, as well as her love for youth. It was for these qualities that she was chosen to lead the first overseas tour for South African women's cross-country. It was Mavis who kept her young 'off-track girls' on track.

It may be a bit ironic that the sport that got her into running is the one thing she enjoyed in which she never set a record or became a champion, but stardom was never the attraction.

For Mavis, It was the uniquely social nature of cross-country that made it far more enjoyable than ordinary track running. *"But in cross-country the spectators are part of the whole thing, the athletes and officials all mix…If there are big runners, you can chat to them, get tips from them."*

Soon there was a league for women, and *"…every Saturday we would be running at a different venue, where different clubs would host it."* Mavis was both an enthusiastic participant and organizer, elected *"secretary for the whole of cross-country and also ladies' convenor of cross-country,"* as well as captain of her own Johannesburg Harriers team in 1964 – most of whom were as young as her own children.

During the 1960s she continued active in cross-country, even after she became the first South African woman to run the standard marathon, and the first in decades to run the Comrades ultramarathon.

Cross-country races were too short for her to be a great and shining light, but she enjoyed participating anyway, as well as helping younger women achieve their potential. Her skills at organization were widely recognized and crucial in the pioneering days of women's cross-country, so much that she was described as the "king-pin behind the success of her province in women's cross-country, as well as that of her club…"

1969: ANCIENT BUILDINGS, MOON LANDINGS AND POP MUSIC

"….. Mavis will our Mother be…"
(from a poem about the 1965 Johannesburg Harriers cross
country team)

Thus it was not really surprising that Mavis was among the first to raise the idea of a women's cross-country tour of the United Kingdom (where women's cross-country had been a recognized sport since the 1920s), that the fundraising efforts she organized in the southern Transvaal were the most successful in the country, or that her committee organized more trial runs for the tour than the rest of the country combined. Nor was it surprising that Mavis was chosen to manage the eventual team.

It was a remarkably young team, and ironically included no runner from Mavis' Southern Transvaal, "which had dominated women's cross-country since it's inception." It might have been otherwise if Anne McKenzie (four times national cross country champion) had not been unable to compete due to knee problems. The four lucky girls were Meryl Hancock (17), Annalie Gildenhuys (21), Beverley Nieuwenhuizen (17) and Maria Koen (16).

Their plane left around midnight. It was the first plane trip for some of the team, and the first time any of them had left South Africa. For Maria the excitement was tempered by the fact that she became airsick. The first stop in Europe was at Luxembourg the next day, where they found it strange to hear that it would be 'sacrilege' to break down any of the 'terribly ancient' buildings they saw. After all, in Johannesburg old buildings were torn down all the time.

Next day they landed in London, where they encountered television for the first time. Mavis was fascinated by the Apollo moon mission, while the

"the girls loved the programmes with the Pop Music." Daily training began – about 10 miles a day – and they all looked forward to their first competition. That would pit the South African girls against the champion English women's cross-country club, a team that included several British internationals.

Mavis and her girls. From left: Maria Koen, Beverley Nieuwenhuizen, Meryl Hancock, and Annalie Gildenhuys. Picture from Dagbreek.

COLD, MUD, RAIN AND SNOW

"Saturday March 1 was the start of our great adventure — our first run against overseas competition. It was cold, muddy and drizzling, as we arrived at the Cophall Stadium which is the Barnet Club's headquarters at Hendon." In other words, they were definitely in England. It was so dark and misty that little of the course could be seen from any one point, and the course had to be marked with sticks onto which colored paper had been stapled.

Mavis had serious misgivings about facing 'this mighty team' on their first outing. But the the South African girls came in first, second, fifth and sixth. *"...we now knew that we would not be outclassed and that we could hold our own..."*, despite the fact that the women they would face were typically in their middle twenties and far more experienced. Mavis could see that Maria had far too much left at the end of the race, but found it hard to get her to change.

A few days later they ran against another English club, and took four of the first five places in bitter cold. Training and running in the snow was a real novelty for girls who'd never seen snow before. But Mavis thought they actually did better *"because they find the climate so invigorating."* Meanwhile Mavis treated all four with home remedies when they got the flu.

But a more more serious test came at Coventry, a week after the meet at Barnet. All the top English women were there, as well as the entire New Zealand team. The field included five from the English International team, and three from the Scottish team. Not surprisingly the four South African girls didn't win this time, but they weren't disgraced. Meryl missed coming second by inches, Annalie was 7th and Maria Koen 18th.

Annalie Gildenhuys runs ahead.

Not a win, but respectable for four young girls against experienced international competition. And this was with only three girls completing the race – pain in her knee had forced Beverley out of the competition. Mavis rushed off to London to get advice from the physiotherapist to the British Olympic team, who told her Beverley had hurt the muscle under her kneecap and would have to rest for ten days.

In a rematch of sorts against the powerful New Zealanders, the three remaining girls next ran as a cross-country relay team against two New Zealand teams of three, and five club teams. The South African team beat one of the New Zealand teams, but couldn't match the 'A' side that included the New Zealand champion. The club sides ran far behind.

It was in Leeds that Bernard Gomersall, well known in South Africa for his Comrades victories, showed them some of the warmest hospitality they encountered. He and his wife gave up their own bedroom, and introduced the girls to English Music Hall.

But the English weather continued horrible. At Bradford they ran a 2-mile road race in a sub-freezing blizzard. Bernard Gomersall ran ahead to 'lead the way', while the girls often ran with their eyes closed, and in any event could seldom see who was in front of them or behind them. Meryl thought it was 'sensational'; Annalie called it 'ghastly', and said *'the snow beating on my face…was just like lumps of ice pounding at you.'* Snow was piled two feet deep at the side of the course, and some of the girls thought the climate was perhaps a bit too invigorating.

Against a field including a Welsh International and the Yorkshire Schools Champion, they took 1st, 2nd, 4th and 5th.

It was their last race. They would not be allowed to compete in the Women's International Cross-country championships at Clydebank in Scotland. For Meryl, this was a special irony since her mother was a Scot.

BARRED

> *"Four South African lassies are likely to be banned from running in Scotland March 22 because the men fear their presence may cause nations to withdraw their official cross country championships…Let the lassies run."*
> *(Desmond Hackett, London Daily Express, Jan. 20, 1969)*

While they were on tour, the Scottish Cross Country Union had finally decided – that politics in the men's championship would dictate who could participate in the women's event. Although the women wanted the South Africans in, the cash-strapped Scottish Women's Cross Country Union had tried to save money (and attract a larger audience) by staging their race on the same day and in the same stadium as the men, with the sponsorship and organization in the hands of the men.

Tunisia and Morocco, who were members of the International Cross Country Union, advised the men's committee that they would boycott the race if any South Africans ran at the same venue. In the official letter, the *"commit-tee has decided they must uphold the wishes of the member countries of the In-ternational Cross Country Union."* Ironically, the countries wanting South Af-rica banned had no women running at all – a different form of apartheid.[1]

Despite the fact that the banning was not popular, and was con-demned in the press as unchivalrous, it was obvious that the 'old boys' of sport had the deciding vote. Nevertheless the South African team took a bus to the stadium, paid for admission and *"...donned our togs and our tracksuits, and...waited, and prayed for a miracle to happen...Then a pistol was fired. To me and to the girls it did not mean the start of a race, but the end of a struggle, the end of all our hopes...We marvelled at the power run-ning of Doris Brown of America, who had won the title twice before...Soon it was all over. The shouting was over, the race was run. Everyone was happy, justice had been done, honour had been satisfied."*

Maria Koen wrote later, *"It was wonderful to see everyone running, but what broke our hearts was to see the medals given out as the countries' na-tional anthems were played. Our thoughts went to old South Africa."*

Mavis commented, *"It's a great shame. What do these girls know of politics?"*

Fortunately, politics hadn't spread to the athletes themselves. Most of the participants came to Mavis and the girls at the stadium, saying how sorry they were that the girls weren't allowed to compete. Fears of unpleas-antness on the bus trip back to the hotel (where the South Africans and all the athletes were staying) proved totally unfounded. They were simply ac-cepted, and were 'all athletes together'. At the official dinner and dance for the cross country runners that night, the actual competitors (including the Tunisians) thought the South African girls' exclusion was ridiculous and 'sneaked them in'. Irony abounded.

MIGHT HAVE BEENS

What would have been the result if they had competed? Judging by compara-tive times in races where the girls ran against women who were allowed to run, South Africa would have come in fourth, behind the U.S., New Zealand and England but ahead of Ireland, Scotland, Wales and Canada. Not bad for a team of only four young untried girls thought to stand 'not a snowball's chance' be-fore they left, denied Springbok colors and derided for undertaking a tour when they were so 'obviously' unready for serious competition. As Mavis put it, "*We showed that we were the equal of the English and Scottish girls. We were beaten a few times by the New Zealanders but never disgraced.*"

ALL TICKETS PLEASE!

Perhaps the final word should be given to a grinning Scotsman who burst into their train compartment as they rode back to London. They were astonished to hear him shout in Afrikaans, 'Alle kaartjies asseblief!' (All tickets please!), and were delighted to hear him say, "I want to assure you that this is not the way the people of Scotland feel about the whole thing. On behalf of the people of Scotland please apologize to the people of South Africa." With that he disappeared.

---

[1]*The South African men's team had been allowed to compete in 1967, but the UK Cross Country Union's committee decided that future South African teams would not be allowed to participate if South Africa was barred from the Olympics.*

Chapter 9: IN THE CYCLE OF THE SUN
"What Makes a Gran Do This?"

*"What moves a human being to run continuously for 24
hours?...But long distance running is more than a sport –
it is a calling, almost a way of life. It demands more than
mere fitness, team spirit and skill."*
(Sportswriter Sam Mirwis, 1971)

ULTRA DREAMS

For Mavis, the Comrades was really too short to bring out the best in her, and she dreamed of running very long distances on the road. But could she do it? By 1971, she had run many races since her groundbreaking first Comrades in 1965, some more notable than others, but none of them longer than the 54 miles of the Comrades itself.

It was time for a new challenge, and somewhat nervously Mavis decided to run in a much longer race to be run around the track of Hector Norris Park. The objective was not only to run a hundred miles, but (for those who were interested or gluttons for punishment) to run as far as possible in 24 hours.

Preparing meant three months of intensive training, which included hours after work on weekdays, and 8 hours a day on weekends.

She said at the time that her training didn't include extensive road work, but that it was usually on the track. Said Mavis: "*I sometimes do a bit of road work, but people pass remarks and some men even try to pick me up – until they see my gray hair!*"

Mavis noted later that this event was really the beginning, or setting of the stage for her really long ultraruns in the years that followed. It gave her confidence, valuable experience, and her first world records.

With Liberty and Toilets for All...Men

> *"How far can a man run in the cycle of the sun?" (slogan for*
> *a 24 hour race in the 1980s – when it was still apparently*
> *unnecessary to mention women!)*

She was the only woman to enter the race, but the 51 men included a number of leading South African long distance runners. Her son Allan, then 22, was also in the line-up but dropped out after about 35 miles due to cartilage problems.

A 'very nervous indeed' Mavis reported for the run at about 12:30 in the stadium. *"I was unsure of my ability to finish 100 miles nonstop on the track."* It must have helped her nerves a bit that family members Ernie, Allan, Ron and Dianne were there as promised to second her.

But there were those who would have preferred not to have her there on that hot August afternoon. Many of those in the world of athletics who knew her thought she had bitten off more than a woman could chew. *"My club was not too happy about my entering. They thought I was a bit overambitious to undertake such a run."*

Jealousy may have played a role as well, as the press were perhaps more fascinated by Mavis' daring attempt than by the male runners who were likely to run farther and faster.

And although this time Mavis was an official entry in the race, the official establishment still had a hard time giving women distance runners full official acceptance. In keeping with this attitude, all toilets near the track were reserved for men only, while Mavis had to leave the track and climb up long flights of steps to the ladies'.

As she ran endlessly around the track under the hot afternoon sun, the naysayers saw Mavis start to set new records for women, first for 25 miles, then for fifty. She was running strongly as night fell, keeping a steady pace in her tracksuit. But she still had lessons to learn. On a really long run, you begin to need refueling. *"I was not feeding at all which was very dangerous."*

Climbing about 200 to 300 meters to the toilet she was permitted to use began to drain her energy. In a considerable understatement, her notes laconically say, *"It was uphill which was not good."*

FEEDING THE RUNNER

By seven in the morning, the officials could see Mavis was in trouble. *"I was not feeling too good at all. Ernie was advised to take me off. I think the race organizers were afraid I would collapse on the track and the race would get a lot of unfavorable publicity."*

Thanks to Mavis' failure to take any nourishment, their fears were not altogether unfounded. After one more climb up the steps, *"I went to the toilet and collapsed. When I recovered, I was lying on a bench in the change rooms."*

But a fainting spell wasn't going to stop her. *"I waited for about five minutes or so to make sure I was feeling steady, then returned to the track to continue."*

The powers in charge got even more unhappy. *"When the officials found out what had happened, they were very concerned. They asked Ernie again to withdraw me from the race. I refused of course."*

Her inexperienced seconds now realized what was causing her condition, and made sure she ate something before trying to go on.

FEEDING THE RECORD BOOK

After 21 and a half hours, she and her seconds realized that she could actually break the 100-mile women's record. Curiously, her only competition was also South African. The inescapable Geraldine Watson had taken 22 hours and 22 minutes to run 100 miles 'on a circular road course' in Durban in 1934 (unofficially of course), despite weather that changed to rain and gale force winds after the first nine hours. More recently, Cathy Burgess had run the same distance on a Cape Town track in 22 hours and 46 minutes in 1963. A heartened Mavis soldiered on to beat both of them. *"You have no idea how I felt when I completed 100 miles in 22 hours 15 minutes and 42 seconds."* Presumably the race officials should now also have felt better.

But she wasn't done yet. In a show of the same determination and stamina that would mark her later ultraruns, *"I then indicated to my seconds that I intended running for 24 hours."* Mavis wasn't tearing up the track with her speed, but at the end of 24 hours she had covered 106 miles and 736 yards. She now held the women's records for 25, 50, 75 and 100 miles (road and track), as well as being the first woman ever to run for 24 hours. With access to a toilet on the track (like the men), there would have been far less time lost. But she still managed several world records, and her fans and family were justifiably proud.

Her effort had earned her the privilege of becoming only the third woman 'centurion' in the world. Those who have that title can claim membership in the most exclusive long distance club on the globe, as to qualify you must run at least 100 miles in 24 hours or less.

Her 400 trips around the track had clearly demonstrated her extraordinary perseverance, a quality that would stand her in good stead throughout her long distance running career, and that set her apart as an athlete. This slightly framed but wiry woman, described at the time by a Johannesburg reporter as having the figure of a 20-year old, wasn't always the very fastest, but she had staying power second to none. The only times she'd come off the Hector Norris track were for badly needed rubdowns of a just few minutes each and for those long climbs up to the ladies'.

Those last miles had been hard, but sportswriter Sam Mirwis wrote that she "gritted her teeth and carried on. In the last 14 laps she lapped one man from Natal seven times."

PASSING OUT WHEN YOU GET HOME

At the end of the race, "*when the gun went off there was much excitement. Everybody was running with me including the press.*" Mavis asked permission to thank her husband Ernie. "*I put a laurel wreath around his neck. There were a few damp eyes while this was being done.*"

Two of the damp eyes belonged to her sister Doreen. Her twin, now Doreen Wilkins, couldn't contain herself and burst into tears when Mavis crossed the finish line. "*It was likely from sheer relief since she worried a great deal about me during the race,*" Mavis concluded. Still very tuned in to her twin, Doreen could literally feel the physical impact of her sister's achievement as no one else could.

Additional excitement was caused by the race officials, who were still afraid that a 'fragile' Mavis might collapse. With stretcher in hand, an ambulance crew rushed onto the track expecting Mavis to pass out any moment. It was typical of her sense of humor that she told them, "*If I want to pass out , I'll wait till I get home!*"

Maybe she should have added that she planned to go dancing with her husband that evening.

Of the 52 who had started the race, 20 men and Mavis finished. She was 47 years old.

DANCING AND GOSSIP

After the race, Mavis *"went home and had a good sleep, woke up and had a bath, then went back to sleep."* By then she was recovered enough to go off with Ernie, and dance at a local athletic club's 50th anniversary dinner. She later commented to the news media: *"Surprisingly, afterwards I did not feel exhausted, though the tops of my legs were sore."*

But she did go home at midnight, as by then she was finally 'rather tired'.

Reporters became so excited about her feat that it may have overshadowed the achievements of the 20 men who'd finished. And her gray hair did not cloud the vision of the rest of her physical self for papers such as the *Southern Courier*. That publication adopted her as 'our Mavis', the pride and joy of Johannesburg's Southern Suburbs, according to an August 1972 writeup. It enthusiastically described her as a "superlative flesh and blood machine. A machine of tireless energy, vitality and strength that can run for mile after grueling mile, hour after hour, in almost perpetual motion with few signs of exhaustion."

This press enthusiasm had unpleasant consequences. She had drawn so much coverage that some of the male members of her club who had 'officially' been in the race became seriously unpleasant. Women also had nasty things to say.

"It was hard to cope with the gossip that followed. I became very distressed about it. But I guess that was to be expected since I had already faced similar nastiness from those who thought I was press hungry, like the one acquaintance who thought I ran just to get my picture in the paper. No doubt she doesn't realize the time and hard work involved. It's just as well I don't mutter when I'm running."

There were many good memories of the ten years with Johannesburg Harriers, and she had worked hard for the club, but the stories of what was being said caused her to *"nearly make myself sick over the whole affair."* She resigned and joined Germiston Callies Harriers, the club where she went dancing after the race.

In later years, she reflected that *"if the same should happen again I would take no notice at all. It would have no effect on me whatsoever."* As she matured and grew a thicker skin, she remembered how much her old club *"has done for me and my running. It is a great club with great people I have a tremendous love for."*

She made a point of mentioning how once again mentor Fred Morrison was very helpful to her, as was Wally Hayward, who was there to start her and the other athletes off. Wally was the holder of the men's world record for the 100 mile and the 24 hour run, set at Motspur Park in Britain 18 years before. He 'blazed through' the 100 mile mark more than two hours faster than anyone before him, and labored onward to complete 159 miles 562 yards after 24 hours. That record would stand for twenty years, and his 100-mile record even longer. He would assist her two years later in her 24-hour walk.

INTERMEZZO – BRUSHES WITH THE 'BROTHERHOOD'

Before and after this landmark race, she'd hoped to participate in a number of runs in the UK: The Two Bridges run in Scotland, the London-to-Brighton walk and London-to -Brighton run over 52 miles, and the 24hr run at Walton-on-Thames where Wally Hayward set up his world record in 1953. But these dreams died when she learned she would not only have to run unofficially, but start at least an hour after the men to erase any impression that she was really part of the race at all.

"The organizers' reply to my inquiries was that women and men were not allowed to compete in the same race and therefore, if women lined up with the men, the race could be declared null and void. They informed me that to overcome that obstacle I could leave an hour after the race started. This offer was meaningless to me. At least in South Africa race organizers would allow me to start an hour before the race. That way, as the race leaders caught up with me, I would be part of the race and my time was taken and recorded."

"I was very disappointed..."

Losing the chance to run in the London to Brighton race must have been a particular disappointment, as this was the unofficial distance running world championship at the time.

Initially it looked as if race walking in Britain might be a better bet.

"...I must mention that when I asked the Race Walkers Organization to allow me to take part in the London-to-Brighton Walk, they were very cooperative

and said that although I could not take part as an official entry, they would look after me on the road. I was excited and started to prepare for the race, following a very strenuous training program for many months.

"But just prior to leaving for England I received a letter telling me their offer to allow me to walk still stood, but that I would have to leave an hour after the race started. The 'brotherhood' had struck again. I decided that the effort, the cost and the distance I had to go to get there and still not to be part of the race was no longer worth it. To my great disappointment I had to let it go."

It was time to try other things.

A 24 Hour Walk

Two years after her 24 hour run, Mavis tried for a double by entering the first 24 hour/100 mile *walk* ever held in South Africa. She'd just run her fourth (and fastest) Comrades, finishing in 9 hours 7 minutes despite a broken wrist.

Press photos of the 24 hour walk. Left:Early in the race..
Right: Exhausted after the finish.

The race began on the afternoon of July 8, 1973 on Germiston's Delville track, with a big crowd sendoff, and volunteers from her new club (Germiston Callies) walking with her at times to help her combat fatigue and boredom.

Participants would be race walking, a rather energy-intensive, prescribed athletic style, very far removed from ordinary fast walking.

Hubby Ernie was there to second her, assisted by sons Allan and Ron. Wally Hayward (who had already completed a 24 hour/100 mile walk himself, but not on a track), and sister Doreen did the lap scoring. Jess and his wife were there to see her off, but soon had to head back to Cape Town, nearly 1000 miles away. He needed to be at work after the weekend.

Another relative was less of an asset. Her brother-in-law Reg Wilkins 'helped' by shouting at her each time her circuit of the track brought her near where he was standing, which Mavis found 'most disturbing'.

As Mavis relentlessly strode around the track, and the sun sank below the horizon, the temperature that winter's night dropped well below freezing, but she was set on giving her utmost.

It wasn't a painless affair for Mavis. One of three well meaning men who walked with her during the night shift to keep her company 'helped' by tightening a loose shoelace a bit too much. She could feel that this was cutting off her circulation, but she carried on, "*telling myself I was imagining all this as I was tired and was looking for excuses. Very foolish of me.*"

After six hours of increasing discomfort, she asked her seconds to loosen her shoelaces while she paused for a rubdown. "*The relief was great but unfortunately I had waited too long. My foot was very badly swollen…*" After the shoelace was relaxed "*I just had to carry on, foot problems or not, which is what I did.*"

As the 'cycle of the sun' brought a new dawn, the cold continued. And as she came near the 100 mile mark, she encountered a peculiarly South African hazard. Seconds and club members were sitting around the fires barbecuing and keeping warm, and the smoke caught her full in the eyes, causing her to falter briefly. Then an icy wind blasted her as she came out of the bend onto the back straight. But mentor Fred Morrison helped her half frozen seconds keep her going, and Doreen and Wally never left their posts though they were more than half frozen at their lap scoring table.

After completing 100 miles in world record time, with 12 minutes to spare, with a foot by now so badly swollen and painful that it took her out of commission for weeks afterward, she limped on for another 340 yards before the 24 hours were up. Fred Morrison described the race as one of her best achievements, and it is hard to say what she might have managed without the injured foot.

One press photo shows an optimistic Mavis with an infectious grin as she strides through the early stages of the race. Another shows Ernie leading an exhausted, pain-racked Mavis away from the track after the finish, wrapped in a blanket. She'd lost the grin.

But again training hard had paid off – she'd averaged six-and-a-half hours daily.

1973 been a truly remarkable year. Besides the 24 hour walk and her fourth and fastest Comrades Marathon, she'd come first in yet another Rand Daily Mail Big Walk – and become the first woman ever to run the 374 miles from the Johannesburg area across the mountains to Durban on the coast. Not surprisingly, people were beginning to suggest her for South African Woman of the Year.

Chapter 10: OVER THE DRAGON'S SPINE
Daring to Dream

"She's the greatest woman long distance runner there has ever been, and only a major injury will stop her from reaching Durban." (Wally Hayward, 24 hour record holder for more than two decades)

A BUMP IN THE ROAD

The 374 mile[1] ultra marathon from the high plateau around Johannesburg, over the rugged Drakensberg (Dragon Mountains) and down to the coast, began with a 'daydream'. *"I was on my way home from a holiday in the beautiful Drakensberg mountains in Natal, when, whilst watching the road, I dreamed of running from Johannesburg to Durban, a distance of about 600 kilometers. A bump in the road brought me back to reality and I relegated the idea to the recesses of my mind, thinking it to be sheer fantasy."*

Like many of her dreams, it didn't stay fantasy, although this was much further than any woman had ever run. A first taste of the real thing came just after she got home. *"I received a phone call from Ian Jardine, a blind distance road runner, to ask if I would join him on his first day of an ultra-ultra-marathon he had planned...the very run that I had been thinking of, a run from Johannesburg to Durban...As a blind runner, Ian needed to be led by a sighted athlete...and I had the privilege of providing that assistance on the first day."*

Mavis naturally mentioned her 'daydream' as they ran, and his response was *"sufficiently positive to keep me working at it"*. Her family responded very differently. They couldn't grasp why *"I wanted to put myself through such an arduous ordeal. They felt I had nothing more to prove."*

The Brotherhood Taketh Away, But the Family Giveth In

Her family's attitude changed after her dreams of UK competition in shorter races fell through. Not long after the above conversations with Jardine and her family, she got the news that race organizers in Britain would not let her participate under conditions she found meaningful.

Ernest could see only too clearly how this setback hit Mavis, and to compensate he finally agreed that they could begin planning for 'the big one', with one slight variation. By this time Mavis had left Johannesburg Harriers to join the Germiston Callies athletic club, and to honor the club which had given her so much encouragement and support they switched the starting point to the suburb of Germiston. The plan was on, but it would still take three years to make the 'daydream' a reality.

Dreaming, One Step At A Time

"I have this desire for achievement." (Mavis Hutchison)

Why did this gutsy gran want to blaze a trail by running a distance no women, and very few men, had attempted?

Her 24 hour run had already established her as a world class long distance runner, but the long lonely miles of the open road drew still drew her. *"What it did for me was to open my mind and heart to the possibility of achieving those hidden teenage aspirations and, in so doing, providing me with a whole new view of, and lease on, life."*

How did she get there? The answer she sometimes gave is a bit less romantic: *"Probably by brute force and ignorance."*

"The lesson I was beginning to learn was that everything is obtained by degrees. I discovered by experience how all challenges can be successfully concluded - simply by moving forward one step at a time."

And so she was going to take another step. She was going to dare to dream. Subsequently, the operative phrase in the Hutchison household became, *"If you want your dreams to come true, wake up!"*

That's what would drive her on until she concluded this giant undertaking that put her so sorely to the test. She told people that she definitely wasn't trying to prove that she was *"better than other women, and least of all that she was better than some men."* It was the challenge itself that drew her. And it was something she could still do in her late forties: *"I decided to do the Durban run because I felt I was at my fitness peak, mentally and physically. To get any reasonable success at running, I decided ultra long distances were my thing, as I did not have the speed of my younger rivals."*

A LATE START IN THE DARK

"I never had the slightest doubt of her success."
(Ernest Hutchison)

At the start of the Germiston to Durban run.
Press photo probably by Frank Black of The Star.

As the clock chimed 4 am on October 14, 1973, the mayor of Germiston and other dignitaries were there in the darkness to start her off.

Mavis was late, which left some of the supporters and spectators speculating that she had got cold feet. When she got there, the collective sigh of relief was audible. Nobody likes to get up for a 4 am event that doesn't come off.

As usual at the start of a long run, she was nervous. *"As with all great challenges, doubts and misgivings fed my apprehension. Had I been too ambitious this time?"* Few thought a woman could actually complete such a mammoth run, especially at age 48, but there were true believers. Trainer and mentor Fred Morrison was one of them. So certain was he that he volunteered to join Ernie on her support team. So did Don Shepherd, one of the handful of men who'd run from Johannesburg to Durban. For a race this long, she'd need seconds, and Don's experience was more than welcome.

She was fit and healthy that morning. The swollen foot that had plagued her in the 100 mile walk had healed, as had the wrist she'd broken earlier that year in a car accident. Her doctor had pronounced her 'in magnificent shape'. She'd trained hard, perhaps even too hard. But this *was* a longer, harder run than any other woman had ever attempted.

As she started off to the cheers of the crowd, carrying a message to the mayor of Durban, she had a prayer in her heart, thinking *"This is it!"*

She had company as she ran off through the streets of Germiston. Many of her clubmates spent that first morning on the road with her. John Ball, holder of the record for the Johannesburg to Durban run, had come from faraway East London on the south coast to be at the start and run part of the first day with Mavis.

Wally Hayward, veteran distance runner and friend, also 'joined the troops' that day, and in the afternoon Springbok athlete Lew Leppan and his wife Trish joined her for a while. They and Dannie Oosterhuyzen *"came out in the afternoon to help me get off to a good start."*

Mavis also had the company of a press team from the Star, a leading Johannesburg daily. Photographer Frank Black and reporter Launa Hickling stayed with her as far as Van Reenen's Pass on the Natal border. They covered the run continuously while other newspapers *"merely sent reporters from time to time."*

It all began so well that it seemed easy.

"I was absolutely thrilled with my first day's performance. Everything seemed to be going right. I came off the road at about 6.30pm, having completed 117 kilometers for the day, which I considered to be an excellent achievement. After having marked the road where I had stopped, we headed to Villiers for the night. I was to spend all my overnight stops at the nearest hotels to the stopping points. In retrospect I realize that many hours were wasted riding to and from these points."

She didn't push too hard the first three days by design, she told the press. She figured if she did she could 'blow up'. *"God forbid"*, she said. *"I have trained too hard for this."*

No Shelter from the Storm

"In all my long runs the weather was to be the biggest obstacle."

Lost time driving to hotels or not, Mavis was on the road again at 4 am sharp. A very strong wind was blowing and her seconds suggested she wait for an hour or two for the wind to subside. Mavis kept on, and it's just as well she did. The howling, icy wind would not let up for days.

The gale-force headwind also *"brought with it a constant drizzle. It was most unpleasant. I had to wear a tracksuit as well as a waterproof suit for protection against the elements."* This was far too much like her first Comrades, and gave her vivid 'flashbacks' of the worst moments of the miserable weather that day. But this time the wind was even stronger, and the blasts of cold wind and rain wore her down steadily.

"My progress was very slow indeed. I just could not move forward at any reasonable pace and felt most annoyed and disappointed. At about 4.30 that afternoon it was decided to call it a day. I was getting increasingly tired , without making much progress. I had completed only 73 kilometers for that day. Not nearly enough! The drive to Warden, where we spent the night, was lengthened by my feelings of despondency. Nevertheless, I had a bath, a substantial meal and went to bed expecting the next day to be better."

It wasn't.

Once more by 4 am the Hutchison team was on the road – wasting precious time looking for the previous evening's finish marker. Mavis knew she needed all the time she could get on the road if she were to make up for the short distance the day before, and was 'most upset'. But this was only the beginning of sorrows.

The fierce wind blew even harder, reaching hurricane force, and the *"wind and rain made it feel as though my face had been torn to pieces. My eyes were bulging out of my head and my general condition was deteriorating rapidly. My waterproof had been ripped to shreds by the wind, offering no protection at all."* And by now she literally did have icy 'cold feet'. Battling a hurricane force (70 mph) headwind was *"making each step an agonizing strain."*

Her state of mind wasn't improved by the fact that she and her seconds had gone ahead the previous night to sleep at Warden, so she still hadn't arrived at what felt like her 'starting point'.

After a seeming eternity she eventually passed Warden and felt a new surge of energy. *"I felt I was finally making some progress"* and the *"utter relief…gave me a new lease on life"* Nevertheless, *"those who saw me at the end of the third day would not have rated my chances of finishing the run too highly."* A worn out drowned rat *can* be less than confidence inspiring.

She herself was also feeling less optimistic.

"Many times that day I wondered how things would end. I ended that disastrous day approximately 16 km from Harrismith, having run 89 km for that stretch. What a relief when it was over."

There wasn't much energy left. At dinner that night, Mavis collapsed from exhaustion at the table. *"A doctor was summoned and I was put to bed. Fred Morrison and Ernest strongly disagreed with each other about what was to happen next. Fred was very worried about the bad publicity I would get after having collapsed at the half-way mark. Luckily the reporter and photographer were not in the dining room at the time to report on it."*

Fred's feeling that perhaps she should withdraw failed to sway her. She was determined to carry on.

But a glimmer of encouragement was in the wings. Overnight the people of Harrismith went to great efforts to obtain a badly needed new waterproof for Mavis. Her old one had been 'ripped to shreds' with the back 'torn right out'. *"This had a wonderfully positive effect on my mental state. It signaled a fresh start."*

They started an hour later on the fourth day, to give her extra rest. But there was no rest from the weather that morning. The wind howled on, and her mood sank again as she ran up to the pass.

By the time she'd completed all her ultra marathons she concluded that she'd been tried and tested to the full by every conceivable weather condition – but she never gave in.

SUNSHINE PASS

Persistence had its reward.

At about 11 am, while working her way through van Reenen's Pass, the sun finally broke through the clouds and the wind calmed. She was smiling once again, and running in lightweight shorts and vest again felt liberating." *It left me feeling as though I was flying, free as a bird. I was rejuvenated."*

But the sun was less a friend than it seemed at first. As she ran down the other side of the spine of the 'Dragon Mountains', her wind- and rain-beaten face and hands began to swell in the bright sunlight. "*I was getting fever-blisters and my eyes were hurting. How easy it would have been to stop all this agony."* Once again she ignored the temptation to give in.

The Other Side of the Mountain

She had crossed into the coastal province of Natal, and the two press people from Johannesburg had gone home, but the people of Natal made sure she felt welcome. About 30 km from the next 'landmark' town of Ladysmith, Piet Cronje from the local athletic club and some of his mates came out the run with her for the rest of the day. The club had organized a barbecue to celebrate the occasion, and offered accommodation for the night.

She didn't just have the goodwill of fellow athletes. Even truck drivers on the Johannesburg/Durban route recognized her, honking and waving as they passed.

But Mavis' heroes were the Natal Traffic Department. As soon as she entered Natal, the Traffic Department took over and "*went out of their way to assist me in every way possible." Never have I experienced anything to compare with the logistical support that the Natal Traffic Department provided."* They escorted her on her way, clearing the traffic all the way to the end, and kept the press and radio informed of her position at all times.

The warm Natal welcome and the amazing Traffic Department were wonderful, but progress was agonizingly slow. "*...I paid the price for the strain of the previous two-and-a-half days. The heat and sun became an especial threat."* She ended the day in Ladysmith having been able to cover only 62 km. "*Hopelessly inadequate!"*

Support from Ladysmith continued the next day, as "*thankfully the runners from Ladysmith came out to run with me."* Company was more than welcome, and the indefatigable Piet Cronje ran with her through the entire day. And the blessings from Ladysmith didn't just come from runners. Ointment from a Dr. Gardner gave her fever-blistered face considerable relief. "*The gratitude I felt seemed to help me regain some of my strength and I was able to complete 85 km for the day, stopping right opposite the Hotel in Escourt."*

Averaging 12 plus running hours a day while at the mercy of the elements was heavy going, a fact the runners in Escourt appreciated. They tried to buoy her up, visiting with her at the hotel, but after supper she had to leave them talking to Ernie and Fred, while she sought her bed. She needed a different kind of buoying up – sleep.

ALL THROUGH THE NIGHT

The customary 4 am opening curtain to the fifth day brought with it a whole bunch of local runners who accompanied Mavis till breakfast time, after which they left to go to work. It was at this late stage of the run that she finally decided to wear dark glasses to protect her eyes from the glare and the wind. When more of her family arrived, they were quite literally a sight for sore eyes.

"By now my eyes were hurting and were very blood-shot. I was wonderfully surprised when my mother and twin sister arrived, traveling from Johannesburg to be with me to the end. The extra moral support was a great inspiration to me." If only they could have brought Beverley and Gayle with them – Mavis was already longing to see her two youngest daughters again.

But seeing her family didn't help her judgement. *"During this stage I also had the additional and unusual privilege of having my twin run with me for a while. Doreen had been crippled in one leg for many years and seeing her run beside me, knowing the extraordinary effort it required, filled me with determination. I subsequently decided not to stop in Pietermaritzburg overnight, but to keep going right through to Durban - a 176 kilometers distance. As we later realized this was not a very wise decision, but at the time I thought it would be to my advantage."*

At four that afternoon, after an hour's rest, Mavis announced her great decision. It wasn't popular. The feeling of resistance was tangible, although nobody said a word. It was 109 miles from Escourt to Durban, and she was in no condition to come anywhere near running it at the pace she'd maintained in setting her record for the 24 hour run. But perhaps that epic feat spurred her on.

Part of what made her night run possible, if not wise, was that Ray Karge, Allen Perry, and Adrian Alexander had arrived from Pietermaritzburg, intending to run with her to their home town. They volunteered to run with her all the way to Durban, staying with her for 27 hours. She was making a supreme effort and they recognized it. They were a life-line and she was awestruck.

"I will never forget the 27 hours I had them constantly at my side providing vital encouragement during this last, long stint. I salute the sacrifice of these three great sportsmen and their wives who stood by me at a time when my team and I were in desperate need of support.

"Whilst their wives took over much of the seconding duties, two of them ran on either side of me; one to protect me from the on-coming traffic and the other to protect me from stepping off the edge of the road, which at times was quite a hazard, especially as it grew darker.

"Allan also had a portable radio on hand for the entire 27 hours he spent with me, which enabled me to hear broadcasts from Radio Port Natal giving regular updates on the race. These were supplied to the station by the traffic officers. That was helpful too."

THE GHOST RUNNER, GLOWING IN THE DARK

At this point Mavis was wearing luminous strips on her running vest and her three escorts held flashlights to ensure they could be seen by passing traffic. Unfortunately, a black cyclist peddling in their direction was hugely unnerved by the spooky effect created by the flashlights and the glow coming from Mavis.

"The bewildered man threw his bicycle to one side and ran off into the night as if his very life depended upon getting away from us. It seemed as though I was mistaken for a ghost. In its own way the incident provided a much appreciated moment of comic relief."

By this time her shoes were in dire need of repair despite changing them regularly – at the half way mark each day - and were difficult to keep on her feet. This seriously hampered her progress. In later runs, she brought more shoes and Ernie became expert at shoe repair.

At about 8.30 that evening the party reached Pietermaritzburg where Mavis was able to take a half-hour breather – by common consent. *"I rested in the car while the rest of the crew stood around waiting for me to reappear. My mom prepared some delicious hot soup in the camper that was traveling along with us, and that hit the spot."*

Help along the road. Top left: Ernie on massage duty.
Top right: Fred Morrison with liquid refreshment on the run.
Bottom left: Portable shade for a sunblasted Mavis.
Bottom right: Ray Karge and Allen Perry helping Mavis get to Durban.
Source of photos unknown

"It seemed only an instant before I was on the road again with my entourage. Meanwhile John Ball had joined me again and Allan continued to do an outstanding job of cheering me up. His continuous chatter kept me awake when I was drifting off and distracted me from a lot of the stress."

At about 4 in the morning her team decided she needed another hour's rest – likely a good decision since she would need every ounce of strength for what still lay ahead. After a short while she took to the road again with the 'Three Musketeers' seemingly glued to her, a position they held right to the bitter end.

After the rest she *"now felt stronger and very pleased to think that Durban was around the corner."* At breakfast time she *"decided not to come off the road...I decided to eat on the run, another unwise move."*

THROUGH MELTING TAR

As the day progressed intense heat became Mavis' mortal enemy. The tar on the road was melting and her damaged shoes were sticking to it, making it extremely difficult to keep them on her feet. The sun seemed to burn right through her, and kept hoping for a few shade trees around the next bend, or a friendly cloud to mask the sun.

Maybe ongoing radio coverage of her ordeals helped to offset some of the hardship. It was clear that the broadcaster, Sarel Marais, had caught the spirit of her monumental effort. During his shift he enthusiastically broadcast a progress report every half hour. As a result the crowds were streaming to the roadside from all over Natal to see Mavis run by.

Sarel made a request for the traffic to give her lots of room and put out a call for Durban athletes to join her on the road. By this time the sweltering subtropical heat was so bad that *"I was doing an energy sapping walk-shuffle to keep my shoes on. I felt as though I was running on stumps."* She was near breaking point, running on empty.

"Could I see this through? My hands and face were, once again, badly swollen and covered with fever-blisters. To protect me from the sun the athletes running with me held a large beach umbrella over my head." Shade that moved with her – what a blessing!

There was no 'loneliness of the long distance runner' that day, but Mavis was too exhausted to acknowledge her fans.

"The crowd was growing rapidly, thronging onto the freeway overpasses. Allan had to wave to the crowds on my behalf as my arms were just too tired and sore to lift. I tried to smile but even that was difficult."

But it was cheering to catch a 'rewarding glimpse' of Piet Cronje again. He'd come all the way from Ladysmith to support her to the finish.

The Natal Traffic Department was still giving her enormous support and protection, and keeping Radio Port Natal up to date. But by lunchtime her flagging energy made her wonder if she'd be able to make it back onto the road. Durban City Hall was near, but still seemed far away.

'DIVINE SECOND WIND'

> *"If you can force your heart and mind and sinew*
> *To serve your turn long after they are gone..."*
> *(Rudyard Kipling)*

Miraculously, energy did come from somewhere, like a second wind from above, but only just enough. *"My progress was now very slow, but giving up was not an option. I was inching my way to the finish, full of aches and pains. The mental agony was as great as the physical. The last hours of the race felt like days."* The runners on the road with her did their best to ease the pressure by keeping the crowd at bay as much as they could, and by telling some 'good yarns' to keep her mind off the pain and exhaustion.

At this junction the traffic was so congested that the officers were forced to divert all outbound traffic, permitting only inbound.

But the end was in sight. Tension was mounting. The crowd was growing and at the stroke of 6 a thoroughly worn-out Mavis arrived at the Durban City Hall where about 3,000 people were cheering her on.

"The people of Natal had taken me into their hearts. As I finished they sang 'For She's a Jolly Good Fellow'. I was humbled by their warmheartedness and the tears poured down my cheeks. I had made it! Kisses, hugs and handshakes were the order of the day. The warmth and love was tangible. My last effort on the road lasted 37 ½ hours, not an easy nor wise undertaking, but with the wonderful assistance from many caring people I had made it."

'SHE'S ALWAYS BEEN A LITTLE CRAZY'

She was overjoyed as she handed the goodwill message from the mayor of Germiston to the deputy mayor of Durban, a joy that didn't fade even as she listened to a Germiston city councilor *"say a few words on behalf of the people of Germiston.*

Her run had taken her 6 days 13 hours and 55 minutes, though she'd hoped to make better time after six months of intense training.

She had missed John Ball's record but beaten the times of the other three men who had run from the Witwatersrand (the area including both Johannesburg and Germiston): Don Shepherd, Alan Ferguson and Ian Jardine. Later she would reflect, "*Not bad for a woman!*"

She duly received a hero's welcome and was appropriately garlanded on the steps of the Durban City Hall in the proud view of hubby Ernie, one of her daughters, a granddaughter and her mom, whose comment to a reporter was:"She's always been a little crazy!.."

TOAST OF THE COUNTRY

"*Three years after I had dared to dream, it became reality. One of my most precious mementos from that run is a letter from Ian Jardine congratulating me on successfully completing the distance. He ended by writing, "You can be very proud of your outstanding achievement, but more importantly, you had the courage to actually undertake to do that which was once only a dream. WELL DONE!*"

Mavis recalls many other encouraging comments: "Only one word for Mavis that is stupendous. I think that it is just about the most wonderful feat achieved by a woman. I think she has got more guts than 99 out of a 100 men." (Sam Mirwis, Sports Editor of the Sunday Express).

Mirwis also felt Mavis had struck a stronger blow for women's lib than Billy Jean King when she defeated 'loud mouth' men's champion Bobby Riggs. He added: "The magnitude of this feat is difficult to grasp," and thought she might well have bettered Ball's record if it weren't for the weather. This could well be true.

Germiston city councilor Gerald Thurley said: " Mavis is one of the most outstanding women of this age. Every age seems to produce wonderful women, we have produced a Mavis Hutchison. Mavis' feat over the last 6 and 1/2 days has been tremendous. I am going to ask the Minister of sport Dr. Piet Koornhof to consider Mavis as a Patron of his 'Walk For Life Campaign."

Radio Port Natal's Sarel Marais reported the following at the finish: "…I feel very honored that I have had the wonderful opportunity of seeing history being made by a very brave grandmother…West Street was like a mirage of lights, with the lights from the cars, the street lights, the traffic lights, and anything that could shimmer and glimmer was being waved around. You knew what you were witnessing was the finish of an epoch-making run…I saw a large banner with the words, 'The Mavis Miracle'. What wonderful words, but they don't say half of what this woman has accomplished. The crowds lined the streets…and now two-three thousand of them are sounding sirens, tooting hooters and singing loudly to give her a most marvelous and wonderful welcome. It is…magnificent to have been part-and-parcel of this whole happening…Our heartiest congratulations to Mavis on behalf of all Radio Port Natal listeners."

A report in The Star at the time also spoke glowingly of her Herculean effort, which sports writers predicted "will reverberate like a thunderclap for years in the athletic world", a view echoed by other sportswriters. After all, her 'blow for women's lib' had definitely surpassed the records of Ian Jardine, Alan Ferguson (7 days, 7 hrs, 45 min) and Don Shepherd (7 ½ days). She stood back only to Ball, who finished 13 hours faster.

Mavis wasn't particularly interested whether or not she struck a blow for women's lib. Like many strong women, she seldom gave the 'movement' a moment's thought.

In an official letter to Mavis, the Minister of Sport and Recreation, Dr Piet Koornhof, expressed his pride:

"I would like to avail myself of this opportunity in congratulating you on your fantastic achievement of running from Germiston to Durban in 6 days 13 hours and fifty five minutes.

You have set a splendid example to the people of South Africa and I am convinced that your achievement will motivate many people to improve their personal fitness…"

Mavis did become a patron of the Walk For Your Life campaign launched by the Minister.

FAMILY SUPPORT, FAMILY PRIDE

Her family gladly shared in her victory. Ernie, whose vigilance and quiet inspiration helped to pull her through, was almost as exhausted as Mavis when she finally reached her destination. He'd never doubted she'd make it, but did make a revealing comment to the press: "Mavis is wonderful, but she has caused me many worries on this route."

His unwavering belief scored him many points with his courageous wife, and so did his unfailing hands-on care: the bathing of her aching feet, the sponging down of her face, the massaging of her legs, arms and back, and the preparation of her meals and drinks.

Among the Durban crowd. after the finish.

The response from daughter Beverley, then 12 years old and justifiably proud of her mom, only added to Mavis' warm glow. Her first words over the phone from Johannesburg were words that would soothe any mother's ear: "I am so glad you are my mommy."

Son Jess, then 26, phoned from Cape Town to add his bit, bearing in mind how his mother loved to have her hair done after a run: "Don't have your hair done. You look great as you are."

Her older daughter Pam, 28 at the time, wanted her anniversary gift to be seeing her mom come in at the finish line.

Her family's support always meant a lot. She remembers times when she just got fed up with the whole thing and wanted to quit, *"but thanks to the encouragement of my husband and kids I got back on the road."*

GIRLISH?

Although Mavis was described by the Women's Daily News in Durban as the 48-year old woman with the 'girlish figure of a 14-year old', she didn't exactly feel girlish after reaching the finish. The race, preceded by more than 3500 miles of training runs over 12 months, was a killer and had taken its toll. In fact it was far worse than she'd imagined, and she wondered whether she'd ever be able to do anything like it again.[2]

After the race she was so fatigued she was dead to the world for many hours and when she finally woke up the next morning she was so hungry that she 'ate her way through the entire breakfast menu'.

Last Words

"There's a stage, two or three times, when you feel you just cannot go on, but you know you have to. This is when you can crack. But it is quite amazing where you get the extra strength and endurance to go on and on."

She would find the same strength in ultra marathons yet to come.

---

[1] *South Africa's transition to the metric system occurred gradually in the early-to-mid 1970s. Chapters 10 to 13 use a mixture of distances in miles and kilometers.*
[2] *One of the throng that met her in Durban said to the press: "South Africa's 'galloping granny told me Saturday evening in front of the Durban city hall that she will never again tackle going the 600 kilometers from Germiston to Durban on foot." Strictly speaking, this was true – she only tackled the much more difficult task of running the other way!*

Chapter 11: AGAIN THE DRAGON
This Time Uphill

<hr>

*"When I run on country roads the grandeur of the scenery
often prompts me to reach down into my deepest self and then
I experience a depth of thought and a closeness to nature I
never knew existed. It sometimes only takes a misty morning
or the warmth of the sun on my back to make that contact.
The result is a profound sense of harmony; a taste of real
freedom like a bird set free from a cage. These are
unforgettable moments that bring you face to face with the
challenge of self-discovery."*

Originally Mavis had planned an even more difficult run for 1974, 914 miles from Cape Town on the coast, over the mountains and up to the 6000-foot elevation of Germiston and Johannesburg on the Highveld plateau. That would certainly have given her ample time to reflect – and not only on the peace and harmony as she communed with the grandeur of nature on country roads. As she would learn again and again, the challenge and pain of self-discovery would always be her close companions on ultraruns.

The run from Cape Town to Germiston didn't happen. Financial backing did not materialize, and the Hutchison family budget couldn't stretch that far unaided.

But the idea of running uphill must have captured her imagination, because what she actually did was reverse her course of 1973 by running the 374 miles from Durban on the coast *up* to Germiston, this time crossing the energy-draining Natal hills and the towering Drakensberg mountain range the hard way.

Perhaps the idea came more naturally because the much shorter Comrades Marathon similarly reverses course every other year – the 'down' run from Pietermaritzburg to Durban is always followed the next year by the 'up' run from Durban to Pietermaritzburg. The 'up' run is harder in the Comrades too, as the record books show.

Mavis knew it would be tough, but felt that with better weather and a bit of luck she might beat her 1973 record. Remembering the hurricane-force headwinds and slashing rain, she told the press, "*I need wind assistance and lots of sun, but if I stick to my schedule of 90 kilometers a day...my time should be very near the mark.*"

But first came the preparation. Newspaper columnist Ian Reid wrote that she trained "six hours a day, five days a week, running around Germiston Lake...to get in form for her 602 kilometer dash from the coast to Germiston". Reid wasn't too keen to try this himself: "If it comes to it, I am not all that keen on Durban. But running all the way back to the Reef from its golden beaches is something I have not even contemplated. Mavis Hutchison, however, is made of sterner stuff." She was now 49 years old.

'THE LIONESS IN WINTER'

> "*People say she's crazy. They say there must be something missing in any woman that ... jogs up and down mountains between Durban and Germiston.*"
> (*press article by Buks Pietersen*)

Mavis remembered the terrible humid heat and melting asphalt of the Natal coast only too well, so this time she planned her run for June, early in the southern hemisphere winter when the climate is much like Florida In December. She also made sure she was well equipped with sun cream and dark glasses.

According to press reports, her original plan was to run the 86 km (54 miles) of the Comrades Marathon as the 'first leg'. As one headline put it, "Mavis Will Just Keep On Running". Saner counsels prevailed. The Comrades pace would have been too fast when she needed to cover at least that distance every day for a week.

Instead she started out as before with a mayoral send-off, this time in the rain. But not in the dark. The mayor of Durban was not about to see her off at 4 am, so she left at 8 in the morning. A few friends were there, including Ian Jardine, and she spotted Don Shepherd, her second the year before. "*I expected him to come over for a chat...was very surprised he did not...*"

As they had on her arrival the year before, the splendid traffic cops of the Natal Traffic Department once more led the way as she set out through the Durban city streets, heading toward the 'thousand hills' of Natal and the distant mountains. Her two-man support team (husband Ernie, and Fred Morrison) traveled in the camper van that served as the team's base of operations.

"The first day went very well", and Mavis and her support team slept the night just outside the Comrades destination town of Pietermaritzburg. As usual, Ernie used *"an aerosol can of paint to mark the road with a large 'M' to make sure we have the exact starting point the next day."*

LIMPING THROUGH THE SNOW

> *"It will be much tougher this time, because she will be climb-*
> *ing most of the way. But she will finish and you can be sure*
> *she will break the record."*
> *(mentor Fred Morrison, to the press)*

It didn't stay easy. As Mavis made her way up and down the endless ridges toward the summit, the total climb was nearly 10000 feet. Her pace slowed, falling at one point to less than forty miles a day, and the initial optimism faded. Mavis had planned on 6 days and 7 hours; Fred Morrison had proclaimed that *"…I have a shrewd idea she will surprise everybody – including herself – by breaking even six days."*

Frustrations mounted as these predictions slipped slowly out of reach, which may have something to do with the fact she *"seemed to be very touchy"*, so that *"Fred and I seemed to clash."* This was highly unusual, since Fred had *"always been there for me, and encouraged me every step of the way."* She blamed herself for the friction.

Time was becoming increasingly precious. She would typically get on the road by about five in the morning, and run for about 13 hours, but every day after the first, time was lost to marking the road each night, finding a hotel, and searching for the previous day's spray-painted 'M' in the predawn darkness. As she struggled up the 'backbreaking hills', the weather became 'bitterly cold' and the daily 13 hours of running began to take its toll.

On the fourth day, disaster struck. *"I twisted my ankle on a very uneven stretch of road. It was very badly swollen again."* It was her 'slow' right leg once more. All her leg injuries in her career were to this leg, which for Mavis always felt 'slower and heavier' than her left. *"I really wasn't looking forward to limping in at the finish."*

And as she struggled toward the top, the headwind intensified, and the weather turned 'bitter cold'. She began to realize that she'd *"misjudged some of the mountains where the pull was terrible."* She was high in the mountains that are the spine of southern Africa, and it was early winter. What had paid off on the coast was her enemy now. *"The wind and the cold were grueling – I just didn't think it could be so bad."* Snow began to blast along the icy wind.

But navigating through the tough stuff was becoming synonymous with Mavis and her quest for that 'indispensable personal growth' she advocated. She didn't reckon on the fierceness of the icy wind, anticipate snow at the top of Van Reenen's Pass, or realize how difficult it would be to keep up the pace as she climbed up to the spine of the 'Dragon Mountains'. But those were the facts and she had to live with them. There was no turning back.

She was now seriously behind schedule, and by day 6 was desperate to make up the time. She felt the burden of her own expectations, and Fred Morrison's very public predictions only made it worse.

Her average of about 13 hours a day wasn't going to cut it any more. In a desperate catch-up attempt on day 7 she set off before dawn at 5.30 and spent a murderous 18 hours on the road covering a distance of about 122 km.

Helping to boost her morale was the company of Dannie Oosthuizen and Norman Jannet, who joined her at 10 am, and stuck with her to the end. When she finally quit at 11:30 that night, she had reached the end of her tether, but she had salvaged part of her dream.

KEEPING ON THE ROAD

Things would have undoubtedly been worse were it not for her adoring husband and trusted second, Ernie, with whom she celebrated her 30th wedding anniversary straight after her hellish journey.

Of Ernie she said: " *I couldn't have done it without him. He has been absolutely wonderful.*" It was Ernie who rubbed down her aching legs, made sure she changed her running shoes twice a day, kept them in repair if possible, cooked, drove, marked the road and encouraged.

But no one could run for her. The back breaking slog was hers to master and the accusation from some quarters that she was just a 'publicity seeker' didn't make the burden any lighter. *"I don't want people to think of me as a publicity seeker. I would do it without any publicity if I could."*

She took pains after the race to make it clear to the media what really drove her. *"I'm not some sort of clown, just someone who wanted to do the run."* She wanted to do the run *"just to prove to myself that I could do it…"*

Mavis had begun as someone who was seen by family as *"a real scatterbrain with no hope at all."* By the time of this ultrarun, this was in the distant past. What motivated Mavis now was realizing her own potential as a person and as a woman, as well as her sheer love of the long road.

It certainly wasn't a 'women's lib' desire to demonstrate some sort of female superiority. Speaking of the 1000-mile run from Cape Town to Germiston she'd hoped to make that year, she said, *"It's not a question of what men can do, women can do better. I love running and I want to show the world that women can accomplish feats which might seem impossible to them."*

There were also those who thought that women who did what she was doing had a screw loose, but she couldn't allow that to deter her and sour her mental attitude. Together with physical fitness, mental attitude was the key to keeping herself moving when running became an agonizing slog, or when the grind of training in addition to managing a family became too much.

THE CHIMING BELLS OF GERMISTON

Once the mountains were behind her, Mavis continued to "'chew up distance" across the rolling Highveld plateau. People came out to meet her, writing their good wishes and congratulations in her notebook, praising her as their 'hero' and an inspiration to their children.

Then it was the last day. As she approached Germiston, and the heavy metropolitan area traffic, police escorts "rallied around her", and runners from her Germiston Callies club came to run alongside and keep her company as she passed by the dull brown and black winter fields.

With dogged persistence, she kept on. The press reported that she was still "looking as fit as a young girl, her long legs brown and slender." She told them how determined she had been to "make up time" so that she could get in by that day.

Ernie sweats along with her on the 'up' run.

Then, nearly 400 miles and six pairs of running shoes later, she was in the streets of Germiston, approaching the finish line. She reached it just after three in the afternoon of Monday, June 10, 1974 , "with the de-termination and grace which has made her a legend in athletics." So the local press saw it, as they stood among the thousands who had come to see her. She had beaten Don Shepherd's record for the 'up' run by more than a day.

No wonder the press could report that the City Hall bells chimed amid a "rising ovation from the large crowd" as "Mrs. Hutchison accepted a laurel wreath from…(the) Mayor, in return for a message from the Mayor of Durban". Mavis sank gratefully into the mayor's 'chair of honor' on the city hall steps, and tried bravely to smile for the "Press and the public who crowded round getting a glimpse of the 'wonder granny' and begging for autographs."

Autographs were difficult that day. As she struggled to sign one schoolgirl's book, she had to explain that she could hardly write as her hands were so shaky and swollen.

DANCING WITH ERNIE, LEARNING FROM FRED

But that didn't stop her from "smiling joyfully at husband Ernie, and sharing an anniversary kiss", as one account puts it. And she wasn't going let tiredness get in the way of her plans for their 30th anniversary. *"Oh yes, we're definitely going out tonight to celebrate…I will rest up tomorrow, but tonight, no, we must celebrate."* This was according to pattern. After finishing her first Comrades, she'd dressed up in her evening best complete with heels; after the 24 hour race she'd gone dancing with Ernie. Fatigue would *not* spoil her plans this time either.

Ernie was clearly thrilled with his wife's achievement. From him came "a gasp, a smile and a huge embrace."(The Star, June 12, 1974). Mavis had again done what some thought impossible for a woman in her late forties.

If the down run was seen as an unusual accomplishment, the more difficult up-run was unthinkable. Yet Mavis was terribly disappointed not to have met the schedule she'd set. *"I hoped to be here a day earlier."*

Fred Morrison had been certain she would finish well. Before the race he remarked: "Mavis does not realize her own…capabilities. She is the most amazing woman athlete in the world and has achieved feats which very few men could accomplish. She will finish and you can be sure she'll break the record". She did, if not in the time he predicted.

Coming from Fred, this was a great compliment. He'd been running since 1930, had come in third in his first Comrades Marathon, and finished that race 10 more times. He had been a member of the Germiston Callies athletic club for 42 years, and it was said that the dark blue stripe across the club shirt was "a Morrison symbol of 'guts'." 'Uncle Fred' was an adventure to know – a man who drummed into her the practical principles of her trade. Even in old age he was "still quick to spot a bad foot fault, or an arm held too high....He is sharp all the way. A critic and a perfectionist." It was said that after "giving up competitive running Fred had probably seconded and looked after more runners than anyone in the world."

In the mayor's chair after the finish, trying to smile.

Running greats such as Jackie Meckler, Wally Hayward and Syd Luyt also felt a deep debt of gratitude to 'Friendly Fred', just as Mavis did. *"Thanks to him I could see through even a rough run."*

And when she got to Germiston it was the end of a rough one. She was happy to be done, and was to write laconically in journal notes that she *"had found the run inland rather tough. Climbing most of the way was not an easy task."*

But it was worth it. The magic of the moment, as the city hall chimes played "Drink to Me Only With Thine Eyes", and the adoring hometown crowd applauded, moved her deeply. The feeling of achievement, shared with Ernie, made the perfect anniversary present.

Soon she was "relaxing visibly", "beginning to chat with all around her", and astonishing an interviewer with her plans to start training again in about a week.

No wonder one article called her 'the woman who doesn't know what it means to give up'.

Chapter 12: CAPITAL ROAD
Learning to Endure a Little Longer

----•◦•----

"My granny couldn't run a ladder in her stocking"
(cartoon caption, 1975)

Mavis was nothing if not forward looking. She began planning to run across America at least as early as 1973, when she became the first woman to run the 400 miles from Germiston down to Durban. But that would remain a dream without backing. Her income as a record sales clerk, and her husband's salary for driving a mine winding engine definitely wouldn't cover the cost. To convince a sponsor she could do it, she needed to prove herself. And she did.

Her record-breaking run from the coast over snowy mountain passes to the high plateau around Johannesburg proved that she was no 'one time wonder' – and it got her a sponsor for the next big step toward her ultimate dream. She would start that race less than 9 months after her rapturous reception in Germiston.

THE BIG ORANGE

This time she would run toward a more distant coast. Hall's Orange, makers of a popular soft drink, would cover the costs of an epic 1000-mile run from Pretoria (South Africa's administrative capital) to Cape Town (the legislative capital), arriving in time for the Cape Town Festival. In return Mavis would run wearing 'Hall's Orange' vests, while the run would be advertised as the 'Hall's Orange Marathon'. There were very real risks to this – in that age of rigid ideas about amateurism she could easily have been banned from amateur running for life.

But Mavis was determined to take the risk of losing her amateur status, and the risk of taking a longer distance than any woman had ever run. Only two men had ever run from Pretoria to Cape Town, Don Shepherd in 22 days and John Ball in 14. Mavis planned on trying to match Don Shepherd's time, knowing that even this would mean covering 44 miles a day over a distance three times as long as she had ever attempted.

Knowing how much stamina this would take, she began training five to six hours a day. Plans came together. Andre Minnie, Les Du Plessis and husband Ernest would be her support crew. And this time they would use caravans for overnight stops – *"no more desperate searching in the small hours of the morning for the previous night's finish markers."*

Helpful supporters made this possible within the sponsored budget. One company provided an 'Autovilla' caravan that needed to be delivered to agents in Cape Town, while *"good friends at Norquay Caravans"* loaned the team a trailer and tow car. In due course, the caravans arrived at the Hutchison home, setting her bemused neighbors abuzz as frantic last-minute preparations were made.

And then the time for her 'colossal adventure' was at hand.

A RABBIT CAUGHT IN THE HEADLIGHTS

> *"Ernie, in his athletic shorts and running shoes, is the*
> *epitome of the trainer with the champ. When he talks*
> *about Mavis on the road, he makes her sound more*
> *like an old car than the woman he married...'*
> *We'll run her until six', he's likely to say."*
> (Johannesburg Star)

Starting time was early on the morning of March 27, 1975. As a warm autumn sun rose over the rolling hills of Pretoria on South Africa's mile-high Highveld plateau, a small but excited crowd of well-wishers looked on as the mayor handed Mavis a letter to the mayor of Cape Town and wished her luck, saying this was one of the most extraordinary duties he'd been called on to perform as mayor. Her sponsors presented her with official running gear.

Mavis looked out at the crowd (including daughters Gayle and Beverley) with a calm that puzzled her friends and supporters. It was easy to be calm, because *"I was a complete blank. My mind seemed to take me nowhere."* Her seemingly nonchalant attitude puzzled the 'excited' onlookers, but *"In truth, I felt like a rabbit caught in the headlights of a car stunned into waiting for the inevitable.*" Then the clock struck seven, and she was off.

Even as she ran through the city she still felt not too sure of her bearings. But gradually she began to find some rhythm in her stride, her thoughts began to thaw, and she began to realize how the huge challenge ahead had numbed her into "*avoiding thinking about what lay ahead. Previous experience suggested that tough times awaited. As the day wore on I could feel the unconscious nervousness begin to dissipate. I was on the long road again.*"

And at first the roads were enough to shake anyone up. Frighteningly heavy traffic roared close by on congested, narrow roads. The sun began to blaze hotter, but "*around midday there was a shower of rain, which was very refreshing*", and cold meat and salad revived her further. Not all the rain that day was a blessing, however. By four o'clock that afternoon, ominous dark clouds covered the sky, and Mavis had to run through two heavy thunderstorms, as every passing car doused her with cold, dirty water.

As she passed through small towns on the way, there were frequent delays for dignitaries handing her "*goodwill messages to be carried to Cape Town, together with expressions of varying degrees of admiration*". This was the densely populated industrial heartland of South Africa, so in each town the local authorities arranged traffic control to get her safely through.

It all took precious time, and by the time Fanie van Zyl, one of South Africa's elite middle distance runners, met her outside Randfontein, it was obvious that this was not going to be a day when the team achieved a large distance run. He ran with her as far as a mayoral reception at the Randfontein city hall, and directed them to an 'ideal camping spot'. Although she'd covered less than 40 miles, Mavis still felt exhausted, and kept interviews with a demanding press to a minimum.

The next day began the normal routine, starting long before sunrise at 4 am. Other athletes kept her company that day. She was excited to have Fanie van Zyl join her for another three hours, and 'extremely humbled' to have a Mr. Carlitz 'tag along' from 4 am until midday. He'd lost his hands in a mining accident, and had regarded Mavis as a role model since he'd begun running. His hands may have been gone, but the rest of him was 'extremely fit'. Young runners from Welkom (and the town clerk) joined her for an hour.

A real highlight was the time fellow Comrades runner Daphne Ledlie spent on the road with her. Daphne had taken up endurance running after beating breast cancer ('to avoid wallowing in self-pity'), and would eventually become the first woman ever to complete ten Comrades Marathons.

RUNNING IN TRAFFIC – AND WITH THE PRESS

Family members also joined Mavis as she fought her way through the Good Friday traffic, feeling vulnerable and small: *"I needed all my concentration focused on the road and the traffic."* One family member's contribution was vital – during the lunch break her oldest son Ronald repaired the gas line that kept the caravan fridge and freezer working.

One member of the press tried running with her too. Raynier Abrahamse from the Vaderland newspaper showed up with his fiancé, having been told to get first-hand experience *"of what demands ultra distance running placed on a person...After about forty-five minutes he was in obvious trouble but did not want to let on so he kept going. He had come totally ill-prepared and before long his shoes were pinching, his shorts were chafing and the sun was burning. His breathing became laboured, at which time he expressed a desperate need to find a hanky. It took a couple of days before he returned."*

Three hours of rain at the end of the day forced an early finish after only 72 kilometers. After only two days her feet were aching, but she diverted her thoughts to the two youngest daughters, wondering how they were managing being minded by their grandmother.

The days now followed a set routine. *"Each day would start at 4 am in the dark. I would run in front of the 'Autovilla' with the headlights guiding the way and the hazard lights warning any passing traffic of my presence. The strain on the support crew during these early mornings was incredible and so we all took a ten minute break at about 6 am Generally, we would then stop again for a half-hour breakfast break at about 8 am During this time I would soak my feet."* She had also learned from her Durban runs that she'd need dark glasses during the day to protect her eyes from the blazing African sun.

After another half hour break for lunch and foot soaking, there would be more hours of running before *"being rewarded with a long rest and a thorough soaking of my feet. At night injuries would receive attention, muscles would be massaged and logistics discussed. It was my job to do the running and the support crew had the thankless task of making sure that I was in the right condition to be able to run."* It became abundantly clear to her that *"even in the pursuit of individual goals, success is often dependent on the commitment and the quality of the support from others."* Without that support, not much would happen.

Too much support could also be a problem. At the end of day four a large crowd came out from Klerksdorp to meet Mavis, and all too many of them decided to run with her. To Mavis it seemed that all the children of the town were on the road with her, and while *"it was pleasing to see so many people interested in my run, I found it very difficult to concentrate on my running as I tried to dodge the hordes of children all wanting their moment of fame."*

A man on bicycle insisted that she had to sign a newspaper clipping about the run – in the middle of the crush, while Mavis worried that in the heavy traffic one of the children might get hurt. In all the distraction, this lack of focus caused her to stumble and twist her ankle. Pain shot through it as she strained a ligament, and painful thoughts of 'catastrophe' flashed through her mind and heart.

But the evening brought more welcome distractions – a visit from her two youngest daughters *"who had been in my thoughts for so much of the time since having left home"*, and a luxurious bath at a cousin's home. But it hadn't been a great day: *"Seventy four kilometers for the day and a twisted ankle. Meager pickings."*

This time her fears proved unfounded. The road was quiet that Easter Monday, her ankle held up, and she enjoyed the solitude – while it lasted. The ex-miner without hands returned, and a young boy from one of the local farms ran two hours with her. The ex-miner had driven far to spend ten minutes with the team, and she felt deeply honored. Raynier Abrahamse had gotten over the embarrassment of his first attempt, and built up enough courage to run the last hour of the day with her. It was a magical, peaceful hour, as a gorgeous sunset painted the landscape. Even the traffic was quiet as the sun slipped away.

Off the road the magic ended. Mavis had sinned by booking in at a hotel opposite where the caravans were parked, and she felt rather lonely as Ernest refused even to eat with her. Worse yet, although the hot bath was 'sheer bliss', she was too lonely to have an appetite, and so afraid she wouldn't wake up on time that she dared not sleep, and left the radio on all night to check on the time.

But she was awake and ready to go when Ernest showed up the next morning, and he and Andre *"tucked in to the chicken I had saved, Andre commenting that cold chicken and 'coffee royal'...at 4.am in the morning was perhaps the right way to get him going from then on."*

The real problem was the traffic. She dared not take her eyes off the oncoming traffic for fear of being hit, especially by caravans that seemed to be swaying the tailwind of the tow vehicles. The invisible but all too audible traffic from behind was even more terrifying. She could hardly stop every time she heard an approaching vehicle because that would have slowed her progress to a crawl. Often she had to step off the two-lane highway altogether as a passing car made *"full use of the breadth of the road"*.

It didn't help that people stopped to take photographs without much consideration for their safety or hers. As darkness set in the blistering heat faded, but increasing numbers of heavy trucks seemed *"not too keen to give me any leeway on the road"*, and both she and her team decided to call it a night before she got hurt. All these things cost time. An average of seven kilometers a day were lost to traffic stoppages, detours and dodging vehicles – and that doesn't count photographers and press interviews, or the drain on her energy caused by the constant danger.

How much time was lost became clear the next day, as Mavis achieved her best daily distance so far despite the time wasted that morning waiting for help to deal with a flat battery. It was *"exceptionally hot and energy-sapping"*, but the lighter traffic made all the difference, although she ended the day *'really the worse for wear'*, with heavy legs and swollen face and hands.

BROKEN DREAMS

> *"She regards Kimberley as the most important stop en route*
> *to Cape Town...she regards Kimberley 'as home' and...*
> *she will make the most of her brief visit."*
> *(Diamond Fields Advertiser)*

But minor physical discomfort seemed very small compared to the excitement of what would happen the next day. She would pass into the Cape

Province, and overnight in the town of Kimberley where she was born and grew up. She had left Kimberley a no-hoper with her tail between her legs. She would return a national figure.

"The excitement in the whole team was unbelievable. I think I was running on air..." A reporter from Kimberley's 'Diamond Fields Advertiser' came on the road for a story. Her mother and sister were coming, and the Kimberley Harriers Athletic Club came out to run with her after lunch. The mayor would meet her at five before entertaining the State President, who was in town to open the 'Kimberley Show'.

"I was looking forward to seeing long lost friends and for the whole day I was preoccupied the for the whole day I was preoccupied with thoughts of meeting old school friend, ex work-mates and friends and many others I had once known in Kimberley. I was certain that this was going to be just like the 'home-coming' events often portrayed in American movies. After all, my father had not only worked for De Beers Mining Company for 45 years, he had also been a local sporting celebrity. I think I was running on air for most of the day. Nothing was going to spoil this wonderful day for me. I regretted that my father would not be there to share this day with me as he had died in 1969. However, my mother and sister would be there. I felt like Cinderella returning as the princess."

The reality was to be very different. For the last 6 miles, she was directed to run on the section of the road that was under construction. *"The loose stones made running difficult and a strong head-wind polluted the air with red sand which soon filled my mouth, nose and eyes. Then it started raining and before long I was covered in red mud. My shoes became increasingly heavy and I could hardly move on the thick slush that, by now, oozed on the road."*

Then she had to move to another section of the road, covered with 'big boulders and rocks'. This was a very dangerous surface to run on, and panic gripped her as her mind filled with thoughts of falling or twisting an ankle. Soddenly aware of how much she was shivering in the cold rain, she draped a towel over her shoulders. It didn't help much. Feeling she absolutely had to get to the City Hall before six, she was really pushing it by this time. Then it happened. She twisted her right leg, and *" heard what sounded like a twig snap"*.

She tried her best to ignore this bad omen and kept going, and her gloom began to dissipate as she saw her mother and sister Ivy, who had traveled hundreds of miles from Oudtshoorn to see her come in.

Dreams are hard to let go, even when covered with grit and mud. As she crossed the railroad tracks into the road leading to City Hall, *"the rain stopped and the sun forced its way through the clouds. My mood lifted. In my imagination I could hear a thousand voices shouting "Surprise!", as I envisioned myself entering the hall."* So exciting was this vision that she was hardly aware of Ernest waving her into the caravan for a quick rubdown and dry clothes before the *"triumphant return of the 'no-hoper' teenager turned sporting hero."*

With two police cars and two policemen on motorcycles guarding her through the intersections with sirens blaring, Mavis arrived at the Civic Center in haze of overflowing emotions, wanting the feeling to last forever. The mayor welcomed her warmly: *"Mavis I won't say welcome to Kimberley -- I will say welcome home."*

But although the mayor and town clerk were there, with her mother and sister and Aunt Katie, her sponsors, the team from Kimberley Harriers, the press and a few old friends – that was it. In the town where she had been born, grown up, gone to school, and where her parents were well-known, respected community members, the old schoolmates, workmates and 'throng of local admirers' in the imagined thousand-voice choir were conspicuous by their absence.

THE ROAD TO HOPE

Her painful childhood memories had not been erased by a roaring welcome, but Mavis received something far more valuable.

"This was to be one of those moments in life when one experiences a totally unexpected life-changing insight: 'Strive to do the best you can in order that you can feel satisfied with your achievements, rather than in to impress others. That way your sense of worth is invested in your own efforts rather than the attitudes of others.'

"In the press the next day the headlines read "Mavis passes quietly through Kimberley". How right they were."

It was also in Kimberley that an an old friend came to spend an hour with Mavis and Ernest. As they reminisced with Doreen Else about old times, Mavis *"began to realize the value of quality friendships as opposed to superficial hero worship."* Painfully, Mavis was coming to terms with what was real, and what had real worth.

Valuable lessons or not, it was with a heavy heart and an injured leg that Mavis left Kimberley, especially when two old friends they met on the way out weren't interested in speaking to her personally. *"Any notion of self-importance that may still have been lingering was finally dispelled."*

And her physical well being, so painfully built up in endless hours of training, was fading as well. It was becoming difficult even to lift the leg she'd injured while trying to run through the rocks, and after only 29 miles the pain was so excruciating that she was glad to stop early.

The next day was no better, and she had to leave the road by 1:30 in the afternoon. Her *"misgivings were intensified when I heard one of the support team phone the sponsors to inform them of developments."* It was one thing to learn that few in her home town were very interested; it was quite another to be faced with the possibility of total failure.

And this was a very real possibility – after one hour and only four kilometers, the pain grew so intense that her team marked the road and rushed to the next significant town in hopes of finding a doctor. What they got was a local GP *"oblivious of the urgency, and so he gave me the 'run around' for an hour until he eventually decided to send me to the hospital for an examination."*

The news wasn't good. Her Achilles tendon was so damaged and badly swollen that Dr. Wiid advised her to rest two days and *"to seriously consider returning home...He had a strong feeling I would have to throw in the towel...I left with prescribed medication in my hand and the echo of stern admonishments ringing in my ears not to overdo things."*

For Mavis the enforced rest was a time to think. For the team it was a time to rest, wash and relax, a welcome breather from the *"hard grind of supporting"* her. Being human, Mavis *"felt rather resentful as I watched Les Du Plessis joyfully soaking up the sun as I wallowed in self-doubt."*

But the pit of despair wasn't a place she'd camp. Her previous struggles to achieve had taught her too much about the power of persistence and the *"untapped reserves that dwell deep within".* In the predawn darkness she was on the road again. Since pain wouldn't let her run, she went back to her athletic roots and race walked instead.

As she passed through Hopetown that afternoon, she wondered whether there might be a hidden message in the town's name. But there were no miracles. Able to move only *"as fast as the pain would allow",* her painful hobbling progress in intense heat (27 miles in more than 14 hours) made Cape Town seem very far away.

The pain remained a close companion the next day, as 15-minute rests every two hours failed to help much. Mavis had covered 38 miles, but it was still far too little.

The next days were little easier, but with leg and foot strapped "*to ease the pressure*", she kept rising at 4 am and limped slowly on into South Africa's Great Karoo desert, passing the halfway mark in Strydenberg two days late. Through the haze of pain and fatigue she still had to pause graciously at each major town to collect 'mayoral messages' for her distant destination.

THE MAGIC POTION, THE WITCH DOCTOR AND THE 'ANGEL OF THE ROAD'

> "*Nothing happens to any man, which he is not formed by nature to bear.*" (*Marcus Aurelius*)

"*On the long lonely roads through the Karoo Ernest met a witch doctor…whom he told about my injury…He gave Ernest some magic potion…*" Instantly a true believer, Ernest eagerly massaged the potion into her leg, "*fully confident that it was going to work its magic on my tired and strained tendons.*"

Ernest and the witch doctor were far more convinced about the effects than Mavis, who got more of a lift from a 'coloured' husband and wife on their way back to Cape Town. They stopped to chat, gave her her homemade pies and fruit, wished her well and assured her that the 'angel of the road' was looking after her. Their assurances that she would make it were a "*version of providence*" that Mavis could relate to rather better than magic potions and witch doctors.

Also soothing was the rare desert rain that set in as she passed through the town of Victoria West next morning – for a while. It wasn't a gentle shower. As the heavy rain developed into a terrifying electrical storm, she could see "*lightning bouncing off nearby telephone poles and it felt as if the lighting was going right through my body.*"

Earlier she had insisted on continuing through the heavy rain against the advice of her seconds. Now as she met them, she felt that this was one time "*I would have immediately responded to the first suggestion of stop-*

ping". But now they seemed to think she'd be able to cope, "*especially since I was being protected by the 'angel of the road'.*" Mavis hated lightning storms, and felt that the pain killers she had to take at each stop were needed not only to reduce her constant pain, but to "*subdue the fear of being struck by lightning.*"

It was on this day of fear and pain that she realized that while it might be a long time before she could really run again, and progress was slow, she could ask her Heavenly Father to help her keep going – one step at a time. Being human, she couldn't help wondering how much further along she might be with a healthy leg, but if she kept on a steady pace she had faith that she "*would see this ordeal through*". This became her nightly prayer.

That night brought a surprise as well as prayer. They'd planned a stop at Three Sisters, thinking it was a town – but there was no 'there, there'. Three Sisters was actually just a road junction with a gas station and a 'supply store'. But there was a place to park, and hot showers which brought such bliss that Mavis exclaimed "*Praise the Lord for small mercies!*" With lifted spirits, the 45 miles she'd walked that day didn't seem too bad after all.

Passing strangers remained a seriously mixed bag. The farm family who invited the team to breakfast gave them "*the unsurpassed hospitality of total strangers who treated us like old friends*" and loaded them up with so many goodies that they had all the supplies they needed for days.

That was a bit of a contrast to the lady who had her family stop their car so she could 'exclaim abrasively, "*Don't tell me you are enjoying this because I do not believe you!*" Mavis really hadn't needed anyone to tell her that her daily pain was at its most intense, or that she was finding the 'daily grind' really rough. But she wasn't about to tell this obnoxious woman any such thing, especially after she "*kept poking me on the chest repeating her statement numerous times, as though she were extracting a confession from a criminal.*"

Mavis never knew what 'strange reason' made this odd lady make Mavis the grindstone for her ax, before (to her deep relief) the family finally drove off. She was just determined not to let these people know how close to tears the unexpected attack had brought her. After the morning's hospitality, she'd expected encouragement, or at worst curiosity.

It felt good to relax that night after another hard day – and another hard-won 45 miles.

ONE STEP AT A TIME WITH HALF A LEG

Prayer notwithstanding, discouragement and despair were never far away, but constantly present enemies to be fought. On one very long hot desert day, as she fought against thoughts that now was the time to give up, she realized, *"I just had to keep going, even if I only had half a leg left."* She thought of how tough things were for her seconds, of how gladly they would have taken turns to do the running and let her rest. This was the day that the train drivers helped her hold on.

For most of the day, the main railway line to Cape Town ran close to the road. Each of the many passing 'train drivers' sounded his horn as he passed, and every one had his own distinctive 'call sign'. This friendly diversion *"helped me to keep my mind off the pain and stave off recurring thoughts of calling a halt to the ordeal."* Prayers are answered in many ways, and not always by taking the trial away.

Something always happened to lift Mavis' flagging spirits each time she reached the depths of despair. As the friendly railway line moved away from the road toward the end of the day, her brother George and his family arrived from far away Oudtshoorn to encourage her, and pain and exhaustion again faded into the background.

It didn't get any easier. On day 15 it took her half an hour at one point to hobble cautiously through half a kilometer. With feet and hands badly swollen, she limped onward, wondering what *"possessed me to do this to myself? Surely anyone with any sense would have thrown in the towel ages ago. How much pain is enough?"*

Her seconds expected her to give in, but said little, *"fearing that I would not cope well with the disappointment."* Mavis simply held on, knowing that without faith and prayer she would come short – but that with them she might still accomplish the seemingly impossible.

And she did. Despite the 45 miles covered on the previous day's painful slog, her astonished team saw their 'invalid' ready to tackle the road once more in the 4 am predawn darkness. *"They did not know my secret, which was to take one step at a time."* A poem by Lucille Boesken had become a central source of inspiration:

One seed at a time
- and the garden grows.
One drop at a time
- and the river flows.
One word at a time
- and the book is read.
One stroke at a time
- and the painting is spread.
One chip at a time
- and the statue's unveiled.
One step at a time
- and the mountain is scaled.
One thing at a time
- and that done well
Is the only sure way
to succeed and excel.
You can write, you can paint,
You can sculpt or climb.
You can do it by taking
One step at a time.

Her leg hadn't let Mavis run since Hopetown, but her experience as a champion race walker meant she could cover much more ground than anyone traveling at a normal walking pace.

And people kept appearing to cheer her. A busload of athletes on their way to run in Cape Town's Two Oceans Marathon (including a junior team from Mavis' own region of Southern Transvaal) stopped to wish her luck. They showered her with plenty of encouragement, and their excitement as they took pictures was so infectious that *"this provided me with sufficient determination to keep going, at least for a while."* Mavis knew how much she needed people, despite the way she withdrew into herself as she ran.

Eight days after the injury, 'miraculously' she was still going, and the pain in her leg began to ease *"or perhaps I was just getting used to it."* Her distance for day 17 rose to fifty miles, and even the chatter among the support team grew cheerier.

For the first time since the less than triumphant homecoming, she knew she would make it.

RUNNING SLOWLY TO JOY

Now she began running again. The pace might be no faster than she'd been walking, but even running slowly felt wonderful after the days of limping. That night there was a hot bath in an actual motel. Bliss was complete.

But the desert still didn't know it was supposed to be autumn, and the intense heat sapped her energy. In the blistering sun, Ernest had to sponge her down every few miles, and Mavis wrapped wet hankies around her hands in an attempt to stem the swelling.

Fear struck outside the oasis town of Laingsburg, where well-wishers told her that she'd have to take a detour because of road construction. Her heart sank at the news, but this detour proved far tamer than the one near Kimberley. And as she climbed a long hill that concealed the town, encouragement from people running with her helped keep her going.

But the climax came at the crest of the hill. What seemed like most of the colored people of the town came from all sides to crowd the road and meet her. There were *"expectant mothers, mothers carrying babies, toddlers, children, fathers...all seemed to be jostling each other in their attempts to touch me...I was being jostled about – they were touching me, pinching me...clapping, shouting, laughing, singing...nonstop...What a joyous experience!"*

Mavis had never seen anything like it, although the formal ritual at the Civic Center was the same as on all the previous occasions. But this time, still buoyed by her boisterous welcome, she made the mistake of shaking hands with the people standing close to the Mayor – and then had to *"shake each and every hand that was present. I am sure many of them more than once."*

Accompanied by a group that wanted to run with her on the last leg of the day, Mavis' euphoria led her to run faster. By late afternoon, once more alone, her throbbing leg forced her once more to face her limits. The day ended in a walk, tired and weary and in lots of pain, and annoyed with herself for not having been more vigilant. After 53 miles, she needed her rest.

'I FIRST WANT MY PICTURE TOOK'

There were blissful moments away from people as well. As she ran along the quiet road early the next day, a wonderful sense of peace and well-being filled her, and just before sunrise the stillness was almost tangible. Anxieties fell away, and she *"felt at one with the miracle of my surroundings, being only vaguely conscious of the droning engine of the support vehicle behind me with its guiding headlights cutting a path through the darkness ahead of me. Then the sun rose with a splash of color rapidly spreading over the horizon accompanied by a cacophony of sound as the birds, the dogs, the sheep and the cattle all celebrated their joy at being alive."* Then she had to focus on crossing the road safely, the moment had passed, and the reality that came crashing into her consciousness *"felt like a coarse intrusion into my blissful cocoon."*

Also intruding was the voice of her anxious husband shouting at her. He wanted her to go back to walking, and she sulked all day as she plodded along desperately trying to recapture the magic of the morning experience. Negative thoughts made the day twice as hard and feel twice as long. But she kept on – one step at a time. One of the secrets of life is to keep moving outside the 'peak moments' when heaven seems near.

Amid heavy traffic, Mavis' glumness was broken with a jolt when she met a large crowd of 'colored folk' *"who had jogged two kilometers out of Touwsriver so that they could boast at having been the first people from their town to have seen me. They decided to make my entry a grand affair by noisily accompanying me into town. The crowd quickly grew and soon it had commandeered the whole road, much to the chagrin of the drivers. The vehicles were beginning to back up, causing a minor traffic jam which people in such remote areas never expect to experience."*

Athletes from the local running club found their more formal welcoming plans completely lost in the boisterous crowd scene. When Mavis asked one of these runners *"to persuade a woman who had entered into the 'spirit' of things far too literally and who was finding difficulty staying on her feet"* to move off the road before a car hit her, the woman refused because *"I first want my picture took."*

In the midst of all this, the chief traffic officer from the next town of De Doorns arrived, reporting that the townsfolk had been camped on the roadside waiting for Mavis. *"He seemed quite relieved that he could go back* with the news that I would definitely be arriving the next day, probably at about 8 am."

Then to her wondering joy, Mavis spotted her son Jess, who stayed on the road with her most of the rest of the day. With the 'wonderful conversation' as they race walked down the road together, the negativity of the day faded away completely. More happy and relaxed than in a long time, she went drifted into a sound sleep realizing that it been a good day.

Through joy in the morning, the gritty slog of life's daily struggle, to joy again in the evening. Life does not stay forever in the valleys, any more than it does on the peaks.

MAVIS GETS A FLAT – AND THE SWEET GRAPES OF SUCCESS

Next morning Mavis kept anticipating an encore of the previous morning's 'symphonic daybreak' as they passed over the mountains and down into the grapevines of the majestic Hex River Valley. It didn't happen, but she felt touched and honored as she passed through the town of De Doorns.

Children had been let out of class for the occasion and thronged the road, calling out, "Oumatjie jy's laat." (Granny you're late). *"They then trailed after me for a long way, again each one seemingly keen to touch me. The townsfolk followed in cars, trucks and on foot for more than an hour."*

She found herself being pushed around, completely overwhelmed in the friendly crush, and tiring rapidly. How could she get them to go home? Inspiration struck with the memory of the intoxicated woman the day before. Mavis got one of her team to start taking pictures. Once the first person had their photo taken they all stopped to have one taken, while a relieved Mavis left them behind.

"By the time everyone's ego-needs had been met I was out of sight and happy to be alone once again. They were happy in the belief that perhaps they would have a moment of fame if their photograph were to appear in a newspaper somewhere." Mavis, once a nobody herself, could relate – but she had to get away.

On she went, through the majestic peaks and green vineyards of the south end of the valley, through winding mountain valleys into another broad stretch of vineyards, and through the old Cape Dutch town of Worcester, with its English name and almost entirely non-English-speaking population. There the local traffic department and police had held the roads clear, waiting patiently as the scheduled hour came and went. One local cop explained her arrival time by saying that 'Auntie Mavis' was only late because she'd had a 'tekkie-burst' (a running shoe blowout).

For the rest of the day, the Worcester traffic department helped her deal with the heavy traffic on the narrow national road. Wine farmers loaded the team with cases of export grapes. One farmer had waited by the road for a long time *"so that he could personally hand to me a very special bunch of grapes. They were so delicious I wondered if this was what 'the sweet taste of success' was like."* Mavis saved a few to savor each morning, wanting to make them last as long as possible.

FOLLOWING MAVIS TO FEEL HER LEG

Another old running buddy now joined her for the rest of the day. Kallie De Jager had run with her in the 100-mile race in 1971, and it was good to see him again. At the farm stall where they stopped for the night, another crowd of well-wishers gathered, including a farmer bringing four bottles of 'prized export wine' that would *"keep the boys happy for a few nights."* Less welcome was an elderly man with two lady friends, who had followed her for some time by car.

"I was chatting to some people in the crowd when I felt someone touching my leg. At first I thought it was one of the support team checking my injury. To my surprise I realized it was the guy who had been following me in his car. I curtly informed him that my leg was in good condition and he said he could see that. This caused much merriment amongst his lady companions who whispered to me that he had been wanting to do that all day. At least one person in the crowd had achieved their goal for the day." The press often commented that she had the legs of a teenager, but this kind of admiration was a bit much.

After three weeks on the road, Mavis was now at the foot of the towering, rugged Du Toit's Kloof pass. In two more days she'd reach the *"end of the lollipop"*.

A BURST OF SONG, AND THE LAST TEST

Mavis knew that Du Toit's Kloof would be her toughest mountain test of the run, so she was overjoyed to see Kallie's 'beaming smile' as she stepped out of the caravan at 4 am. His pleasant company seemed to add to her sense of well-being and comfort that warm, moist morning as she walked to the foot of the pass, then began to run up the winding road into the mountains. An unusual touch was the group of Gospel singers who serenaded them near the top.

Then Kallie left to go to work – and the coastal weather hit on the downward slope. It turned bitterly cold, and swirling hurricane-force gusts of wind made it hard to stay on her feet, much less run. *"When the wind blew from the front I had to lean right into it, fighting hard to progress at a snail's pace. As it turned to blow from behind it blew me over. But it was most frightening when it blew from the side."*

At times she was sure the wind would blow her right off the mountain into the canyon below, especially since she had to run on the edge of the narrow roadway so that she could dodge the heavy oncoming traffic. Narrow and only two lanes wide, this mountain road was the national highway from Pretoria to Cape Town, with traffic to match. And all of this had to be done on an injured leg which had been badly stressed by the climb to the summit. Mavis was petrified, and even the press found it impossible to take photographs in the howling gale. They also seemed strangely reluctant to be blown over the edge.

By the time her team stopped her for a badly needed early breakfast break, she was shivering so badly that not even warm food and drink, massage and wrapping herself in eiderdown could stop the shakes for the hour she was off the road.

Still shivering, she drifted on down the pass wondering why she was being tested so hard again, and how she would combat the cold for the rest of the day. She didn't have to. She surfaced from her dazed contemplations, imagining the worst, to realize that the wind had dropped and that the sun was *"beginning to peep out from behind the clouds"*.

As she stripped down to running shorts and top it seemed almost as though what she'd experienced a few miles earlier had merely been a nightmare, replaced by a feeling that a burden had been lifted – with a pleasant surprise.

A less pleasant one awaited. Her seconds had moved on down the road, and children playing in the fields near the foot of the pass decided that it would be fun to throw rocks at the *'slightly built, grey-haired grandmother jogging past…The 'galloping granny' had become the 'artful dodger'*.

Mavis never did figure out why they did this – she was just glad to leave these unruly children safely behind. Running was now relatively easy as she moved over a gently rolling, often flat landscape of fields and vineyards. That night she was unable to get a straight answer from any of those who'd come out to see her as to how far it really was to Cape Town. If her guess was correct – only about forty miles – she was almost there. For the team, a long day got longer when the sponsors insisted they clean the mud off the team caravans so they'd sparkle for the grand finale.

TABLE MOUNTAIN AND MOTHER CITY

> *Cape Town is called the 'Mother City' because it is the oldest*
> *European city in South Africa, founded by the Dutch in 1653.*

The big day was at hand. The traffic was denser than ever, but posed no threat as three patrol cars moved with her. With their protection, the only problem from the crush of vehicles was that the thick fumes made it hard to breathe. As she ran in the heat, *"majesticTable Mountain...in the distance...seemed to be gesturing to me to join it in enjoying the glorious Cape sunshine. The mountain looked as if it had been scrubbed and polished for my entrance into the Mother City."*

Mavis had no need to rush. It would be eleven that morning before the mayor would meet her at City Hall. This may have been just as well. There was again road construction to deal with as she passed, but this time *"the road workers all downed tools as I passed to cheer me on. The cars honked as they passed with the occupants leaning out the windows shouting encouragement."* The South African Broadcasting Corporation had sent Gerhard Viviers to interview her as she and her seconds relaxed on a grassy spot by the roadside, and the excitement built steadily.

As they moved deeper into the city with only six miles to go, the support team had to leave her. Mavis soon missed them, as the heat left her desperate for some water and a sponge. In spite her discomfort it seemed that Table Mountain was glowing – just for her.

It hit home that another major milestone was near enough to touch after enduring the long painful road. At five minutes to eleven she spotted the clock in Adderley Street, and knew that City Hall was just around the corner. *"Five more minutes and it would all be over."*

As she remembered the many times along the road when she'd been 'certain it was over', the feeling of having achieved her goal was 'real magic'. She realized *"the Lord does not give us more than we can endure...I had learned the importance of 'staying with it just a little longer'...".*

She 'felt like Superwoman', with all the hardships forgotten. One step at a time for a thousand miles, with faith, prayer and encouragement from those around her, had brought her all the way to the end – only 4 hours over her planned time of 22 days.

Then suddenly she was on the old military parade ground before City Hall, where more than a thousand people were cheering her on. She addressed them from the balcony, and the mayor presented her with a medal and a bouquet. Her Hall's Orange sponsors presented her with a silver tray, the support team members got 'festival ties', and tea at the reception attracted a deputy cabinet minister as well as a Mr. Cruizwagen from back home in Germiston.

The press and radio were there for interviews, but Mavis wandered through the rest of the day in a dazed trance, barely noticing what was happening around her.

Running toward the finish on Cape Town's Grand Parade.

'ONE OF THE MOST FANTASTIC WOMEN IN THE WORLD'

As she flew home the next day, what she had achieved really began to register. Over and over she read the front page report of her run on the front page report on her run, finding it difficult to accept that it was her they were writing about, to say nothing of the suggestion that her feat made her a worthy candidate for Woman of the Year. But there it stood in black on newsprint: "Mavis arrived on schedule at 11 am in Cape Town today. From the balcony of the City Hall she told the thousand strong crowd that when she saw Table Mountain she knew she had met the challenge she had set, and notwithstanding the tribulations, it had all been worthwhile. She is definitely not merely the 'Galloping Granny' of the press, she is something more…Wally Hayward, one of South Africa's greatest long-distance runners, when asked prior to the run said she would do it, 'She has the determination, the dedication and the will-power. She is one of the most fantastic women in the world…' "

Running through Mavis' mind were the words of Rudyard Kipling's "If':

> *"If you can force your heart and nerve and sinew*
> *To serve their turn long after they have gone,*
> *And so hold on when there is nothing in you*
> *Except the will, which says to them: Hold on.*
> *If you can fill the unforgiving minute*
> *With sixty seconds worth of distance run,*
> *Yours is the earth and all that's in it*
> *And - what's is more - you'll be a man my son."*

She might not be a man, but she knew first hand what Kipling meant. With these thoughts, she drifted into slumber. She had indeed learned more about enduring a little longer. Moving past self-importance, need for recognition and self-pity, she'd become nationally famous for self-discipline. As one *Sunday Express* writer put it, she'd run nearly the distance of a Comrades ultramarathon a day for 22 days, and her time would have been 'world class' even for a man. No other woman had run half that distance.

For months she'd sweated through five hours of training runs a day. Defying the rules forbidding women to enter, she'd conquered the Harrismith Mountain Race three times. The very next year she'd run to Cape Town again, smashing her own record by more than three days.

Of course there were limits. It was far too soon after the run from Pretoria to Cape Town that Mavis had her first chance to run the Comrades ultramarathon officially. She couldn't bear not to take the chance, but her body simply could not run fast enough to finish in the allotted time. Not long before the end she dropped out, for the first time since 1961 and the last time ever. But her wornout body had to force her to stop – mere hardship wouldn't make her give up.

"It's not the suffering that is important but the objective. if you knew anything, sir, about the pains of labor, you would know that the moment the child is born, all labor pains are forgotten,. They become irrelevant. It is a moment of great joy. That is how it is with my running."

True grit, true class, true faith.

"If Mrs Hutchinson can do it so can we . . . Are there any athletes here who'll join me on a quick marathon from Cape Town to Pretoria?"

Chapter 13: RUNNING WITH FAIR LADY

———•◆•———

*"I thought at first she had done it to avoid the unfitness that
accompanies flying, but she told me she loves flying and didn't
know why she had run all that way, except it was the furthest
she could go without running into the South Atlantic. The
furthest my two grannies ever ran was after my grandpas,
and when they caught them they stopped dead."*
(Cape Times columnist John Scott)"

'I'D RATHER WEAR OUT THROUGH USE THAN THROUGH RUST'

Her pluck and passion for running were going to be tested once again as
she set her sights toward bettering her time to Cape Town. This time her
1471-kilometer adventure would start from Germiston, some 18 months
after her ground-breaking run the previous year. It would be another step
in getting ready for the 'dream' run across America, and in attracting a
sponsor with deep enough pockets.

After a warm sendoff at 10 on the spring morning of September 22,
1976, the 'running wonder' settled into her customary stride, accompanied
on the first day for part of the way by fellow athletes from her club. Traffic
police escorted her through the crush of vehicles on the roads in the opening stages. Under these conditions progress of only 39 km on the first day
was not unexpected. It was very different after that.

Starting her days at 4 am became par for the course once again, running in the beams of her team's headlights until dawn. Despite blisters, the
next day's mileage rose to nearly twice the total on the first day. Blisters
continued for a while, but the first stages of the race, sponsored by leading
women's magazine Fair Lady along with BP Southern Africa, went without
any major hitches. She would often cover 30 or more miles before lunch.

She would run till 8 am, have breakfast and a breather for an hour and
push till 1 pm. At that point she'd have a bite and rest another hour before
hitting the road again till sunset. During the breaks, one of Ernie's duties

was to pop her blisters. In the evening he'd rub her down with wintergreen.

As the running routine settled into a rhythm of its own, she crossed the Vaal River into the Orange Free State, where intense heat sometimes made running more uncomfortable – but by this time she knew how to deal with it. Dark glasses and goggles, protective sun creams and 'about 10 different foot salves' followed her everywhere in the two caravans driven by Ernie and his assistants Paul and 'Ampie'. These two young men had once been among the neighborhood children who ran after 'Pied Pipers' Mavis and Ernie in the evenings. All three helped keep their 'star' on the road.

By now she knew how to protect her feet as well, changing shoes and socks at least three times a day. She was prepared. She had trained about 35 miles a day, so extending this to 50 miles during the run wasn't too much of a stretch.

In the diary of her friend Jean Blake, who looked after domestic matters on the trip, it's clear that the race was going as planned, despite the heat often giving way to cold and rain in the unstable weather of spring. On day seven Jean wrote that "Mavis is running very well with no trouble...very fit."

Being caught by 'terrible rain and hail storms' near the Free State capital of Bloemfontein on the afternoon of day 8 was a bit of a bummer, but not the end of the world. It was better than the hurricane-force headwinds and driving rain and snow of the Drakensberg range, and Mavis had already covered well 50 kilometers that morning. The storms didn't go away – two struck the next day – but Mavis ran on undeterred. As she continued on toward the southwest, her daily mileage gradually rose.

FAT OF THE LAND

The Free State farmers appeared to be remarkably wealthy – Mavis noted they all seemed to be driving Mercedes Benzes. One farmer posed an unexpected culinary challenge when he invited them to dinner. What appeared on the table were masses of lamb chops, farm sausages, steaks and fried bread. Mavis knew that she couldn't tuck in to this rich feast if she wanted to cope with the next day's running. 'A tricky social thing', Mavis remembers.

Fortunately Ernie saved the day. He found her some fish, which she could enjoy with a little fruit. "*Hopefully the farmer wasn't too offended and I didn't have to compromise my performance on the road.*"

A lot of her running energy came from raw honey together with vitamin supplements, raw fruit and veggie salads. Heavy fatty foods were not for the road and there was still a lot of road to cover, with unexpected challenges likely.

Much of that road would take her through the energy-sapping heat of South Africa's Karoo desert.

HAIL AND RAIN, HEAT AND SAND

The hail and rain of the Free State caught up with Mavis again in the desert, but it didn't bring much relief from the heat. Near Beaufort West, "she ran piled high with windcheaters that didn't allow her body to breathe and caused the sweat to pour off her…" On day 13, she fought a terrible head wind so strong that she had a hard time running against it.

Jean Blake and her improvised thornbush washing line.
Picture from Fair Lady.

But mostly it was just hot, although in the early coolness before dawn, the beautiful starlit sky of the Karoo made a spectacular canopy when it was clear. In an article titled "The Puzzle That Refuses to be Solved", a writer for the Johannesburg Star gave a memorable description of her trek through inhospitable desert terrain.

"The sight of this slim woman merging with her own mirage as she appears on the horizon of a vast, empty landscape is heart stopping. Those slender legs, bronzed like an advertisement for suntan oil, belie her 51 years.

"She's definitely not the 'galloping granny' of the Press, a sobriquet she loathes. Mavis is something more.

"Vulnerability is marked by continually having to get off the road onto the gravel verge each time a truck, petrol tanker etc. bears down on her, putting her off her rhythmic stride and causing her to cringe away from the roaring whoosh of air and vibration."

It was precisely this kind of hazard that brought Mavis in crushing contact with the tarmac. She stumbled on a stone which brought her flat on her face and resulted in a badly swollen nose and scraped knees. Her lip was already throbbing with a fever blister.

To add to her discomfort her grazed hands became very swollen at times – in fact so swollen and sunburned that Ernie again had to come to the rescue by wrapping two of his handkerchiefs around them.

But her aching feet, although carefully smeared with the hordes of salves carted along to protect these vital running 'assets', just had to wait till the end of the day before she could soak them in a well deserved tub of warm sudsy water.

By then her running shorts were drenched with perspiration and provided the finishing touch to the picture of a fighter - but a fighter who had not lost her sense of femininity as the 'Puzzle' article made clear:

"She looked at her weather beaten face in a cracked silver hand mirror painted with a design of yellow roses and fluffed up her hair."

She had come a long way, so the the final destination didn't seem quite so far away any more to the woman in the mirror. But rain, hail, and wind, broken by spells of scorching heat, would pursue her all through the next 150 miles of the long stretch from Leeuw-Gamka to well past Touws River.

Fortunately the endless slog now began to be lightened by groups of fans along the way. As she passed, the local 'colored' communities turned out en masse to cheer on 'Aunty Mavis', sometimes running with her. Jean Blake preserved a careful list of 28 runners' names.

'Fair Lady' in the Desert

It was also a bit past Leeuw-Gamka that Flavia Pascoe and photographer Peter John from the magazine Fair Lady caught up with Mavis. In her article, 'The Unstoppable Woman', Flavia wrote:

"'Where's Mavis?'…We looked up the hill. The white figure seemed slanted in the refracted light on the tarmac: then Mavis emerged; slight, insubstantial in the endless expanse. We ran to meet her.

"It was somewhere between Leeuw-Gamka and Prince Albert Road.…It was the fourteenth day of her marathon run and the weather hadn't been kind. Rain, hail and high winds preceded the heat of the Karroo. Victoria-West was a memorable experience, sloshing through inches of water — but Mavis went on doggedly, never varying her pace. She was walking now with short fast steps, much faster than ordinary walking pace and only a little slower than her own jogging trot.

"Mavis slowed her stride to match mine. She started to tell of the anxieties that had built up before she left from Germiston City Hall…The track suits hadn't arrived until the night before…Running shoes, ordered six months before, hadn't arrived and another supplier had to be found to provide 12 pairs of size six shoes…

"These last-minute anxieties tell on Mavis. She is a woman who loves order; she tries to prepare things well in advance and leave nothing to chance. But she can't control everything. The anxieties caught up with her on the day the run began. She looked very relaxed and happy when she left, but 39 km later — less than half the distance she normally runs in a day — she had to stop. The beautifully controlled body let her down just once. 'I had a terrible bilious attack.'…

"I'd wanted to talk with Mavis from time to time to try to tune in on her mind to reach the profundity of thought believed to be released by pushing the body to extremes. But alas, on that first day my thoughts were for my inadequate breathing and the pain in my calf muscles.

"And there was Mavis, eating up the kilometres at seven an hour, completely freed from physical considerations for much of the time. She'd daydream about her children —Ronald, Pamela, Jess, Allan, Gayle and Beverley. She'd keep count of the kilometres as she passed the markers on the road, and think about breaking her own record set 18 months previously. And she'd think about herself. A kind of confrontation.

"...She hates the epithet 'Galloping Gran'. She neither gallops, nor is the image grandmotherly. On the road she looks like a girl with her long legs, beautifully shaped and toned, her golden tan offset by short white shorts and vest leaving her slim arms bare.

"...Her team stop her often. Ernie sprays her with anti-sunburn lotion; Paul and Ampie take turns in feeding her cups of orange juice. Her sun-swollen hands are wrapped in handkerchiefs. Cars come uncomfortably close to the running figure. Mavis stops until they pass. Long distance drivers have passed the caravans several times; they toot encouragement. Some drivers give her a wide berth; others intent on reaching their destination seem not to see her..."

Galloping or not, she finished 51 miles that day. Jean Blake recorded that a very fit and brown Mavis "had a good run...in the terrible heat."

It was the next day that started to test her resolve. The road led from Prince Albert to Laingsburg, and it was narrow with constant detours. Mavis had already fallen twice by the time the journalists from Fair Lady caught up with her, shaking her confidence. When would the next fall come?

And after more than two weeks of pounding the asphalt long hours in all sorts of weather, thrown off balance by shock waves from passing traffic, her 'slow' right leg was starting to give trouble.

Against a very strong head wind, she made progress by race walking some of the time to ease a sore foot that was also putting her off her stride. Her mileage for the day was down to 47.

'IT IS THE MIND THAT IMPLES HER ON.'

The Fair Lady team was based at Matjiesfontein, a quaint little Karoo village established as a model 'refreshment stop' along the railway line. The luxuries there induced guilt.

"We'd drive back to the hotel in the heat of the day for the icy refreshment of a swim and a quick nap. We felt guilty, thinking of Mavis.

"Her ordeal wasn't purely physical. She is so fit and finely trained that she can forget about it unless something happens to cause pain and discomfort; it is the mind that impels her on. Mavis has to have will to continue running when the sun is hot, when she's becoming tired, when everything in her calls out for rest. At one stage she said: 'One of the things that keeps me going is the thought of just half an hour in the sea.'...

"That second night in the Karroo…I sat on Mavis' bunk. She had washed her feet, sponging them again and again, and was resting while she ate a cup of asparagus soup. She looked young and gentle, like a child ready for sleep after an exciting day. She was tired, but communicative…"

Mavis spoke about her future plans and her ambition to run across America, which would call on all of her talent for order and organization.

"It's a chaotic and disorderly world, but Mavis has chosen a field where order is paramount.

"She has tuned her body to perfection; she knows exactly what she can do with it and how far she can push it. She plans a trip like this one months in advance and if things go wrong — as with the running shoes —it isn't her fault…and her shopping list included everything down to the last bar of Kitkat chocolate.

"There's not a millimeter's difference between the length of each step she takes and she knows exactly what she wants at each four-hour stop. Woe betide all if it isn't there. She knows if she packed it and there it must be.

"Suddenly I lost Mavis. I could see it in her eyes. I got up quietly and left, and I'll swear that as I closed the caravan door she fell asleep."

OF TWINS AND RUNNING

"Why does she set herself the punishing, and seemingly pointless, task of long distance running. I don't believe there's a single answer, but another clue came from Jean Blake who told me that Mavis is one of identical twins.

"…she is as alike Mavis as a mirror image. They have uncanny empathy — they feel each other's pains and fears even when they're continents apart. Doreen suffers all the aches of a marathon runner right there in her home near Vereeniging.

"And after Mavis had fallen during her run, she heard from Doreen that on the same day she had fallen too.

…Their mother confirmed that Mavis and Doreen became one word, one concept.…but in their twinship they must have lacked personal identity. Mavis has found a separate identity."

When Mavis thinks back today about her late twin, she agrees with Flavia.

'LIKE A CHAMPION'

> *"I suppose that when I fell heavily…I struggled to regain my
> composure. But one of the most difficult periods was during the
> final stages when I was hampered by strained tendons. That was
> when I found it really hard, especially when going down hill."*

Back on the road, the leg problem became acute when after a 3:35 am running start on day 16, she pulled a tendon in her left leg. Ernie insisted she
race walk again rather than run.

Although obviously in pain, Mavis covered over 12 miles before the
sun rose, never altering her pace. Flavia wrote of this day: "You only have
to walk with her to realize how fast and steady it is. It was a beautiful day,
but scorching. Her hands were puffy and even early in the morning she
looked tired. But she came down the hills outside Laingsburg like a champion – no one who didn't know about the tendon would have guessed she
was in anything but prime condition. "

But Mavis thought otherwise. For a time the pain forced her to slow to
only 3 miles per hour, and this kind of pace just wasn't in her plan. She'd
intended to cover 62 miles that day, and she wasn't going to make it. Flavia
believed that it "wasn't humanly possible". Mavis wasn't a great believer in
limiting the possible. She had about 180 miles to cover in a little over three
days, and she wasn't going to be late. She speeded up through the pain,
covered 52 of them, and paid the price.

The Fair Lady team were no longer quite passive onlookers. "Our involvement with Mavis' quest was growing; we began to care deeply, to
share her need to arrive in Cape Town on time. Ahead of her, a long way
ahead, lay the Hex River Mountains and the even more formidable Hotten-
tots Holland range traversed by Du Toits Kloof…My sunburn and those
aching muscles became a touchstone to bring me closer to Mavis, to identify with the pain she must have felt in her leg; to feel with her the fever blister the sun had brought out on her lip; to care about each of the hundreds
of kilometres.…She and her crew never doubted she'd make it; or never
showed it if they did. We weren't so sure."

The desert landscape softened as the day drew on, and there were more
spring flowers. The desert hills grew into mountains. A strong wind sprang up,
giving a foretaste of what might meet Mavis in the mountains ahead.

16 hours after her start, she came off the road at seven, "under a sky turned a brilliant pink." Her Fair Lady chronicler adds: "She looked up as she stopped, allowing herself to be absorbed in the beauty around her. Piebald horses chomped gently by the road; a hedge of tamarisk lent a silvery pink to the darkening ground. It was a restoring moment. Mavis talked briefly as she washed her feet, then closed the door on us and the sunset."

'SHE'LL MAKE IT.'

> *"...true enduring represents not merely the passage of time,*
> *but the passage of the soul...With enduring comes a willing-*
> *ness...to "press forward" even when we are bone weary and*
> *would much rather pull off to the side of the road."*
> *– Neal A. Maxwell*

Mavis described the last days of her gut wrenching undertaking as sheer torture. Her super fitness couldn't dull the terrible tendon pain. For that a special kind of tenacity was required: moving right through the pain and the disappointment of a slower pace than she thought she should achieve.

A worried Ernie wanted to make sure Mavis didn't burn out in a bright flame of determination. "Athletes can't think for themselves. If I let her run, she'd run hour after hour. She ran for 37 hours when we did the first run to Durban. We didn't know any better then. She'd burn herself out. We'll just start earlier and earlier each day. She'll make it."

That proved true. The first of the mountains came that day, and Mavis took the Hex River range in her stride as she "gobbled them up and strode triumphantly down into the valley." Full of new fire, despite a 2:30 am start, she "forgot about her tendon, the sunburn, the painful, swollen hands."

Her son Allan accompanied her at least part of the way, and the colored population of the town of De Doorns were just as enthusiastic as on her run the previous year. To escape the mob scene, they once more used the 'picture trick'. Jean Black writes: "We took two photos and then bluffed them we were taking more so that they could let Mavis and Allan go on their way."

After De Doorns, she moved past more vineyards green with spring leaves, over the mountains at the south end of the Hex River valley, and on through the relatively flat Breede River valley and the town of Worcester.

Just before Worcester, her tendons started giving her more problems. "*This time it was both heels.*" But she'd again covered 52 miles.

'IT WAS THE WORST EXPERIENCE OF MY CAREER.'

When Mavis, Ernie, and Jean, and their two younger teammates got to the foot of rugged Du Toit's Kloof Pass, the goal was almost close enough to touch. But here, on the narrow road winding up through towering crags, the Fair Lady run turned into something no fair lady would choose.

"*Du Toit's Kloof was a real nightmare. It was raining again and the wind the strongest I had had to battle through. It kept changing direction. There were a few photographers trying to take photos – they eventually gave up. At times the following wind was so strong I felt as if any moment I would land flat on my face. The next moment I had a head wind where I was unable to move forward at all. Then again I was almost blown into the side of the mountain.*" It was so cold that her rest break in a warm blanket helped very little. As she got back on the road she was still shivering.

The Fair Lady crew left another vivid description. "Freezing at the foot, Mavis walked in a tracksuit. By the time she reached the top of the pass, she was sweating furiously. She abandoned the tracksuit, dropping it where she stood for the crew to pick up as the passed, and braved the downward climb. There was a gale blowing and Mavis became icy cold again as she struggled against the wind to put one foot in front of the other. She felt the pull of the cliff, a sheer drop, and was out of touch with her crew because a caravan cannot park on the mountain. The fear of cars was heightened by the narrow road."

But what impressed the journalists most was the *way* she conquered the pass. "She just kept up that unflagging pace, faltering slightly in the tunnel before Du Toits Kloof — scared that a driver might not see her in the dark —but she took the kloof with amazing vigour."

All the same, Jean Blake was probably right when she wrote: "I am sure she was glad to see the bottom of it."

The last lap that day was one she didn't have to do alone. For the miles across the Cape winelands to Paarl beneath its famous rock, her son Allan joined her again. This was no longer the desert. "The lush landscape seemed to swallow up the runner and her entourage. She seemed less vulnerable than she had in the lonely Karoo."

Through the pass

'A REAL TRIUMPH OF MIND OVER BODY'

Ernie's cautions about burning out had all been aimed at making sure Mavis had enough left for the final push. She had.

The last stretch from Paarl to Cape Town called for an all-out effort, and so she pulled out all the stops. That meant hitting the road at 1:45 am, once more running in Ernie's headlights as she often did to catch the cool of the predawn hours and to make up time when necessary.

The Fair Lady duo saw her going down the highway as if driven. "The mechanical perfection of her steps was like a drumbeat – soundless to all but those of us who had grown to care so much...Mavis never faltered."

As so often, there were "*a lot of road works going on*". With officers protecting her from cars and trucks, she slowed the traffic coming out of Cape Town quite a bit. Some were less than charmed with the slowdown, but others were enthusiastic. "*There was a lot of hooting and waving from the motorists.*"

During the last miles, with the end then firmly in her sights, her spirits lifted. "*I suddenly just thought it was over and that a wonderful finish was waiting.*"

Flavia gives a flavor of the finish: "She ran up Adderley Street, into Darling Street to where a cheering crowd waited...I felt a lump in my throat. Mavis had made it, minutes before eleven o'clock that Monday morning. The marathon had taken her 19 days and 50 minutes. She'd broken her own record. It was a real triumph of mind over body. And maybe that's what it is all about; that's what makes Mavis run."

The new record was an improvement of more than three days over almost the same distance as the previous year's run from Pretoria. She'd averaged about 50 miles a day, about like running a Comrades Marathon every day – 19 days in a row. It was true heroism, a victory of the spirit and will.

WITH A SMILE AND A NEW GRANDSON

As Mavis took her final strides toward Cape Town City Hall on her 'pilgrimage-for-fun', wearing her last and 12th pair of running shoes, she still managed a smile.

Reporter Andre van der Zwan captured it well on that 11th day of October when he said: "Her short cropped gray hair glittered with perspiration as she collapsed happily into the arms of her husband. It was a stirring occasion. A stunning achievement.

"Cold chills went down my spine at the mere thought of trying to emulate this feat. In fact, not many males have the 'true grit' to even attempt to tackle the course…"

In answer to a question about whether he could equal his wife's doings, Ernie was ready with an immediate response: " No sir, I know of easier ways to travel to Cape town." He said just driving the car and caravan on the trip tired him out.

In reality, this 'epitome of the trainer with the champ' was more fit than he admitted – quite capable of sticking with Mavis for 10 miles or so. And he was the one who had to keep her at a schedule her body could stand. As he saw it, she might be 'perpetual motion' in a 'magnificent human machine,' but the machine needed to be carefully controlled to reach the end of the line without mechanical failure.

When she finally 'machined' into the finish, the welcome was sweeter than usual because she could share her triumph with her beloved sons Jess and Allan.

But the crowning joy was the presence of Jess' wife with their nine-week old baby boy David, her most recent grandchild at the time. He clearly stole the show and granny's heart. Forgotten for the moment were her badly swollen ankles and sun-blistered mouth that made verbal communication a bit of a strain.

BED AND HONEY

Baby David's quiet gurgles and the poses with grandma for photographs could not delay Mavis' need for replenishment forever, however. Fatigue was taking its toll. While still cuddling the infant, her answer to a question made her immediate desires clear: "All I really want is a nice soft bed."

Some even joked that she'd done her bit for energy conservation by using an alternative fuel at a time of gasoline restrictions – Mavis ran on honey.

Chapter 14: NORTHERN LIMITS
The Last Warmup

———————•·◆·•———————

*"The puzzle which obstinately refuses to be solved, is that spe-
cial quality that takes a woman over peaks blanketed with
cloud, that makes the impossible dream possible..."*
(Johannesburg Star)

Messina's mayor fired the starting shot, punctuating another celebrity send
off for Mavis, as midst well wishes and cheers she commenced one more
practice run for her much anticipated trans-continental trek – a daunting
prospect beyond the ability of most distance runners, and for which she
had to be in peak plus condition. Vanda Cosmetics had agreed to be her
sponsors for an America run in 1978, and she had to be ready.

It was also a chance to complete her survey of her country on foot from
north to south. Messina was on the northern border with Rhodesia (now
Zimbabwe), about as far from Cape Town as you can get without leaving
South Africa.

It was about 548 km from the northern border down to Johannesburg.
It proved to be better training for America than she knew, as the incessant
rain made for days of soggy running in wet clothing over hills and mountains. She also completed her 'warmup' in good time (seven and-a-half
days), with daily totals much like those she'd need for a trans-America run
in the 10 weeks she planned for. At the end all seemed well enough for the
following year's gargantuan undertaking.

RUNNING WITH MR. GOODSPONSOR ON A BAD HAIR DAY

Drizzle introduced her departure on September 22, 1977, but didn't succeed in dampening the spunky lady's spirits, a humidified hairdo notwithstanding. The 'do' had been a 'must have' the previous day. *"Got to
look good for the run, right,"* was Mavis' sentiment the day before. But on

race day vanity had to take a back seat.

In spite of the wet weather, which got worse with a heavy downpour in the afternoon, good time was made and she completed 65 kilometers, averaging 8 km an hour. Fred Hattingh from the cosmetics company sponsoring her US crossing joined her in the rainy run – the company wanted to see her in action.

After all, 'Mr Goodsponsor' had a vested interest in making sure the prize performer was up to scratch. Fred ran with her a number of other times during the race when he wasn't fulfilling his driving duties for the Hutchison team, which this time included Mavis' nephew Clifford, engaged as a co-driver. Fred must have been underequipped for the running side of his mission, as he borrowed a pair of Mavis' sponsored athletics shorts – an unusual fashion statement.

OVER HILL, OVER DALE

Day two proved to be another US training opportunity, with more rain, strong wind and mountain terrain. But 'super granny' was fighting fit and there was bite to her 'gallop'. At the end of the stretch she was able to tick off 73.2 km.

The following day another 4am start put her ahead of schedule even before she stopped for breakfast. She was already in Pietersburg by early afternoon and finished the course with a total of 76.5 km - good going by anybody's measure.

On day four she cleared Potgietersrust by lunch time. She was, however, slowed down considerably by more rain that seemed to come down in buckets at this point. Apparently the buckets didn't agree with her, 'sexy rain short pants' notwithstanding. By the day's end she wasn't feeling well at all, and had clocked only 62 km.

But the next day things looked up, and again the marathon woman was ready to hit the road running. The predawn hours saw her striding along smoothly and thinking clearly – about America, not surprisingly – and other practical matters. So Naboomspruit and Nylstroom came and went, but reminders for hubby didn't leave her mind: *"Please tell Ernie not to forget a bucket for Jean on the America trip and don't let the eggs roll around in the caravan."* That's woman for you – and Mavis stayed true to her gender.

Fred Hattingh from sponsor Vanda Cosmetics runs with Mavis
in a warmup for the Trans-America race.

Day five was also not without rain, but the distance covered was back up to 71 km. The team celebrated and Mavis summarized it thus: "*We all had a lovely bath, went out for supper and hit the sack by 8.30 that evening*". As always, small things meant a lot on ultraruns.

Although the sixth day had a wet start, drizzle finally gave way to sunshine and a suitably warm welcome to Warmbaths where Mavis was eagerly greeted and cheered on by fans. But most importantly, it put on record her best daily distance for the entire excursion – despite some steep hill climbing on the way in. The completed mileage was 78.5 km.

She was near the finish, but on the second-to-last shift Pretoria's city traffic sabotaged her pace badly. It took her a whole hour to get through it. She would have liked to do better, but 63 km had to suffice once again.

The last leg to Johannesburg presented far less traffic hassles, thanks to a helpful officer who came to her aid. It was clear from a newspaper report later that it was a real thrill for him to assist the famous grandma. She arrived at City Hall early in the afternoon on day eight, having logged another 60 km in far less than a full day. Happy with her 'try-out'; she felt ready for America .

'ON HER TWO FEET?'

But the 'try-out' wasn't only remembered for the training it afforded. Nephew Clifford preserved a memory of a different kind, a reminder that not everybody runs hundreds of miles for fun. Approaching Cliff in the Messina Municipal Caravan Park, he asked a natural question for a town on the border:

"Excuse me, son, are you on your way to Rhodesia?

"Reply: 'No Sir, I am helping my aunt who is leaving Messina on Saturday to run to Johannesburg.'

"A glum look fell over the gent's face and all of a sudden he replied: 'On her two feet?'"

Chapter 15: AMERICAN DREAM I
Out of the Smog, Across the Desert

"When people ask me why I do such endurance running, in their voice is a hint of ridicule. My comeback is - I would rather be worn from using than from rusting. That usually shuts them up."

"Yes, there ARE flights across the US. Why d'you ask?"

FINDING MR. GOODSPONSOR
"When I first had this idea I didn't think it would happen."

Mavis had dreamed of crossing America for years, and planned her five years of long runs across South Africa's plains, mountains and deserts as training, but it was a daunting thought. No woman had ever run across America, and only Barbara Moore had walked the distance, taking a bit more than 85 days.

It would be six more years before women would be allowed to run an Olympic marathon, and that was a distance less than a hundredth as long as a trans-America journey. The idea of Mavis running across the American continent frightened prospective sponsors, who feared being associated with a disaster.

One was only willing to be involved if Mavis would guarantee that she'd make it. He begged off when she would only say that she would do her considerable best, and that if she failed it would be under conditions that would prevent anyone from finishing.

She finally struck gold after the Fair Lady run from Germiston to Cape Town in 1976. *"Dolf Marmetschke, managing Director of Vanda Cosmetics invited me to have tea with him. Dolf asked me about my American run and he also asked me what such a venture would cost. I estimated the cost at about R25,000. Without even blinking an eye lid he said 'You're on; Vanda will sponsor the run.' You can imagine the excitement, delight and surprise of such an outright commitment."*

Vanda got worried later, and asked Mavis if she would reconsider, since as a South African running on public roads she 'would be a target for anyone who wanted to sabotage the marathon'. This seemed like the end of the whole project, and an very 'disappointed and upset' Mavis contacted international sports personalities for advice and guidance. Being who she was, though, she decided to take the chance – and the managing director kept his word, although he was worried enough to insist that Vanda would take no active part in the venture, footing the bill but getting little or nothing out of it themselves.

In tackling the trans-American run, Mavis became part of a colorful history. The idea of *running* across the continent seems to have begun when C.C. Pyle promoted a trans-America foot race from L.A. to New York in 1928. Cash prizes up to $25000 (very serious money when a dollar day could hire a laborer) attracted 199 competitors from over a dozen countries to this 'Bunion Derby', including Arthur Newton from South Africa. Following the runners in their grueling slog were two busloads of press, 50 officials, 100 trainers, and (almost unbelievably) a carnival.

The 22 finishers were naturally appalled when it turned out Pyle had no money to pay the winners, but a California millionaire named Gunn came to the rescue. The next year Pyle promoted a race from New York to LA, which also ended in financial disaster. Pyle was broke again, and the admission fees from the crowd at the stadium where the race finished were seized by IRS agents to pay Pyle's back taxes. Not until the 1990s would the idea of a Trans-America Footrace be revived.

In the mean time, many *men* had run the distance solo. Among them was the remarkable South African Don Shepard, who ran unaided and unsupported, carrying clothes, money and a running shoe repair kit in his belt pack.

But no woman had done it. Mavis was determined to be the first, or collapse trying.

CHASING THE MUGGERS, AND BEING CHASED

That meant she had to be fit, and she spent many hours in training. This was not without its hazards. As she was running across a vacant lot toward the 'main Heidelberg road' near the local slaughterhouse, two young black men came toward her. One drew a knife and held it against it against her while the other grabbed her bag. Mavis wasn't so worried about the bag as about the expensive 12-hour stopwatch in it. So she held on to the bag, saying, "*Let me have my stopwatch – you can have the rest.*"

They didn't say a word, and the one kept on pulling at the bag while the other pressed the knife against her. At this point reality set in, at least for the moment. "*I was hoping someone would see us from the main road as there were cars whizzing by, but it was in the veld on an open stand, and I realized I was in very real danger.*" She let go, and the two men ran off.

Still determined to get that stopwatch back, she chased them into the trees 'near the old City Deep golf course'. When she shouted to an older black man to stop them, "*he apparently thought discretion the better part of valor and did nothing. And perhaps I could not blame him with those two young men armed with the big knife.*" Soon after, the chase ended as Mavis fell into an ash dump. By the time she got up, covered in ash, the two men were off in the trees and she gave up the chase. The danger of being knifed finally outweighed her desperate desire to get the stopwatch back.

This wasn't the only time she found herself in danger as she trained, but at least she didn't chase muggers again. When she noticed a black man following her early one morning, she "*put on the pace thinking he was also perhaps going for a run.*" He kept following her, and every time she crossed the road or changed direction he did the same. When he got closer, she " *ducked into a house and…asked the lady whether I could stay for a little while.*" After the would-be mugger disappeared, Mavis then continued her training.[1]

It was hard to discourage Mavis for long.

MAVIS WE WISH YOU GOOD LUCK FOR AMERICA (1978)

*"She is now preparing herself for the greatest run of them all.
The gigantic run across the continent of America. It will he
the realization of what once seemed to be an
impossible dream." (press article)*

The epic began March 12 at Johannesburg airport, where the support team came together for the first time, together with their extended families, assorted well wishers, the sponsors (plus entourage), and journalists from women's magazines and the local press. This *"made a sizable crowd, which suggested there was a lot of interest in my departure."*

The support team included three who'd been with her on previous runs: Jean Blake, Raynier Abrahamse from the newspaper Die Beeld, and her husband Ernest. One new member was driver and route planner Dennis Clayton, who had hitchhiked all over America – the only team member who could draw on any knowledge of the country where they were about to spend months on the road. The other new team member was a journalist from the Johannesburg Star, Lucy Gough-Berger. At 9:45 that night they started the long flight on Air France.

To every venture fall the mundane preliminaries, and the first days in Los Angeles went to renting two motor homes, and learning how to manage them. This included getting used to driving on the right side of the road and – especially vital – practicing navigation on the obligatory trip to Disneyland.

Nobody forgot what they were there for, however. *"Each day I arose early, drank my magic potion and went for a two-hour run. Lucy did some public relations work. Jean, Ernie and Ray organized the supplies and Dennis did a reconnaissance to make sure we could find the Town Hall and find our way out of L.A."*

On the side of each caravan, the words "MAVIS HUTCHISON: TRANS-AMERICA MARATHON" announced their intentions to the world.

Meanwhile, American athletes Mavis had met the year before at the World Masters' Championships in Sweden came to visit, easing the pre-race jitters and imparting local knowledge that helped in planning. A member of the South African Information Service from the consulate in L.A. also helped out where he could.

People who hadn't met Mavis found her a bit different than they expected. *"We also attended a number of social functions where, it seems, many of the guests were expecting to meet a muscle bound 'Amazon woman', who was going to conquer the continent. Were they surprised!"*

Packing shoes before departure. Over two dozen pairs were needed to get her from L.A. to New York.

Final preparations kept the support team busy and focused, but for Mavis the jitters came back as the starting day loomed closer."*I seemed to spend the final day of preparation in a stupor. The ambivalence of wanting to get started versus the fear of what lay ahead kept me in a state of suspended animation. The distance was three-and-a-half times longer than my previous longest run. Were the difficulties going to be proportionately greater?*"

They would, but her spirit would carry her through.

At the Starting Line

> "*I know exactly how a journey of a thousand miles feels. It hurts.*"
> "*My mind was going round in a state of panic…*"

The day began with '*typical frenzy, trying to get to the start on time, dealing with the press and TV, greeting the supporters and well-wishers, planning the route…*" In a daze she accepted running vests from local athletic clubs, while fighting "*overwhelming feelings of inadequacy and fear*".

It was the greatest spiritual and physical challenge of her life, and now it was unequivocally real – and about to begin very publicly. She was in front of the press on the steps of the Los Angeles City Hall, and it was too late to back out. "*It was my greatest ambition, but I felt so apprehensive. Would I really be able to do it? What lay ahead of me Was I strong enough? Had I prepared properly? I wished I'd had enough sense to have stayed at home.*"

This cost her a few minutes. "*As I set off I glanced up at the City Hall clock through the haze and realized that I was seven minutes behind schedule before I even started.*" Confusion set in immediately, as the local runners with her decided there was a quicker route out of the city, causing the support team to lose track of where Mavis was.

Anxiety prevailed, especially with her husband Ernest "*whose stress levels remained high for the rest of the journey. The tensions were exacerbated by Ernest's shouting that I was running too fast causing me to lose concentration, stumble, fall and graze my right knee and both my hands. The drivers of the second caravan, Lucy and Dennis, briefly lost their way, leading to further panic and so when in the height of the rush hour traffic it was decided I should stop for the day, I was much relieved. Surely from here on things could only improve!*"

Anybody who knows L.A. traffic will sympathize.

Getting out of the massive urban sprawl took a couple of days, putting things further behind schedule. As the team struggled to establish a daily routine, problems persisted. Heavy vehicles thundered by on the narrow road the team had chosen, making running along the side of the road more difficult and dangerous.

Dennis (the designated navigator) damaged one of the caravans and had to change a tire. That made him miss his scheduled linkup with the rest of the team, "*resulting in pandemonium as we needed him to keep us on the right route.*" Unlocked cupboards led to bottles of Worcestershire sauce, wine and rum smashing onto the floor. "*The rather 'spirited' cleaning frenzy worsened when the food that was put on the table joined the wine and the rum on the floor. Comedy on the run!*"

But for Mavis, all this helped keep her mind off herself and the heavy trucks zooming by a foot away.

One thing was certain – nobody was going to let Mavis navigate. "*My sense of direction is not so good as you well know. When Allan* (her son) *was packing I offered to help him get to Benoni. I took about 90 minutes. Going via Kaalfontein, Kempton Park. My theory is that I always get where I want. It only takes me a little longer.*"

Well-intentioned supporters turned up at odd moments. "*A woman I met on the road gave me four dollars and informed me that she had been waiting for me, that is, if I was the person who was running across the continent. With the four dollars was a note that informed me that she would be praying for a safe journey for me.*"

Sometimes Mavis wondered which she needed most, divine protection from the vehicles on the road or from the antics of her team.

None of the six people packed into two modest caravans was ready for sainthood, and nerves were already fraying by the third day. Ernest was complaining about being behind schedule, Mavis was complaining about the constant heat (although the true desert was still ahead), while Raynier complained about Mavis' complaints and Dennis complained about the difficulties in finding the best route. Only Mavis' friend Jean "*…just smiled and tolerated our complaints as she rubbed thick layers of barrier cream on my neck, legs and arms.*"

Ernest may have been the lead complainer. According to Lucy he was the 'classic pessimist', starting and ending every day with a moan. More entertaining was the way he showed "*a touching tenderness towards his wife one moment and unconsciously referred to her as an old car engine the next*".

So far the 'old car engine's' legs and feet were holding up. Unlike Don Shepherd she'd brought 25 pairs of running shoes and rotated them in strict sequence after every break, with her husband keeping them in repair.

Hoped-for sights along the way didn't always materialize, even for those not running 14 hours a day. *"I think we were all secretly entertaining wild fantasies about who we were going to bump into at our next overnight stop - Palm Springs -playground of the stars. I was jarred into reality when I was instructed by the traffic police that I would not be allowed to run on the freeway and consequently had to take a 39 mile detour."*

Naturally the detour roads were terrible, and they spent the night at a campsite in the desert.

HEAT AND DUST

> *"I never took my eyes off the cars and trucks. It was the traffic from behind that scared me half to death…at times they would be so close that I could touch them."*

> *"At times her burning lips were swollen with fever blisters and her hands and legs smarted from grazes where she had stumbled and fallen. In the pre-dawn darkness, with never a murmur of complaint she would leave the security of the team's two motorised unit homes to tread the unknown road in the slender beam of the headlamps." (Lucy Gough-Berger)*

With the crossing of San Gorgonio pass, the true desert slog began. Nothing in Mavis' experience had quite prepared her for the 'freezing cold starts' and 'blisteringly hot days' of the Mojave Desert. Keeping her in running condition drained the crew's own energy. Mavis needed constant sponging and cold fluids to run long hours, and the heat brought *"more regular stops, more complaints, more stumbling, more injuries."* Mavis had been the first woman to brave the heat and mountains of South Africa's Karoo marathon, but this was like running that desert distance every day.

Mavis saw a bit of the non-tourist America as she ran by, but there was no time to figure the country out. *"We came across a family living in shacks; I don't know which group was more astonished, them as they contemplated the senselessness of a gray-haired woman charging across the country for no ap-*

parent reason, or us as we mooted the reason why anyone wanted to endure such harsh circumstances in the 'land of plenty.' " They knew shacks as a feature of Africa, but hadn't expected them here.

'Wild West' movies had *traveled* worldwide, and toward the end of day four she drifted into *"imaginings of the old 'wild-west' days and the cowboys chasing Indians on horseback, dressed in their war regalia and chanting their war cries as they fired rifle shots and arrows at each other. I was jolted into the present with shouts from Ernest that I should immediately come off the road. The light was fading rapidly and I was in a state of exhaustion."*

It was the second time that day. A press report noted that Mavis started to wander across the road just outside the little town of Mecca, prompting Ernest to insist she come off the road and rest for half an hour.

The real America wasn't always quite as she imagined. She looked forward to majestic sunrise scenery and 'sparking colors' in the Painted Canyon one morning, but *"…the vista was marred by the mounds of debris scattered next to the road from years of passing motorists discarding their litter; petrol cans, old tools and the like."* Nobody bothered much about cleaning up around the by-roads Mavis ran on once the freeway was built. Even today the little town near this canyon has been considered possibly the most littered in America.

Uphill through a formidable desert pass.

The heat continued, and her friend Jean Blake came up with a practical housewifely remedy, turning *"face towels into mittens which were soaked in water and then taped around my wrists to keep my hands cool."* Minor frictions proved the team all too human. Ernie was cheerfully chatting with two officers in a patrol car when the women of the party told him that one of the 'policemen' he was chatting to was a woman rather than a man.

"When we pointed this out to him, he became quite irate for the rest of the day, which may have influenced his decision to take me off the road earlier than I wanted." This was a bad omen for the future, but Mavis decided not to argue and wrote poetry in her caravan *"reflecting my experiences of the Painted Canyon."*

The beauty of the canyon had been there, behind the trash. The *"vast cruel angry mountain ranges"*, the magical beauty of the canyon, and the peace, quiet and shade filled her with gratitude to her Lord for being allowed such a 'moment of bliss', and a desire one day to share her feelings about her day in 'this wonderland', despite the *"roads not very easy on which to run"*.

It wasn't just rough back roads that could be a problem. There was no vehicle wall insulating this solitary, slightly built grandmother from the rougher human side of America, something a woman on her own might fear. On one lonely desert stretch, with the support team out of sight, *"I came across a rather primitive looking campsite close to the road, The residents were unshaven, untidy and unfriendly; I felt vulnerable. My vulnerability leaped into panic when three vicious-looking dogs came bounding towards me. Many years before I'd had a traumatic experience with a dog while running, and ever since then I've become petrified when I cross paths with untethered dogs. Disaster was avoided when they were called back by the owners. I tentatively walked for some distance not averting my eyes from them until I felt safe to start running again."*

It didn't help much when a passerby warned her a little later to look out for rattlesnakes.

'ARID ZONA'

"The heat was a shocker…"

"As the trucks passed going either way, I would be lifted into the air, then come down hard on my right heel. I was beginning to feel some stress.…"

Occasionally the grind of the daily routine was relieved by events like the celebration of Jean's birthday, when the team sang 'Happy Birthday' throughout the day – and pleased her even more by dining at the Coach Inn in Quartszite, which meant that the camp cook was 'excused from duty that evening'. Still cheerful for the most part, the team had taken the blowing of horns by passing truck drivers as part of the day's festivities.

The routine ground on in the second week, except that more truckers somehow needed to stop to inspect their tires as Mavis ran past, and felt so sorry for her that they typically offered her a lift. Her standard reply: "*No thanks; I'm in a hurry!*" Some wanted to know whether she'd been kicked out of one of the team caravans, while others thought maybe her caravan had broken down and she was running for help.

Passing motorists were just as clueless, but sometimes less polite. Offended by her refusal of a lift, they often responded with "*Are you expecting a better car?...I judged their level of annoyance by the speed with which they pulled off, or the noise level of the screeching tires.*" These 'diversions' broke up the boredom of the endless slog, but one of them caused Mavis to fall and injure her right leg.

Logistics were often an issue, and could cause loss of time. The team stopped early one day next to a gas station -- even though it had already closed – because they thought they might run out of gas before getting to the next town. The half dozen venturers were on their own; there was no safety net if they got it wrong.

The roads got narrower and the traffic denser as they proceeded deeper into Arizona. Mavis found she had to run on the gravel shoulder because the roads were simply too dangerous. "*One incident found me landing on my back in a ditch trying to avoid a speeding daredevil who had decided to see how close he could get to me as he passed.*"

There were also physical warning signs, as she began "*to feel weary as my body suffered the constant pounding day after day.*" But she did get to see her first real cowboy as she passed by. Mavis was clearly a veteran of many a cowboy movie, and this was a genuine compensation for the strain.

A new adventure awaited her outside Phoenix. A 'less busy road' through Goodyear turned out to be a dead end "*which sent everyone scurrying around to find the way out. The best we could do was for Ernie and me to scamper along a dry river bed,*" while the vehicles looked for a way around.

This meant an extra five miles of rough running, and Mavis was 'spitting fire' by the time everyone met up again, but there was one compensation. In the river bed there was no traffic!

That was certainly not true as she entered Phoenix on an eight-lane freeway. *"This made the traffic of the previous few days feel like child's-play. In a terrified state I reached the City Hall where a TV crew had set up for a live broadcast. It was difficult for me to suppress the ordeal I had just been through and I wondered whether the viewers thought that my nervous jig and chattering teeth were some sort of African ritual. At least it provided some mirth for the rest of the team as they watched the interview. We all needed a good rest."*

After fire came the first brief trial by water. Rain cooled things down, but the constant spraying from the wheels of passing vehicles left her 'drenched and dispirited'. Constant stopping to change her waterproof gear added to the feelings of time pressure and discouragement.

Heat reasserted itself in Mesa, 'the Caravan Capital of the World', where Mavis saw more caravans than she had ever seen in one place. *"Almost as though it was accommodating the wishes of the many caravaners, the clouds disappeared…"*

But she was soon in darkness. There was no way around the quarter-mile Queen Creek tunnel, and it felt to her as though it took an eternity *"to get through this dark, dank, dungeon-like experience."* Her mood lifted on the other side as for the first time she saw a largish house on its way toward the tunnel on a flatbed trailer. *"I found it humorous contemplating how they would negotiate the tunnel, and even funnier when I was informed the purpose of the man sitting on the roof was to ensure that there was no snagging of overhead electrical wires with the passing house. It's amazing how relative things are, instantaneously the challenges I was facing did not seem so bad."*

For a while her *"plodding changed to prancing"*. Fantasies enlivened the journey. After a photo session with the FBI and the sheriff at Apache Junction, she *"drifted into dreamland for the night with various fantasies involving the police and FBI."*

The 13th day of the journey was a Friday – and it stank. *"Dennis decided that he needed to repair one of the caravan toilets by pushing a wire down the pipe to clear it. In his enthusiasm he pushed too hard on the bowl which responded by crumbling beneath him and, in turn, caused some of the con-*

tents in the storage tank to spill out over his prostrate, writhing figure, The scream he let out was deafening, but the accompanying smell from the spillage was even more disabling. Lucy attempted to assist him by hosing him down but he ran around like a headless chicken until he had washed himself and his clothes to excess in a nearby stream."

When a local radio station manager interviewed Mavis as she ran north that day, she just hoped Dennis didn't show up as she'd last seen and smelled him. To her relief no Dennis appeared, cleaned up or otherwise. In a scene to be replayed elsewhere, radio listeners started 'stopping for a chat' on the road, and a crowd in the town center waited to cheer her on.

INDIAN COUNTRY

"I felt pretty dwarfed among God's creations. I didn't realize the U.S. was so big."

Tensions flared later that day with the news that they couldn't sleep over in the White Mountain Indian Reservation, meaning that they'd need to travel elsewhere for the night and come back the next morning – and the morning start didn't go well either. *"The moon shone from behind, silhouetting me against the black road snaking into the distance. However, I soon found that the lack of adequate verge space made it impossible for me to continue running in the dark. So, after covering all of 2 miles I decided to climb back into the caravan and wait for sunrise."*

After sunrise things went better. With little traffic to worry about in this remote, rugged corner of eastern Arizona, Mavis could enjoy the *"awesome panorama as I glided down the mountain pass."* Even better was the pancake breakfast waiting at a few miles on at their overnight campsite.

But the fun stopped there. Ahead was an unexpected 3700-foot climb up another pass. Planning an unfamiliar route with nothing but flat highway maps can lead to surprises. But Mavis won the gold watch for perseverance. *"With my gaze planted firmly six-foot ahead of me, I gritted my teeth and accepted the challenge of conquering this mountain -- after all I was going to climb it only once. Keeping my nose to the ground (or is it grindstone) had its benefits. I picked up a gold watch engraved with the words " I found gold in them there hills".*

This kept her entertained the rest of the day wondering where the watch could have come from, but the pass had taken its toll. Only the cold evening breeze nudged her from her plodding stupor toward the end. She was completely exhausted after only 39 miles, and was more than ready for her first shower since Apache Junction, 145 miles to the southwest.

Meanwhile Ernie and Jean had finally gotten to meet some Indians – three local Apaches who answered Jean's innocent question about 'the real things to buy to send home' by telling her that *'nobody could buy that because the most precious thing the Apache have is pride.'*

They'd come a long way to get to the small town of Show Low, high on the forested Mogollon Rim, but their progress didn't look very impressive on her American maps as Mavis tried to convince herself that the next day would be better. They were behind schedule, and she couldn't stand the thought of disappointing those who'd believed in her dream.

And people back in South Africa were following her progress, kept abreast of events by the two journalists in the party. *"Some nights, after supper, Lucy would come for a chat. One night she arrived unexpectedly and found me on the toilet. She announced that she was the only person who had been allowed to have an audience with the Queen on the throne. Ray generally interviewed me whilst he was driving the caravan that accompanied me most of the time."*

Up to now, the trial had been heat, but at 6400 feet above sea level the grass was white with frost. Warned that an even colder front would be coming through, Mavis put on two tracksuits, gloves and a knitted beret. This extra weight slowed her down, but the real burden was psychological. *"I was becoming despondent because my daily average was falling way below the expected 45 miles per day. I could not understand the reason for my lethargy but kept forcing the negativity out of my mind by wondering what the folks back home where doing. This required of me to calculate the time difference, a sure way of diverting my attention from the tedium of the road."* It was a battle of mind and spirit that only she could win, with many weeks still to come. Occasional relief was welcome, including a brief stop at an Indian trading post for a hot drink and a cookie.

It was a tougher battle because her team was fragile, and that included her husband. *"One of the many struggles between Ernest and me erupted as he broke my trance by calling me off the road. I wanted to do at least 32 miles before lunch and was way short. I was not happy about his decision. But as happened on most such occasions, I gave in to his decision in order not to disrupt the tenu-*

ous harmony amongst the team. The tension between Ernest and me made the afternoon stint even more difficult than the inclement weather was making it to be. The wind and the cold caused me to take shortened strides and an arched stance to minimize the effect of the wind. The inevitable hill presented itself at the end of the day, just to add salt to my wounded pride. To compound matters, just as I felt I was beginning to loosen up and deciding that I still had a good few miles in my legs for the day, Ernie decided it was time to stop."

Everybody had an opinion about how Mavis' run should be managed, and that included stopping early at the ghost town of Vernon. *"The emptiness of the small village of ten houses, (eight of which were unoccupied) symbolized the hollow feeling and shattered expectation that had consumed my thinking. It was Easter Sunday and I was oblivious to it."*

To make up the time, they would try an early start. But it was hard to get moving. Lucy summarized what it was like.

"It was the shock of the predawn forcible awakening that was the worst thing of all. If you could survive that you could survive anything.

"From outside the camper in which we three women slept Ernie Hutchison knocked sharply and shoved three cups of coffee through the door before we'd even struggled into our clothing. I say clothing, because in the dark you felt around for the gear you'd cast off the night before and stowed under the pillow. Ten minutes later when Ern shouted 'We're moving!' before you could taste the hot strong sweet coffee -- Baby, you'd better move."

This morning it took more time than that. It was 5.15 am before Ray switched on the headlights to light up the path ahead, and *"the snow on the mountains and the accompanying cold seemed to affect Ernie's thinking as badly as it affected my running."* After only four-and-a-half miles he pulled her off the road again until dawn. There was no reason for this that Mavis could see. *"When I returned to the road I contemplated whether the gloom of the day was depressing my mood, or whether my despondency was causing the day to appear gloomy."*

LAND OF ENCHANTMENT?

"...there were no easy days..."

"The motorists passing me really thought there must be something wrong with me. What kind of crazy person goes on the road on a day like this far away from everything?"

But there's nothing like progress to alleviate depression, and she snapped out of her misery for a while when she finally saw a road sign saying "Welcome to New Mexico - Hasta la Vista."

New Mexico brought another new experience – a chance to win over the reluctant husband of another woman who wanted to run. "*...he promptly came out to see for himself and ended up running, (carrying his baby) a good few miles with me. After the obligatory photo session we left them...full of enthusiasm and encouragement for the wife's newfound hobby. That night they arrived at our campsite with a book on long distance running which they presented to me.*"

But the heartwarming mutual encouragement didn't take away Mavis' constant worry about why, as she saw it, she was still underperforming. She knew that her friend Jean Blake's notes painted a far more positive picture. Jean's notes were generously sprinkled with "Mavis looks good," "She's running well," "She's strong," "She's fit," in stark contrast to Mavis' own thoughts. As she ran through the western New Mexico highlands after a typical 4:15 start, she "*concluded that the best days were those that were behind me because I would not have to run those miles again.*" For the rest of the day, Mavis slogged along on 'automatic pilot', not thinking much about her running.

Meanwhile the team had company. A local school principal and farmer brought his family along, and "*spent much of the day accompanying the team, finding out about us and arranging for Ray to give a talk about the run and about South Africa at the* (Quemado and Datil) *school the next day.*" New Mexico hospitality could be a bit different, as "*the day ended with the family providing pickled cactus and deviled eggs to supplement our evening meal. Jean was given hard-boiled eggs in lieu of the Easter eggs she had missed out on the previous day.*"

Ray was supposed to sleep late the next morning so that he'd be fresh for his talk at the school, then catch up later – but it didn't work out that way. Dennis flooded the engine of the caravan that was supposed to light the way so Mavis could start running before sunrise, and nobody could get it started. "*This meant that Ray had to be awakened from his promised cozy lie-in to swap caravans. We left him on this bitterly cold morning in his barely-adequate tracksuit whilst we rode off in the dark with his warm bed and well prepared speech...*"

That was only the beginning of sorrows, as Ray then got lost after finally getting the second caravan started. "*Luckily a local garage owner spotted him running round in all directions trying to find his bearings.*" The run was big enough news in this small isolated town (population 1500 today) that the woman who owned the garage guessed who Ray was and knew he was late. In spite of losing his way and his notes, his talk inspired a number of students to visit Mavis, eager to talk more about the run.

For Mavis it was another cold, wet, unpleasant day, bundled up in "*excessive layers of clothing to help achieve diminishing returns*". Her anxiety was rising as she fell even further behind schedule.

PLASTIC SACKS ON THE RIO GRANDE

"I did not know so many plastic bags could be in one place...It looked really gross."

Optimism could surface, as it did the next morning when the 'ever menacing trucks' magically disappeared. Despite the bitter cold of the High West in late winter, and the heaviness of the extra layers of clothing, the day was going well enough until a strong crosswind began blowing this 'wisp of a woman' dangerously into the road. Fighting the wind sapped her energy and optimism, although the team "*attempted to buoy me with constant encouragement.*"

To make matters worse, heavy rain began to pour down, and "*looking and feeling like a drowned rat*" she decided to pack it in for the day. All she could remember of getting to the campsite in Socorro was a surreal glimpse of a fence that had been completely covered with plastic bags blown against it by the wind. As soon as Ray helped her stagger into the relaxing warmth of the caravan, she was out like a light.

The plastic bags were still there in the morning. It wasn't just a bad dream of home in South Africa, where plastic supermarket bags caught in fences have been called the 'national flower'. But Mavis was feeling optimistic about the day, especially after a good sleep and an early breakfast. An interview for the team with a local radio station gave her company: "*a horde of school boys deciding to run with me through the town.*"

'Fame' also brought a contribution (of sorts) to the venture's finances. "*When we turned onto the highway we met a couple who were holidaying and had been waiting to watch the procession. After taking a photograph the wife was heard saying to her husband, 'You never know, she could become famous.' and then instructed her husband give to Ernest a dollar."*

Undisturbed by this sudden wealth and with no mountains ahead for the moment, Mavis ran north up the Rio Grande valley, mildly pleased after covering 42 miles and happy to 'call it a day'.

The team met all sorts on their slow traverse of America. "*At the campsite we met a man called Joker who had arrived on a motorcycle. He chatted with us briefly and then did the rounds introducing himself to fellow campers. Not long after his arrival the serenity of the campsite was shattered by the screams of a husband watching Joker ride off into the night with his newly found friend's wife.*"

For Mavis and the team things were less eventful, and as they crossed the Rio Grande early the next morning, "*Ray predicted that it was going to be a good day.*" Even more encouraging was the news they had now completed 1313 miles, or about a third of the distance in less than a third of the allotted time.

But optimism faded even before breakfast. "*Sadly, Ray had omitted to check the weather report and what had started as a gentle breeze soon was gusting at about thirty miles an hour. Three hours into the day and the heavens opened, forcing me to wear two weatherproof tops, a tracksuit and a hat which I had to tie down using a scarf. What a sight this must have been for passing motorists, many of whom, ignoring the accompanying caravans, stopped to offer me a lift. The tumbleweed that came whooshing past me seemed to be teasing me to try to catch up.*"

No wonder that she fell asleep immediately after breakfast, only to be brusquely awakened after a short nap with a reminder that a climb through the Manzano Mountains lay now lay ahead. "*Almost in a stupor, I mechanically began fighting my way through the physical, emotional and spiritual battle that was on offer for the day.*" Having been "*tossed around by the wind for most of the day*", she was happy to reach Mountainair that night, even if it was only 40 miles from the previous night's stop. "*I took the strain one step at a time…feeling my strength and stamina leaving me by degrees. It was sheer will power that got me through the day.*"

INTO THE SEA OF GRASS

> *"On the road I was a person who did not talk much…I am in a world of my own, a world it is difficult to share with the team."*

"If you ask me how Mavis felt about the run, I couldn't tell you. From the moment we left Los Angeles and even before, Mavis withdrew mentally and physically from the group…Even if she shared the caravan with…Jean Blake and me her spirit was far away. Yet over the whole run her presence was tangible even if she was out there on the road." (Lucy Gough-Berger)

The team were now beyond last mountain range they'd encounter in the West, and as Mavis started running further she reflected *"on how the loneliness of the running had made me quite insular. I never spoke much to the team and expected that they would anticipate my needs."*

At times she even found it hard to share what she was experiencing with her husband, while she knew *"most passers-by questioned my sanity, especially when they saw me running past wearing a French Legion hat and my body covered with milk-of-magnesia as protection from the sun. Anyway, I was happier now that the Colorado and Mojave deserts were simply a memory. I got to thinking about the only other woman to have completed the coast-to-coast journey on foot, Barbara Moore. She had traveled in the reverse direction to me and spent about six months doing it in an attempt to prove that she could survive off the land."*

Actually the Russian-born Moore had taken 85 days to make her epic walk, fuelled entirely by nuts, honey, fruit and vegetable juice. Rumor had it that she was a 'breatharian', nourished entirely by air – and she did claim to survive for months on melted snow. Mavis favored honey and fruit on long runs but never claimed to be able to get by on water alone.

The days drifted into sameness, punctuated by minor disasters. *"April 3rd began with a car that refused to start and then when we eventually set out to locate the previous night's marker…we had a lot of difficulty finding it."* It meant a late start and lost time, along with Ernie using *"some choice words about getting up in the middle of the night all for nothing".*

Ghost towns were a feature of the journey in New Mexico, and Mavis was relieved to leave the last one behind. More exciting was the thought of a town called Vaughan, where she wanted a souvenir because Vaughan was her maiden name. Souvenirs were in short supply in Vaughan. *"I need not have bothered because the best we could find was a pencil with the town's name inscribed on it."*

Over undulating grassland with an occasional distant mesa or mountain, the run continued cold and windy. The weather and the lack of mail *"heightened the strain on the team who were beginning to become homesick."*

The team had also had enough of 'the middle of nowhere' for a while, and looked forward to reaching Santa Rosa, the biggest town since Socorro. For the team this meant Dennis and Lucy going ahead to plan a route through town (and make sure Mavis would be allowed to run on the famous 'Route 66', while for Mavis it meant the *"return of menacing trucks as companions"*. She found herself becoming quite irritable after the relative quiet of New Mexico's back roads, but managed 20 miles before breakfast, and another 16 by lunchtime.

This was cheering, but Mavis had trouble with socializing after her long day on the road. *"I was just settling down to rest for the evening when Ernest, who had been socializing with fellow campers, informed me had accepted an invitation for me to go visit with them. Having to walk quite some distance to their caravan and back took the shine off the occasion."*

In its way this was a symptom of a deeper problem that would cause more friction over the weeks ahead. To manage her exhausting routine of 14-hour days on the road, Mavis *had* to draw inward and focus her spiritual, emotional and physical resources on the task at hand. But for the others on the team, her isolation looked like self-centered obsession, and the routine was killing.

Lucy Gough-Berger put it this way: "For the team, it was monotony gone mad. For 70 days we were prisoners of the road, while Mavis ran free. Within the confines of the caravans, tempers frayed. There was no time off. Somewhere along the line the fun went out of the trip and conversation simply dried up…Seventy days is an endurance test for people from different backgrounds and interests, confined without exercise in such a claustrophobic atmosphere."

Considering the strain the team were under, with all the 'stardom' reserved for Mavis, it is a tribute to their character that "duty triumphed over boredom" although "everything was sacrificed to Mavis' Holy Grail quest." But if Lucy's comment that it 'was a marathon for us too' is entirely valid, so is the fact that without Mavis' determination their would have been no marathon run, no team, and no achievement at the end.

Distances continued to lengthen as they moved east toward the Texas border. Mavis covered 45 miles on her last full day in New Mexico, *"the best we had done for a while"* , despite the constant threat of injury on a narrow road 'with no shoulder to run on' that was especially dangerous at dusk. There would be 14 miles of similar conditions left to be tackled next morning. The team often had to divert to secondary roads more or less parallel to the highway when traffic on the main highway became too dangerous.

---

[1] *Sam Mirwis, Daily Express, January 29, 1978.*

Chapter 16: AMERICAN DREAM II
The Struggle

———•◆•———

"This was the loneliest and most dangerous marathon of my life."
"My mind was very well trained and I was able to relax at
night, or for the odd half hour during the day. This relaxa-
tion got me through each day."

LONE STAR

"The eyes of Texas are upon you." (popular song)

A return to better roads meant a return to trucks and traffic. *"Day 26 we got off to an early start and just as the conditions started to get under my skin (or rather under my feet) we hit the highway once more."* After crossing into Texas, they were in a new time zone, and Mavis wanted to use the extra daylight to run a bit further. But Ernie stopped her after only 43 miles for the day, and a heated argument made her more aware of the rising tensions among the half dozen South Africans generally. Her suggestion that Ernest *"allow pairs to take alternate days off to give them a break"* was met with *"Request denied!"* Part of a woman's gift is to sense emotional undercurrents and atmospheres, and Mavis could see what her husband could not.

Rebellion and blowup ensued. *"During the early morning stage he and Ray went ahead to get some rest and he left the others with me until we caught up with them. This presented an opportunity for Lucy and Dennis to dart into Amarillo to check for mail. When Ernest found out, the resultant explosion sounded like an atom bomb..."* Nevertheless, the mail from home did help considerably to ameliorate the growing stress. The 47 miles covered that day also helped.

Amarillo could have been a problem. It had 1.5 million people, and Mavis was definitely not allowed to run on the freeway through town. Dennis and Lucy saved the day, however. They found a route only 1.5 miles longer than the freeway mileage – and *"through the most beautiful part of town. I enjoyed the scenery so much that I stopped to pick some blossoms from a tree and then skipped along shouting out 'It's spring, it's spring!'"I needed that bit of upliftment to steel myself for what lay ahead."*

What worried her wasn't the *"usual barrage of interviews and TV shots that seemed obligatory at most sizable towns".* After all, before too long they were out on the open road again. Nor was it just the many miles to go. Texas has tornadoes.

"We started hearing tornado warnings over the radio. Not having had any experience in such things it sent us all into panic mode, especially Ernest." Dennis was sent ahead to *"locate a safe haven... With each broadcast of a warning the tensions rose, until Ernest could take it no longer and decided to stop at the first building we came across. This happened to be a dilapidated house close to the road and next to an open field."*

It was at this point that Dennis returned to tell *"Ernest that he had located a safe location further along the road and had ordered dinner for the team. Ernest was so agitated that he forbade anyone to leave the 'shelter', even at the cost of missing their meal."*

Only Ernest thought the abandoned house was a great plan. *"Jean was not happy about the location as she thought that the water tanks close by were gas tanks and feared that they would explode should the tornado arrive."* There was heavy rain, but the only tornado was *"the one created by Ernest."* Mavis' above-average run of 46 miles that day, despite the interviews in Amarillo and the early stop caused by Ernest's panic attack, had passed unnoticed.

What made Mavis desperately conscious of each day's progress was partly anxiety about her ability to accomplish her transcontinental dream, partly her sense that the backup team was fraying badly, plus ominous warning signals of pain and exhaustion.

"The heaviness of the previous day was beginning to feel like an omen warning me of the difficulties to come. The accumulation of the struggles to date seemed to be reaching breaking point. My right leg was beginning to hurt. The bad roads, the wind, the rain, the stresses within the team were all screaming at me. The camber on the road exacerbated my feelings of despair. In a state of numbness I willed myself on. Oh how I wanted to have a decent rest but I kept having visions of the L.A. City Hall clock ticking incessantly

away and knowing that it would only stop once I reached the New York City Hall. At McLean, where we were due to camp for the night, the unevenness of the brick roads sent pain shooting through my right leg, just as a reminder that this was no task for a mere 'wisp of a woman'."

After 45 miles, she was thankful to stop and have a chance to elevate her leg to ease the pain. But elevation made the pain worse.

That night *"howling wind and the din of rain being slammed against the caravan"* kept her from sleep. It was so cold that morning that it was snowing in Amarillo to the south. Mavis had to wear two tracksuits and a 'waterproof' that made her feel 'like the Michelin man'. Despite the additional weight and the discomfort of the extra clothing which made the going tough, she tried not to limp on her painful leg in order *"not to discourage the team. Luckily the rain camouflaged my tears."*

Her 'Michelin suit' not only increased her wind resistance, but *"seemed to assist the extra wind caused by the passing trucks, to lift me and then dump me either on my hurting right foot or my hurting pride as I stumbled forward. How much longer could I endure this agony? Just before I reached the end of my tether, a secondary road appeared next to the highway, as if by miracle, to offer me some respite from the buffeting wind caused by the trucks. I graciously accepted the minimal improvement in conditions and plodded on."*

AGONY AND DETERMINATION

"You don't know Mavis. She never gives up!"
(Jean Blake, friend and team member)

"I prayed often for courage to bear the pain."
(Ensign magazine, January 1980)

That night they camped just across the Oklahoma border at the football ground in Erick, and the mind games had to begin in earnest.

"It was St Patrick's Day and everyone was celebrating, except me. My daily mileage was a pitiful 43 miles. My thoughts kept reminding me of all the possible obstacles that could lay ahead. I tried to resist these intrusions with forced visions of beautiful green cornfields and the road winding through undulating countryside. We had crossed into Oklahoma and I used that as a good reason for improving my expectations."

Trying to ignore the increasing pain, Mavis took to the road at 4:45 that morning, just as "*streaks of light began to edge over the horizon. I kept telling myself the new dawn represented a fresh beginning, but the pain in my leg reminded me of the distance I had already traveled and the even greater distance I still had to run.*"

Jean was the first to notice that something was wrong, but soon communications between the other team members "*suddenly dropped to whispers. I felt like they were all just waiting for the last gasps of an ailing invalid. I kept to myself the real extent of the pain and I declined the offers to be taken to a doctor. I could clearly hear my inner voice remonstrating with me to at least rest my leg by staying off the road, but preferably to go home and stop the madness.*"

Now began her return to race walking for long stretches at a time to ease the jarring impact of each step. Other than aspirin, she refused pain killers because she feared that by numbing the pain she might do even greater damage to the injured leg. Like some of the exhausted pioneers who dragged handcarts west, she would find a landmark a short distance ahead, "*urging myself to only make a decision about continuing once I had reached the marker.*"

Often the markers were only cracks in the road "*There were times when I thought I could not run another step but would set my goal as the next crack in the road – and so I ran from crack to crack.*" Marker by marker she got through each day. Packing her leg with ice Ray had managed to find helped a little for a little while, but the pain always came back.

Pretending became the new psychological game. "*I pretended that the pain was only marginal and the team pretended that there was no tension in the camp.*" The team rushed back and forth between towns to see if a 'magic potion' could be found, something of a forlorn hope perhaps in rural Oklahoma. Constant massage seemed to help little physically, and constant jokes "*in an attempt to distract thinking about the reality of the situation*" did little to lift the team emotionally or mentally.

What was truly constant was pain. The pain in her swollen leg would be her "*constant companion for most of the rest of the run. It felt as though there was a clamp around my leg which was being screwed tighter and tighter and then as if a red-hot poker was being forced up and down the inside of the bone in my leg.*" Even race walking was now so agonizing that it "*…took* *all my concentration and determination not to scream out in pain, let alone continue the agony of walking."*

Finally one day she refused to budge another inch after only forty miles, which worked out in a practical way because just at that moment a local farmer's wife passed by and offered a place to park for the night. For the Mavis the last mile had felt like ten.

In her pain and discouragement, she was deeply grateful that the farm family felt "as unsociable as I did and left us alone." Perhaps they felt their night visitors were a little too outside the ordinary, especially when they saw Dennis practicing his ballroom dancing on the concrete drive with his imaginary partner. The team reacted differently. His "joyous expression as he waltzed his way to ecstasy" touched them all with a reminder of happier things.

Next morning the run stopped. *"The bandages that had been wrapped around my leg for the night were taken off just prior to my taking to the road. I was quite horrified by the amount of swelling and as I started out all I could manage was a few hops on the left leg to avoid placing any weight on the right one. In the headlights of the early morning ritual it must have seemed as though I had decided to emulate Dennis' antics from the previous evening. The horror on Ray's face reflected the gravity of the situation and I could respond only by throwing my arms into the air in despair. In silence, Ernest came out and escorted me back into the caravan and declared the day to be a rest day."*

For Mavis this seemed like catastrophe, and she took her *"heightened emotions out on Ernest. I argued that after a short rest we needed to attempt to get to Binger, only 10 miles away. He would not have a bar of it. I turned to the rest of the team for support and all I got was the cold shoulder. Ernest thought that it was safest for him to disappear for a while so he took Jean shopping for supplies and he went for a haircut. During their absence Ray had a heart-to-heart discussion with me, trying to point out the foolishness of hiding the injury from them for so long. Blinded by my fear of not being able to achieve my goal, I responded with every lame excuse I could find."*

Defying her pain and her own doubts, she proclaimed that she WOULD get to New York on time – no matter what. Her dream would not stop in Caddo County, Oklahoma. *"I explained to Ray that if I complained every time something worried me I would not have much time to run...each day I asked the Lord for guidance and the strength I need to see me through..."*

For the first time, the team saw the sun rise from the same place as on the previous day. Progress was slow as Mavis limped slowly onward, her speed controlled by the level of pain, and her right leg dragging so badly that her right shoe needed constant repair because of the extra wear. Fortunately there were 25 pairs, which meant there were no delays while the shoe-cement set hard.

Ernest not only had to do constant shoe repair, but massage her legs every two miles. In spite of what he could do, "*The leg swelling increased progressively as the day lumbered on. The 'tightening clamp and red-hot poker' experience was being repeated. The constant doubt about completing the journey was temporarily relieved by the conversations during the breakfast and lunch breaks. I was reminded of the joke about the person who kept bashing his head against the wall because it provided such relief when he stopped.*" In Union City, the negativity was sidetracked when a group of children on their bicycles arrived to give her support, and showed the team a sports field where they could camp for the night.

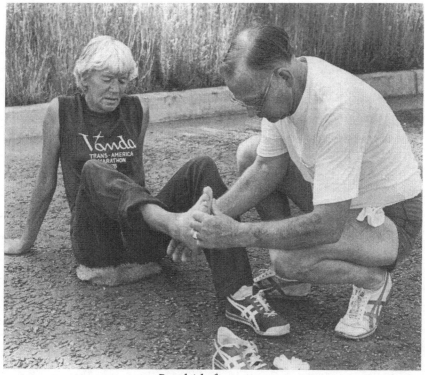

Roadside foot care.

More children provided 'medicine for the soul' after the 33 agonizing miles covered that day when forty of them arrived for a chat at the campground. Full of exuberance and energy, they wanted to know all about the run as well as 'all about South Africa'. In return they offered horror stories about the local drug scene and Ray had to decline their contributions to begin his own stash. One offer of cocaine and marijuana came from a boy of eight.

By the next morning Mavis had resigned herself to pain and discomfort for the rest of the journey. It was still raining that morning when she got on the road, which merely reinforced her dismal outlook. Nothing went right that morning. One of the two camper vans had a flat battery, so the two drivers and vans stayed behind in the predawn darkness while Ernest had to accompany Mavis on foot *"to support me through the puddles, the narrow roads, the heavy traffic and the constant stepping on and off the curbstones. His incessant nagging about needing to slow down, being cautious of the traffic and the wet grass, and not tripping over the curb, stopped only with the arrival of the vehicles."*

As they crept through the urban sprawl of Oklahoma City, Mavis kept going with the aid of frequent stops for a quick massage, and ice packs during the longer breaks. A visit from South African friend Colin Cumming (studying at the University of Oklahoma) lifted spirits – and his gift of ointments and a heating pad was more than welcome. But only 33 miles were covered that day, and New York seemed very far away.

The next day began with 'very attractive country'. Tall green trees lined each side of the very narrow road and what looked to Mavis like 'pioneer houses' seemed to reflect the name of the town – Frontier City. Minimal traffic was a welcome relief, and balloons floating high in the overcast sky gave her a feeling of freedom – but not freedom from pain.

The pain was worse than ever, and *"I confided in Ray that I would not be able to reach New York in 70 days as planned."* That day they passed the halfway point at the little town of Luther, but *"tremendous ambivalence filled each member of the team as we achieved the milestone."* Celebration was muted. *"It was exhilarating to know that I had run over 1500 miles, but this was tempered with the knowledge that it had taken two days longer than scheduled and, because of the injury I was carrying, the likelihood of completing the journey at all, let alone the scheduled time of 70 days was fast becoming a pipe dream."*

INDIAN PRAYER

Despite being frightened she would not be able to cope, Mavis started the next day at such a brisk pace that by nine 'the adrenalin had dissipated' and her badly swollen leg was giving her severe pain. Ernest had tried to warn her. Regular ice-pack treatments began again, and a crosswind from the left forced her to use her right leg as a brace to keep from being blown into the road. At times was the wind was so strong that she walked doubled over, almost falling to the ground. When she told Ray how painful the leg had become, the three men in the party decided she must come off the road immediately.

With 1500 miles to go, they were afraid that if she didn't stop for another day's rest she would risk becoming totally incapacitated. Mavis saw all her dreams crumbling before her, and for the first time *"really broke down in front of the team. I promised to walk very slow, but…with the tears streaming down my face I begged the team to allow me to stay on the road. The team was very close to tears as well. I pleaded to be left alone for a while."* As she lay on her bunk, she alternated tears with asking her Heavenly Father to guide and direct both her and her team. She was then moved to pin the 'Indian Prayer' above her bunk, hoping the team would read and understand – 'Do not judge another until you have walked a mile in his moccasins.' [1]

It took some time alone to work through her emotions, but eventually she *"was ready to talk rationally to the team."* Walking steadily but at a very slow pace, she surprised them and herself by completing 40 miles that day. *"Everyone was left with a new sense of optimism having realized that even during our darkest moments we can still make progress towards our goals."*

From this moment onward, optimism began to creep back. By the next morning, Dennis had calculated that they only needed to cover 43 miles a day to get to New York on time. If Mavis could cover 40 miles on a really bad day, this was still manageable.

Both swelling and pessimism were down, and *"Dennis, Lucy and Jean happily went through to Tulsa to plan the route through the city and the next few days after that. I was more relaxed and therefore so was the team. My progress was slower than I would have liked but it was steady. Had it not been for bad light at the end of the day I would have accomplished the required daily average rather than the 42 miles I had completed"*, despite heavy peak hour traffic coming into Tulsa. Long hot showers for all at the caravan park that night were a cheering extra bonus.

The tide had turned. Before the crisis in Texas and Oklahoma, her team thought she could make it if things went well. But in *"the depths of the emotional and physical despair everyone began to realize that failure was never an option for me, irrespective of the circumstances."* Her five companions now realized that Mavis was determined to make it whether things went well or not. That *"meant instead of looking at the obstacles, they were now looking past them, as was I."*

Since the six South Africans now radiated determined optimism rather than fear of failure, the press began asking how soon Mavis would get to New York, rather than whether she could make it there. It didn't hurt that she felt and looked much better, and even a long TV interview slowed her surprisingly little. In spite of the hour lost, the cold, having to wear several tracksuits, and heavy traffic, she beat the target that day by a mile.

Nor did things slow down the next day. In bitterly cold weather Mavis started off at a quarter to five in the morning, and covered 21 miles before breakfast. No wonder she *"was feeling very pleased with myself."* A bit of farce ensued when two people from a local radio station invited her into their car for a telephone interview. *"My expectation was that they had a car telephone and that the interview would take place in the car. As soon as I climbed in they sped off to find a telephone with me screaming at them to drop me off. Bewildered they stopped the car and I informed them that I would walk to the nearest phone where they could have their interview."* By this time there were more local journalists waiting for more interviews, and *"to cap it off Ernest overslept at the lunch break and I lost another half-an-hour."* In a different category were the mother and daughter who had waited two and a half hours so they could take pictures of each other posing with Mavis. *"I felt humbled by this request and this spurred me on even more. Notwithstanding the delays we had completed 47 miles—my best for some time."*

Having other people place confidence in you can be a powerful motivator.

SPRINGTIME IN MISSOURI

> *"As she sits quietly on the couch in the rear of the motor home sipping Coke...Mavis Hutchison doesn't look like she has just run 45 miles. This is partly because...she has the determination of an army tank."*

As she race walked from Twin Bridges on into Missouri, the landscape gave her another lift. There were more trees than they'd seen for a long time, and the *"apple orchards were covered in pink blossoms which the wind carried across the road showering me in pink"*, which led to thoughts of confetti and *"fantasies about being a spring bride."*

But during the break Mavis noticed that the team members were far less buoyant, *"struggling and going about their work with a lack of passion. Jean and Lucy, in particular, seemed to be under a lot of stress."* Mavis tried a new strategy. This time she got Ray to persuade Ernest that the two women needed *"a few days respite. Not long after 2pm two happy ladies were being chaperoned by Dennis to Springfield for a short break. We would pick them up on the way through."*

For Mavis the day was less relaxing. There were no shoulders on the narrow roads, which were flanked by hedges so that 'unsympathetic vehicles' passed *"menacingly close to me as they raced past."* And the day wasn't over when the running was. Two journalists showed up for interviews, one an elderly reporter *"from a tiny mining town who took photographs with a vintage camera probably acquired at the time of the establishment of the town."* Since this town of Gabriel was said to be the 'first mining town in America', the camera must have been seriously antique. And Dennis returned with news that the hazardous narrow roads would continue for *a* 'fair distance further' in the morning.

The men got so engrossed with a discussion of whether it would be safer to start at daybreak rather 'running in the headlights' before dawn, *"that they were oblivious of the ingredients they were throwing into the dinner pot. It ended up being a rather formless, but tasty concoction of mush…they could manage without the women."*

Mavis was less impressed with the men's cooking the next morning. Breakfast was boiled eggs and soup, and she started regretting the absence of the womenfolk. Despite the extra sleep, she found struggling mile after mile along the shoulderless road with traffic 'far too heavy for safety' a miserable experience. When the road's shoulder finally reappeared, it was a narrow sandy footpath – and at the same time the rain began pelting down in torrents. *"The rest of the day was punctuated with alternating downpours and sunny breaks. This meant I was constantly changing into and out of waterproofs."* Nor was the day improved by her swelling ankle and the need for icepack treatments.

ALARMS AND EXCURSIONS

At lunchtime the men decided that they and Mavis could also use a treat. Mavis would stay in a motel room, which *"conjured up images of a long soaking bath followed by a plush comfortable bed and a night of undisturbed sleep."* Dennis would indulge his passion by twirling the night away on a local dance floor, while Ray and Ernest would find a good restaurant.

Dennis found his dance floor, but the rest found the night a little different than they had imagined. Mavis found that her room had no bathtub, and *'the resident cockroaches kept fluttering around to remind me of their presence in a way that seemed to claim ownership of the room."* There were no restaurants in town so *"Ernest and Ray had to be satisfied with some grub from the bakery next door to the motel,"* before returning to the caravan parked right outside Mavis' door. *"But excitement they did have when the one baker shot the other one...Soon after their return to the caravan someone broke down the door of one of the motel rooms, leaving a woman shrieking in fear of her life. This all resulted in police cars careering up and down with their sirens blaring for much of the night..."*

No wonder that the morning could not come soon enough, or that the team was totally unified that there *"would definitely be no more luxurious treats – like booking into a sleazy motel."* Springfield's underside might not have been much of a treat, but Mavis reflected on what she had to be grateful for, thanking God that there had been no accidents so far, and asking 'for continuing traveling mercies'.

SAND, STONES, AND A PINK LADY IN SHORTS

> *"The roads have not been kind to me...loose stones especially.*
> *I must literally watch where I place each step."*

With the next day's dawning, *"Jean and Lucy rejoined the team obviously happy that they had managed to enjoy some shopping therapy."* They also brought the news that departure would be delayed (with the accompanying risk of increased traffic) because a TV crew would be arriving for an interview. It was not a great success. *"Tensions arose when they insisted that I should run for the camera, without due consideration of my injury. I managed a semi-shuffle which displeased both parties, The team because I was trying too hard and the TV crew because I was not trying hard enough. I wished they would film Dennis's dancing with his phantom partner instead."*

At least once they left town, Mavis felt the road was a good omen. *"This was day forty-four and we were on Route 44 – surely this was a sign that good things were going to happen."* They didn't, although *"on the bright side, we were still creeping forward in spite of needing to take an early break-fast and an early lunch to tend to a fast swelling ankle."* Only her continuing to race walk kept the pain bearable. And the pleasant experience of moving along a road with a wide shoulder came to an abrupt halt after two hours. There was once again no shoulder along the highway, and the side road found by the team was not only miles longer, but sandy and full of stones. Apart from the slower pace, it made her leg hurt even more.

It was a small setback but seemed much larger at the time. Her mood sank through despondency toward depression and the fragile harmony among the team sank with it, straining *"the already jaded relationships amongst the team to breaking point."* Relief came in the form of *"a stocky middle-age woman, comically dressed in pink shorts far too small for her oversized frame, arriving with a truckload of children who had all come to join in the madness of a galloping granny attempting the crazy task of trav-ersing the whole width of the continent."*

They soon discovered that galloping across a continent was harder than it looked, as *"…their enthusiasm exceeded their capacity and they were soon dropping off like flies."* Unlike Mavis they had options, and *"they then decided that riding bicycles would be far less demanding, so they all scurried off to return in greater numbers now proudly able to keep up with the pace. This continued until the end of the day when we graciously accepted the offer to camp at the 'pink lady's' homestead."*

They never saw the 'pink lady' again once they'd set up camp, but far more serious was the fact that the support team were over the horizon al-most equally quickly, desperately searching for diversion.

One brief break for Lucy and Jean was nowhere near enough, and Mavis could see and hear the rising tension only too clearly as she listened to the team discuss their problems and clear the air as best they could *"Living in each oth-er's pockets for such a long time was taking its toll and so I again urged Ernest to schedule alternating respite days for the team but he was not interested."*

The media were certainly interested in the run, however. Mavis was *"going well and striding with a purpose"*, and was now well past the halfway mark, and *"the feeling was she is going to make it injury and all."* The day after the 'pink lady' saw two radio and two press interviews *"which although flattering, impeded the pace of progress."* But Ray Hick from the radio station in Rolla spent so much effort on preparing and conducting his interview that Mavis and the team felt it was the best interview in the 45 days of the journey. It reveals something about Mavis that she especially valued the the chance *"to thank the public for their support and the truckers for their friendliness and interest, as it was they who would radio ahead to inform locals that I was passing through."* More 'amusing' or perhaps alarming was a lady journalist who insisted on taking pictures while lying down in the middle of a dangerously busy freeway.

Rolla also brought a reminder of a previous South African transcontinental runner. The owners of the Country-Aire motel next to their camp showed the team a picture of John Ball posing with them, reminding Mavis how John had joined her for the first and last day of her first really long run, when she became the first woman to run from the Johannesburg area to Durban. *"With these images in my head I drifted off to sleep accompanied by Ernest droning on in the background about my having to concentrate on my running and not interfering with the team logistics."* It was a speech she was to hear more than once.

As she walked through the predawn darkness in the light of caravan headlights the next morning in light traffic, Mavis was sure it was going to be the perfect day. There were only a hundred miles to go to get to St. Louis, and *"although the energy within the team was beginning to flag, the thought of soon being able to receive mail from home helped everyone to keep going."*

All went well until at lunch she encouraged Lucy, Jean and Dennis to spend the afternoon exploring some caves Jesse James had used as a hideout, which they happily did. Mavis could see only too clearly that they needed a break, but this *"sparked Ernest's fervor for continuing the diatribe he had begun the previous night about our respective areas of responsibility. For the rest of the afternoon I had to enduring being admonished about not concentrating on the task at hand and interfering with team organization. According to Ernest this was the root cause of all the ills that had befallen us, from injuries to tensions within the camp, from reduced mileage to reduced hairlines and increased gray hair. It was all my fault. According to Ernest our fortunes would change if only I would concentrate on my running (or, at this stage of the proceedings, my walking) and just leave him alone to organize the team."*

But as can happen, getting rid of his pent up emotions helped him to see more clearly. By the time the team returned a bit before six, Ernest was worried and had become genuinely concerned about the well-being of the team. There was peace that night at a local service station which doubled as a caravan park.

Things seemed brighter for a while after that. *"Fresh but not too cold"* spring weather brought good progress the next morning, and green grass and flowers along the road were a cheering contrast to the deserts of the West, although most of the flowers in the gardens were artificial. As the day grew hotter Mavis began to wilt, but friendly motorists who had seen a TV segment about her the night before honked and waved. Dennis announced he'd found a good route through the 'maze of streets' of St. Louis – but she and the others could not hide their disappointment that there was no mail from home. Ray got a bonus that day, when Mavis gave him a 'very nice scarf' she'd found on the road. *"I picked up all kinds of things on the road from time to time"*.

RUNNING THROUGH FEAR

> *"This is sure a wide river. It took Mom nearly three*
> *quarters of an hour to get over it."*
> *(letter from Ernest Hutchison)*

Well before sunrise the next day, Mavis was once again running in the beams of light provided by one of the vehicles, and concentrating hard as *"the unevenness of the running surface was often quite deceptive and the headlights of oncoming cars were frequently blinding"* while wearing two layers of tracksuits to stave off the morning cold. When a booming voice ordered her to stop, she froze *"like a frightened rabbit caught in the headlights"*. She could now understand the instruction being bellowed out to approach the police car, but remained petrified in fear until Ernest arrived and escorted her there.

Actually the police turned out to be friendly and *"enthusiastic about the run. They wanted to check that things were all right with me and that the motorists were accommodating me appropriately on the road. In fact they returned twice more during the morning in the belief that their presence would enhance my safety."*

By daybreak they were approaching St. Louis at last, and Mavis' *"heart palpitations had still not eased."* It didn't help that Dennis' carefully plotted route through the 'back suburbs' and byroads proved to have traffic as dense as it had ever been at its worst. The caravans couldn't keep her in sight or help her in the press of vehicles and she felt isolated and afraid, as well as amazed at the sheer size of the city. It was a bit different from the lonely plains and mountains of New Mexico.

Now she had to face one of her worst fears. Because the new bridge over the Mississippi had no space to the side of the traffic lanes, and pedestrians were therefore forbidden, she would have to cross on an old three-mile bridge which appeared rickety and ready to collapse. At the sight of it, the *"scared rabbit quickly turned into a blob of jelly...The girders of the bridge had small gaps through which I could see the river below so I painstakingly inched my way across the bridge. Every minute movement was filled with terror"* as she imagined falling into the river. Mavis was 'petrified of heights', and the heights were all too visible.

Her painful progress across the bridge was so slow that the press decided to come to her instead, expecting her to smile for the camera and to comment on the run. *"All they got was an icy glare and a mummified grimace as I deliberately placed one foot ahead of the other with not the slightest intention of diverting my attention from the next girder. I remember briefly wondering whether a stiff whiskey would have been helpful -- for a teetotaler to have such thoughts is indicative of the anxiety I was experiencing. Every time a vehicle used the bridge the shaking and rattling convinced me I was about to crumble into a heap of dust and remain there for eternity. Luckily no train crossed while I was on the bridge. All around me people were exclaiming the wonders of the views from the bridge and exhorting me to look up and enjoy the scenery. All I could be amazed about was the fact that I was still on my feet."*

At the end of the bridge, she was unable to go on without a break, and it was there that the journalists had their interviews and two policewomen stayed a while to chat. Fatigue could also be a useful ploy, as Mavis dodged answering her first question of the journey about racism in South Africa.

But dodging questions didn't help her own fears of racial hostility, perhaps fueled by the two incidents with hostile black men in South Africa during her training. East St. Louis was a black area and not considered very safe, and she was told by the police not to stop at any stage while passing through. In fact, two police cars stayed with her for most of the day, *"afraid our vehicles would be a target and would be overturned by angry mobs."* It didn't happen.

The people turned out to be very friendly. They'd seen her on TV, and wished her well as she passed. One man who owned a saloon even invited her in for a drink. But *"Ernest almost burst a blood vessel"* when a group of young men *"much the worse for what they had been drinking...decided that it was imperative for them to wish me...luck on the road ahead."* After all, she must be important. They'd seen her on TV!

Meanwhile, Jean, Lucy and Dennis had gone back to St. Louis to buy supplies and check once more for mail from home. When Mavis heard that she had mail but that they couldn't collect it without Mavis' written permission, the *"nonstop flood of my tears convinced Dennis that he needed to return to the city for the third time rather than have them forward the mail to Columbus"* in Ohio as the Post Office intended.

---

[1]*This is possibly a conflation of the familiar maxim about not judging a man until you've walked a mile in his shoes with a Cheyenne saying: "Do not judge your neighbor until you walk two moons in his moccasins."*

Chapter 17: AMERICAN DREAM III –
Neither Snow nor Rain Nor Gloom of Night

———————◆•◉•◆———————

"Mom is running a bit just to try the leg out. It seems to be OK
but I told her to take it slowly."
(letter from Ernest to daughter Gayle)

POLICE AND SNOW

"I was on the road very early – it was bitterly cold."

Although spring 'disappeared as fast as it arrived' after crossing into Illinois, at first there were trees on both sides with pink and mauve flowers showing that spring had been there. Mavis began to try running a little more each day, although her leg was still stiff and painful and the extra weight of cold weather gear made moving difficult. She didn't get much of a welcome to Illinois roads. Once again a policeman stopped her, but not with words of encouragement. *"I got the fright of my life...I was told in no uncertain terms to get off the freeway at once."* So concerned was he about the sacred Illinois rule that pedestrians were banned from the freeways that she had to get into a caravan without a moment's delay, and she was lucky that an offramp to Route 40 was right there at the spot.

It kept getting colder, and with two tracksuits and a hat to keep off the cold and wind, it felt like running in her sleep on the wet, muddy roads. As always, reporters who came out onto the road for interviews slowed her down. Mavis might have finished days earlier without them.

It kept getting colder. As temperatures plummeted further on her last day in Illinois, bringing snow and frost, she looked 'like an Eskimo in the snow', as she battled against icy headwinds in her *"Michelin-man routine with layers of tracksuits and a bright orange waterproof, fur hat and protective goggles"* to keep the wind from burning her eyes. With the wind so strong that she felt as if she were pushing a heavy weight ahead of her, Mavis felt exhausted well before noon, and asked her support team every few minutes how much distance she'd covered.

"Some nights I came reeling off the road like an old woman."

It kept getting colder, and with two tracksuits and a hat to keep off the cold and wind, it felt like running in her sleep on the wet, muddy roads. As always, reporters who came out onto the road for interviews slowed her down. Mavis might have finished days earlier without them.

It kept getting colder. As temperatures plummeted further on her last day in Illinois, bringing snow and frost, she looked 'like an Eskimo in the snow', as she battled against icy headwinds in her *"Michelin-man routine with layers of tracksuits and a bright orange waterproof, fur hat and protective goggles"* to keep the wind from burning her eyes. With the wind so strong that she felt as if she were pushing a heavy weight ahead of her, Mavis felt exhausted well before noon, and asked her support team every few minutes how much distance she'd covered.

After only 20 miles, she was *"ready to call it a day…when I expected to have done much more. I felt like giving up. I reverted to 'one step at a time' thinking to see how long I could last."* Physically and mentally at the end of her endurance, she pressed on although by the 30-mile mark she *"would have given anything for a rest."*

And the reward came. As she continued she began to feel better mentally and knew she had won not just the mental and physical struggle, but a spiritual victory as well. But the day was not over. The last few miles went through a neighborhood with a multitude of dogs, another of Mavis' fears since she'd been bitten while training. Dennis had to accompany her armed with a stick that looked like a bush. She'd made it forty miles through cold, wind, snow and fear.

Climbing that figurative mountain made her so happy that evening that she bewildered the team with her cheerfulness. It didn't hurt that on this 'bitterly cold' night she could have a good night's sleep in a soft clean warm bed in a comfortable motel room, awakening occasionally with brief pangs of guilt, thinking how cold the rest of the team must be in the caravans parked outside. Dennis' inability to find an RV campground that night had brought Mavis and Ernest a bonus.

PLAYBOY IN THE RAIN

> *"She had a smooth and steady gait, this incredible woman,*
> *and the sleekness of an animal honed to do the thing it*
> *likes best. In this case it is running. And run she does,*
> *though even her husband is at a loss to know why."*
> (Plainfield, Indiana newspaper press report)

Indiana began well. The sun came out, and she was able to shed her extra layers of clothing one by one. Sun brought hope, and she was able to run part of the time, unburdened by the weight of cold weather gear. Covering 47 miles that day gave her such a lift that she decided to go shopping with Jean, and that evening atmosphere at the appropriately named Mount Comfort camp was lighter than for some time. "*Good dinner, good chat, good shower, good sleep. I was content.*"

It didn't last. "*Sadly, every up-beat must be followed by a down-beat. We awoke to torrential rainfall and I instinctively knew this was going to be a tough one.*" It was. "*Two layers of tracksuits and two waterproofs could not keep the wet out nor the warmth in. This, in turn, meant regular stops to change out of wet clothing and frenetic activity by the team to keep a regular change of dry clothing available.*" With a cap and flap protecting her neck, topped by a plastic hat, she 'looked a real sight'.

Her team grew tired, wet and discouraged, and Mavis didn't want to make it any harder for them by complaining. She knew only too well the strain they were under. Meanwhile she experienced the "*amazement of the American people seeing this apparition on the road*". They were sure she was in trouble and running away from something, and were horrified or offended when she declined their offers of a lift.

After breakfast she was stumbling along the road, finding it very hard to stay focused. Extra rest in the lunch break made no difference. As she plodded along, soaking wet and exhausted, she tried to keep the team from seeing her distress, knowing that this would only increase the general anxiety.

But the day had one highly unusual feature. Terry Fisher from Playboy Magazine had been searching for Mavis for two weeks, and was waiting for her at one of the 'change into dry clothes stops'. *"There, in the disarray of the caravan, strewn with wet clothes and crowded with helpers all trying to conduct their activities, I spent over an hour in a most engaging interview…"* while worrying about the lost time and thinking that this was one article she'd never see – Playboy was banned in South Africa. She'd felt sorry for Terry Fisher after his long search, but when radio and newspaper journalists showed up as well that day, she was *"more curt than I intended to be"* in her exhaustion.

After only 37 miles through the pouring rain, she was too worn out to go any further. The support team were even wearier, and everyone was relieved when Ernest decided *"enough was enough"*.

Even through the gray curtain of fatigue, Mavis knew where she found the strength to keep going. *"Ray could not contain his wonderment at how I was able to continue. I reassured him that my strength came from my creator whose power was limitless…The Lord guides me."*

But the Lord wasn't changing the weather. *"I strained my ears to hear the weather report above the noise of the pounding rain, - more rain."* Meanwhile 'Campers' Haven' provided a bit of entertainment for the team, although Mavis slept like the dead from the end of supper onward. While the men played slot machines or table tennis, Jean and Lucy spent the evening socializing with the owner. Conversation with people outside the claustrophobic atmosphere of the narrow team circle would have been a tension reliever.

Tension relievers were needed.

Stresses were not diminishing because New York was now only 700 miles away. *"This time it was Dennis who exploded, accusing Lucy of not feeding him properly. Ernest was frightened into taking sides as he realized that we had become very dependent on Dennis's planning skills and could not afford to lose him."* Ernest's new attitude of 'resentful tolerance' toward

Dennis appeased neither party, and did nothing to produce any real reconciliation. It's no wonder that the tense little band hardly noticed their crossing into Ohio.

THE DOGS OF OHIO

"For the first time in three days there was a little sunshine, but most of the day was cold and misty with light rain."

"She wore 25 pairs of shoes in rotation, and had repairs made 40 times…One raincoat would keep her dry for exactly one hour; she wore two. Together they kept her dry for four hours."
('Three-thousand Mile Lady', Ensign magazine, January 1980)

As Mavis ran in the dark with the headlights of the caravan showing her the way, mulling over events among the team, her tension spiked as she *"became aware of a giant white dog storming toward me with its teeth gnashing"*. The dog *"went for her a few times growling"*, then jumped at her in attempt to bite her in the face, but was foiled by Mavis' instinctive turn away from its teeth. Meanwhile Ernest had jumped out of the caravan and raced toward Mavis, angrily pelting the dog with stones. He knew her terror of dogs, and managed to distract the animal enough that she could continue down the road 'in a state of shock'. But the fun wasn't over.

"*Before anyone in the team could regain their composure a speeding car swerved to avoid a stationary vehicle and in the process narrowly missed me. I jumped out of the way and tumbled down a steep embankment. The team members thought I had been hit and as I looked up the embankment, all their ashen, wide eyed, wide mouthed faces appeared simultaneously in disbelief that I was attempting to clamber up the incline. I must admit the thought crossed my mind that it would be better to just stay where I was.*" Initially both Mavis and her team believed she really had been hit. On this 'shaky day', which included being chased by a second dog later on, she carried on to reach a total of 45 miles.

Most of the team was hardly in a mood for adventure that evening, but Dennis had Ray drop him off at what he believed was a local dance hall. It turned out to be a bar *"where the locals danced – not what Dennis was looking for."*

Mavis was now moving well again. The daily stress of the painful leg, the danger of traffic passing all too close, the constant rain, the weight of double tracksuits and waterproofs, and the long days on the road *"did not seem to matter any more as long as I could have a decent mileage on the road for the day."*

That wasn't always easy. At each break she would sponge down with water heated by Jean, and it became hard to dry wet clothing in the damp, musty caravans. It was often difficult to run in the mud, and Mavis figured that she lost a good four to six miles a day to the weather.

That weather included thunder and lightning one morning before sunrise, and Mavis was almost as frightened of being on the road in an electrical storm as she was of dogs. It seemed to her that the lightning went right through her – but after the breakfast break she sneaked back onto Interstate 70 for fifteen miles of good running conditions, and for once the highway patrol didn't shoo her off the road. After that it was back to moving at a snail's pace through the 'quagmire', wearing two tracksuits, two waterproofs, two pairs of gloves, a cloth hat, a southwester waterproof hat, and a pair of goggles – in a hailstorm. After 47 miles they rested in an old garage off the exit into Quaker City.

THE MOUNTAIN MAMMA MOMENT

> *"It was difficult to focus and get my mind right. I would ask*
> *myself how I would manage. The first ten minutes or so*
> *were never easy. After that I got myself into gear and would*
> *plod along accepting whatever the day had in store for me."*

Ohio gave her one more golden moment when the highway patrol kicked her off the interstate again, forcing her onto narrow, uneven roads that strained her injured leg. Then she was in West Virginia for – for fifteen miles. Then she was in Pennsylvania, and soon back in West Virginia. She never did figure out 'why it happened this way'. All she was aware of was that she had to complete the day with as much distance as she could manage through the neverending rain and slush. An exhausted team spent the night at a 'hillbilly camp', 45 miles closer to the Big Apple.

Chapter 18: AMERICAN DREAM IV –
From Sea to Shining Sea

——•◆•——

*"When running a marathon in which you are struggling you
reach a stage when you know that despite the difficulties,
you have passed the threshold of doubt and will be
able to endure to the end."*

A NEW HORIZON

*"The team could not wait for the end of the journey. By this
time it felt like monotony gone mad. They were prisoners of
the road or so it seemed..."*

Mavis no longer doubted that she would succeed. But as her own confidence increased in the teeth of obstacles, she became more worried about the team, *"the people who keep me going"*. In the constant rain, *"they were more confined than usual and the duties they had to perform to keep me on the road increased exponentially. Every time I stopped for a break my injured leg needed treatment; hot and cold packs, massages, shoe repairs, change of clothing. When entering any of the freeways there was the inevitable negotiating with police patrols about whether or not we were allowed to use the freeway and if so, under what conditions. When we were ordered off the freeways, finding the best alternative route became a point of contention. Jumping in and out of caravans in wet weather, preparing food, finding a place to sleep for the night – the tedium of it all was getting to everyone except me, because I knew I was doing what I needed to do to achieve my goal."*

She had accepted the constant physical pain, but the emotional pain of seeing the cohesion amongst the team disintegrating was getting to her: *"I felt saddened by my helplessness to provide the support that each team member now needed and I became increasingly conscious of the great sacrifices that they had made to help me achieve my dream.* Even for Mavis it seemed like a 'forever struggle'. Buffeted by winds, on roads in shocking condition, putting one foot in front of the other was a real effort – although every step taken was one that didn't have to be taken again. But for the team, it was even worse than before, as the police insisted that the caravans had to crawl along ahead or behind Mavis at all times – for 17 hours a day.

And now the climbing came back, as her leg had to take the strain of getting her to the top of the endless ranges of Pennsylvania hills. More important though, was the courage and willpower needed as the eternal cold rain poured endlessly down, depressing the spirits of every one of the six. It was at this point that Mavis called the team together to share a poem she had written, born of despair and determination alike:

> *A new horizon is what I seek*
> *I'm very tired*
> *And very weak.*
> *But I must stand and face the day,*
> *There is no time to turn away.*
> *Lift up your head.*
> *Move on, Move on. For there to be progress I must press on.*
> *There are many more miles to be run,*
> *Please, God, give me the strength to do just one.*

God gave her the strength, and on she plodded through the eternal rain, over the hills to Chambersburg and and (illegally) up the interstate toward New York. At any moment they expected to be chased off by the police, which would have led to panic because there was no alternative route. And giant trucks were out in force long before dawn. It got too dangerous to run before sunrise, when "*at any moment a truck could collect me from the back*". She decided to start at daybreak, when she could at least see the hazards.

One psychological lift came as she struggled to cross the last mountain range. When she started to doubt that they would ever see the sun, and began to feel sorry for herself, she "*again began reflecting on the sacrifices that had been made by the members of the of the support team, and my melancholy soon dissipated. These were people from very diverse backgrounds who had sacrificed earnings and home comforts to be cooped up with others for seventy days for no tangible benefit. They had to endure a marathon of a very different kind and in the end would be the unsung heroes. The thought of their unselfishness and my deep indebtedness to them helped propel me up the last of the mountains we needed to traverse."*

Powered by the need to make sure that these sacrifices would not be in vain, she refused to let up until she'd covered the scheduled 46 miles for the day. She knew it would be all downhill from there.

IMAGES OF VICTORY

"The slipstreams from the mammoth trucks buffeted the caravans. I was like a small insect being tossed about by them."

Excitement grew as they drew closer to New York, but the difficulties increased. The traffic intensified further, although *"the buffeting from the slipstreams created by the passing trucks and caravans took their toll but could no longer suppress"* her.

There were no good choices of route. The shoulders of the secondary roads were crumbling, making Mavis wonder if they were ever repaired. But on the freeways the support vehicles couldn't stay near her, leaving her completely alone most of the time – running along the shoulder of the freeways was illegal in any event.

Changes were made at short notice to accommodate local conditions. Mavis kept herself going with images of *"how the team members would celebrate their new-found freedom once we reached the end"* and hoped desperately that her *"orange waterproof was bright enough to be seen through rain-drenched windscreens."*

The press from Harrisburg also distracted her, staying with her on the road for *"a long while"*.

TRIUMPH IN THE SUN

"It was a very lighthearted day."

And after three weeks of perpetual rain, the clouds parted. As she ran in shorts and an athletic vest for the first time in weeks, she was able to soak in the beauty of Allentown and the Delaware River instead of having the constant downpours soak her. Overjoyed by the sunshine, her spirits were further buoyed by a familiar face from Virginia -- Bob Boal, whom she'd

Leaving New Jersey on the toll road, at the 'outer bridge'.

met at the World Master's games in Sweden. Mavis was so bubbly at this pleasant surprise in the sunshine that she insisted that everybody *"celebrate the occasion with a toast of orange juice."*

In her notes, *Mavis didn't even bother to note the hills of western New Jersey. After the Rockies and the Appalachians, a few sun-kissed slopes just didn't seem important. There were only 51 miles to go from the old town of Lebanon with its 18th century Dutch Reformed Church, and Mavis knew she could push all the way to New York the next day. But it was not to be.*

After an early start, they got word from the Mayor of New York that he would only be available to receive Mavis at noon the following day. Since the team now had time on their hands, they accepted an invitation from Jody Levin, a road runner who owned the 'very posh' Red Bull restaurant in Summerville. It was exciting to get a medal and a Red Bull mascot, but Mavis was 'quite exhausted' when she got back on the road.

Too much excitement was draining her energy, and when she reached what she thought was the Verazzano Bridge, she went into the caravan for a rest. After all, that was almost at her destination. But when she came out, the local people who greeted her let her know that this was the 'outer bridge', and the Verazzano was 16 miles further. Mavis was in shock, but refused to come off the road. *"I immediately sprang back into action with the team members in tow trying to convince me that there was plenty of time for a rest. Stubbornly I insisted on continuing even though I was in a state of near exhaustion."*

Protected by police cars in front, behind and at her side, she 'chugged' her way across Staten Island to the real Verazzano Bridge, through traffic far worse than anything she'd ever seen. Being Mavis, she spent the night *"calculating how much earlier I could have finished had it not been for all the mishaps."* The fact that she would finish her run well inside her originally calculated time counted for nothing. She knew it could be done faster.

Now there only twelve miles to go, but one more fear to face. She had to run across the longest suspension bridge in the Americas, where for the first time ever all traffic on the lower bridge had been stopped for a single athlete. *"Although the views were breathtaking, with the ocean way below, splattered with ships crisscrossing in a seemingly chaotic pattern, the Statue of Liberty in the distance and New York sprawled ahead, I was petrified with vertigo."*

She was far ahead of schedule, so they stopped for breakfast and chatted to children playing baseball, accompanied by police on horseback, until it was time to cross the Brooklyn Bridge. It was a cloudless day, *"the kind of day that makes the city come alive. Refracted beams of light glistened"* on the breathtaking skyline of lower Manhattan, and 'in a blink' she was at City Hall, still twenty minutes early.

At 12 noon sharp the mayor arrived. Vere Stock from the South African Consulate was there in a pink suit he might not have worn in South Africa, as was pioneering ultramarathon runner Ted Corbitt. The grandson of slaves, he had set new American records over 25, 40, 50 and 100 miles, as well as in the marathon. Nina Kucsik (the then American 50-mile record holder) was also on hand, and Mavis felt honored by her company as well as Corbitt's.

Even her sponsors were there now that Mavis was at the finish line. But Mavis was "only vaguely aware of the dignitaries who had come to welcome me…" She wasn't at all put out when TV crews who arrived late "*coerced me to run the last 100 yards over again. I ended up finishing five times but did not object because I could relive the completion of a mammoth ambition on each occasion. Sixty-nine days, two hours and forty minutes[1]; six million footsteps, and now it was all over.*"

What didn't enthrall her was repeating the ceremonial side of the finish: "*Each time I was loaded with laurels and medals and cups and gifts from various firms and had to shake the mayor of New York's hand. It was so embarrassing. Quite uncanny!*"

But of course she was already calculating how she'd lost three hours to time zone changes, and at least four days to injuries, not to mention the time lost to endless media interviews. If she could find a sponsor, she'd do it again.[2]

Meanwhile, she and the team stayed in two penthouses provided by Vanda Cosmetics, and Mavis tried to adjust to the idea that she'd actually fulfilled her dream. She slept 'like a baby' that night, and next morning the whole team dealt one last time with logistics. They had to drive fifty miles to Long Island to return their Winnebagoes, then make their way from the station where the caravan people had dropped them to the flats where they were staying.

It was the next day as she had her hair done that Mavis realized that there was a lifetime ahead of her, and that she needed new goals, more ambitions. This could not be the end.

Without new goals she might end up like David Warady, who would win the 1992 Trans-America Footrace and say a year later: "*It was difficult. Here I had finished this great thing, I had all this incredible energy and power and feeling that I could knock the world dead. But I went from Superman to Superman looking for a new adventure. I still feel that way. I have all this incredible ability and foresight and energy, but I don't have anything to channel it into.*" [3]

In the introduction to Tim Noakes's *Lore of Running*, he says this: "Beyond each academic or sporting peak there will always, indeed, must always, be another peak waiting to be tackled. Mavis Hutchison realized this the very moment she had completed her life's ambition – to run across North America."

Though she didn't know it, the next peak to be tackled was just around the corner, courtesy of two young men who would knock on her door after her return.

Meanwhile she had a chance to see a bit of America while not running through it, including Greenwich village where she had never seen so many hobos in her life, beggars, dozens of people sleeping on the sidewalks, drug sellers on every corner – and Chinatown, which she found the people very friendly.

It was time to leave, flying home via Paris and Brazzaville. Family, friends and sponsors met her at the Johannesburg airport. "*It was great to be home again – now for a rest before I make any plans.*"

Praise poured in from her countrymen. From the government gave her the State President's Award. The Johannesburg Star named her their Sports Woman of the Year.

Mavis' most finished account of her American epic ends with these words: "Thanks team!"

---

[1]*Allowing for the time zone changes and the switch to daylight saving time, her true elapsed time would have been 68 days, 22 hours and 40 minutes. In the quote above, Mavis is also not allowing for her late start, which cuts the time to 68 days 22 hours and 33 minutes. This would of course have been reduced by more than half a day if the mayor could have received her the day before.*

[2]*Had a sponsor materialized, Mavis planned another US run in 1983, hoping to cut at least five days off her record. Sadly, it never happened, and the Hutchisons certainly lacked the resources to try it without a sponsor.*

[3]*From a Los Angeles Times article of June 18, 1993. Of the first three finishers in the 1992 Trans-America Footrace, David Warady was unable to run effectively again until May the following year, Milan Milanovich said nine months after finishing second that he might never run again, and Tom Rogozinski of Maryland finished third after "running much of the race with stress fractures in his feet". In the next year's Trans-America, 35-year-old Lorna Michael became the first woman to finish, and the first to run across America faster than Mavis. She took 64 days, or roughly what Mavis thought she could have done without injuries.*

Chapter 19: SPIRITUAL HEIGHTS

———•◆•———

"Does the road wind uphill all the way?
Yes, to the very end…"
(Christina Georgina Rossetti)

1978 was Mavis' watershed year, when the same spiritual strength that propelled her across America helped her begin the spiritual marathon she pursues to this day.

Within a month of her return, her chance to peel back a new layer of self-discovery arrived when a pair of young men appeared on her doorstep, wanting to talk with her about their church. Mavis recalls they had a "soft patient teaching manner", and she felt God was saying to her, "Now is the time for you to grow spiritually."

WITH THE SPIRIT ACROSS A CONTINENT

Mavis still keenly remembers the first set of young missionaries from the same church, who had caught her right in the middle of frantic last-minute preparations for the great trans-America saga.

All she could think of then was that she was about to fulfill her biggest dream, her greatest ambition, something so big that at the starting point in LA she wished she'd had enough sense to stay home. At that moment there was no doubt in her mind that she was facing the greatest physical *and* spiritual challenge she'd ever had to meet.

In fact, she was going to have to tap into every bit of spirituality she possessed to pull off the physical challenge. Running across a continent was one thing, and she had prepared for that, but the spiritual aspect was quite another.

Still, for Mavis they were intimately intertwined. After all, she was a woman of faith who knew that reaching the outer limits of her physical and mental endurance would push her into a sphere above and beyond where the rational mind could reach.

At more than one point in the race the excruciating pain of shin splints took her to that space. "*I prayed often for courage to bear the pain. I didn't ask God to take it away, but just to help me bear it.*" Prayer was the order of the day and many times throughout the journey she pled with her Heavenly Father:

"*Please God, give me the stamina to fight the wind, the endurance to stay the distance, the willpower to keep going.*"[1]

Reflecting on those moments so many years after the fact, she recognizes that He did help her. "*At no time did I ever doubt that I would finish the distance, but I can assure you that there were times when I didn't know how I could finish the day or even the next hour. And then I prayed, in the words of John Henry Newman's beautiful hymn, 'Please, God, I do not ask to see the distant scene. One step enough for me.'*"

Looking back on the odyssey and how she had to lean on her Maker in her extremity, she feels it all helped to prepare her for what the missionaries would share with her. She was ready to expand within a wider truth, to grow beyond her wildest dreams.

The long and lonely road and its *"purifying solitude"* that taught her nothing is impossible if you're prepared to work hard enough, that there are no barriers and handicaps, opened her mind and her heart *"to the hidden reaches of a hidden existence,"* where she found a deep joy.

DISCOVERING HERSELF

"*I was ready to discover myself,*" she told the late E. Dale LeBaron, who presided over the missionaries of The Church of Jesus Christ of Latter-day Saints in South Africa at the time Mavis joined the church. In an article authored by LeBaron he described her as someone who "honored the truth and despised sham."

With this kind of disposition she became keenly involved in discussions with the young ministers. She greatly enjoyed their visits and felt *"sure that they would keep coming indefinitely."*

One of the visiting elders was Claude Behrman, now an architect near Cape Town. He recalls Mavis vividly. "From the beginning we were received in a most cordial and friendly manner. From the outset she seemed very curious about the church. She was impressed by our values and the emphasis on the strength of the family."

She was likewise impressed with the sacrifice of early church members that came to her attention during discussions.

"I believe that her extended marathon across the US, much of which would have been through landscapes like those the early Mormon pioneers trekked through on their way from Nauvoo to the Salt Lake valley, gave her an empathy for their sacrifice."

Elders Behrman and Wheeler met regularly with the Hutchisons over a period of about two months, at the end of which daughter Gayle joined her mom in the eventual baptismal plunge on September 30. Although Ernie never joined the church, Claude recalls that he was always very supportive of her involvement.

But aside from gospel exchanges with the family, Claude has fond memories of running with Mavis. "My companion and I used to go jogging with her on preparation days. She was very accommodating of having us along and we would run for at least two hours. Both of us became very fit as a result."

Today the members of her Fish Hoek congregation praise Mavis as an inspiring speaker, and when she tells her conversion story they learn of her first shocked response to the Behrman/Wheeler baptismal invitation: it was a resounding 'no' since the proposed date was the very next Saturday after the invite!

BUSY ON SATURDAYS

"I was completely stunned. I made sure that I was busy the next Saturday – and the next, and the next."

Even so, she knew she was just making excuses. *"I also knew that if I chose not to join the church I would lose my way again, for I knew there was light in my life that hadn't been there before."*

She hung on to that light and the knowledge that *"God knows who I am and what I need. I've gained so much additional understanding that helps me appreciate how I fit into the scheme of things and that there's a relationship to be enjoyed with Him. It drives all my actions."*

She will always remember when she prayed about her decision to make the spiritual leap. *"I felt the Spirit of Heavenly Father telling me that I must do the right thing"*, but that *"only I could make the choice."*

When the defining moment arrived she was ready. It was almost an emotional replay of the LA count down: *"I was very nervous and very unsure...Had I prepared properly? Was I doing the right thing? It was an enormous commitment – would I be able to keep it?"*

She recalls the moments after her baptism clearly. "*When I came up out of the water it felt right, like when the gun goes off and I start to run.*"

Of course not everybody felt that what she did was right. But she was a woman of conviction and that carried her through.

Many of the members of her current congregation may not even know she was once considered a legend, but that doesn't bother Mavis since she doesn't care much about fame. She just wants to serve and blend in with her fellow members, who "love her to bits and speak very highly of her".

Mavis in the late 70s, when she made her spiritual leap.
Picture from The Star.

---

[1]('Three-Thousand Mile Lady', Ensign magazine, Jan. 1980)

Chapter 20: BATTLE IN BRITAIN
Beyond the Limits

———•◆•———

*"If certain race horses…develop an inferiority complex and
suffer a nervous breakdown, this could be directly attributable
to Mavis Hutchison…Mavis, you see, is currently doing her
training on a horse training track close to her house. Mavis is
running between 35 and 40 kilometers each day, and if this
doesn't make the local race horses feel like a bunch of sissies
nothing will."*
(press article in the 'Courier')

After the run across America (not a job for sissies or race horses) Mavis got itchy feet for a new adventure. *"I just had this tremendous feeling of achievement that I felt afterwards. I remember thinking to myself that I had achieved a goal of a lifetime and yet I still had lifetime to live."*

What she decided on wasn't a new idea. Beating the women's record for running the length of Britain was a challenge that had attracted Mavis since her first Comrades Marathon run in 1965. Five years before that Comrades run, Liverpool hairdresser Wendy Lewis had set a record of 17 days 7 hours and 43 minutes that would stand for 20 years, trudging on through rain and snow and not sleeping at all for the last 48 hours. Wendy was 18 years old as she stood 'like a drowned rat' signing autographs at the finish.

HOT FRUIT

Mavis was 55 as she stepped off the plane into a sweltering mid-July London. Her only previous visit to London was in winter, when her cross country girls learned about training in the snow, so she was surprised that London could be so hot that many men were walking around stripped to the waist. The price of fruit was even higher than the thermometer – *"prices seemed to rise even as I stood there watching the laden barrows."* This was serious stuff for a woman used to running on a fruit-heavy diet, and at these prices she wondered if she'd have to change her plans.

This time her husband Ernie wasn't there to 'wind her up and put her on the road'. She'd miss his experience and support. *"He helped me through my difficult runs and I just wanted him to reassure me."* But Ernest's 94-year-old mother was in the hospital with a broken hip, and for the first time he wouldn't be there with her on the long road. An occasional phone call would have to do. This time her team included Dirk Mostert and Butch Smith from the South African Broadcasting Corporation, and Mavis' daughter-in-law Dianne. There were plans for a documentary.

It was a fairly public arrival. Mavis was sure she could beat the record by two days *"which the London papers duly splashed all over their sports pages, leaving me feeling rather tense about meeting expectations."* The South African Minister of Sport sent her a telegram encouraging her with the promise of a reception at the South African Embassy if she succeeded. The South African Ambassador, a former member of the national rugby team, said he'd try to join her at a later stage of the run.

Also with her was Philip Jones of the Sunday Times, who'd *"committed to run with me intermittently so that he could send a first-hand account to the readers back home of the trials and tribulations of the expedition. Philip had completed his first Comrades marathon two months prior and felt well prepared to complete the assignment."* He'd find it a lot harder than he thought, but he did make it possible for readers of the Rand Daily Mail and the Sunday Times to follow Mavis every step of the way.

Mavis, meanwhile, was so fascinated by the Olympic 800-meter final between British runners Sebastian Coe and Steve Ovett, scheduled for the day after her arrival, that she decided to rent a TV so she wouldn't miss it.

But the heat wave didn't last. As her team headed north, overcast skies with rain and thunder set in, and Mavis found herself hoping that her five 'rainproof tracksuits' would be enough. She also *"reflected on how close the run had come to being called off because the sponsors, Ronnie Bass Sigma, vacillated before finally agreeing to back me."* For her it was always 'no sponsor, no run'. She hoped she was ready, whatever the weather.

The omens were not good as they drove through the rain toward the northern tip of Scotland. When a 'flying stone' cracked the windscreen of one caravan, they had to wait for a replacement. The other caravan then broke down outside Newcastle, and they waited there for hours before repairs could be made. Mavis was getting anxious, and had had only eight hours of sleep in three days.

Without Ernest to challenge her decisions, her support team were unable to get her to agree to delay the start for a day or two. She *"knew the only way to relieve the anxiety was to start running, so I ignored their pleas"*. Later she would know she'd made a poor decision in her sleepless mental fog, but by then it would be too late. She drove on alone to the start, knowing her seconds would catch up.

WHEELBARROWS, BEER AND FOG

At John O'Groats she and her team discovered they were hardly alone on the southward trek to Land's End. According to Philip Jones, people began the pilgrimage down the length of Britain "every day through the British summer or lack of it…There are experienced runners and there are novices. There was the man who walked all the way on his hands, another who walked barefoot, and a chap who went on a monocycle."

On the day Mavis started, *"four men were attempting to push a wheelbarrow to Lands End, well fortified by their sponsors, a local brewery. They had two barrows and the pairs alternated between pushing and resting in the barrow (with the accompanying refreshments)."* Mavis was the only Latter-day Saint in her team, so they cheerfully accepted the beer this group 'showered' on them, and it kept them in 'high spirits'. Besides the wheelbarrow team she noticed two youngsters trying to break the tandem cycling record and a solitary walker.

It was 1:15 in the afternoon on the scheduled day when she finally got going, and TV cameras and press photographers captured her disappearance into the Scottish mist. Friendly motorists who could actually see her through the rolling billows of fog waved as she pressed on for nine hours, but she certainly missed the scenery. What Mavis hoped was that the traffic would miss her. The fog was a 'traffic hazard, and she often had to jump smartly out of the way as cars pressed close.' (Philip Jones) Her experience dodging traffic came in handy on the very narrow Highland roads. *"This was the height of the tourist season and the Scottish roads were jammed with cars. Constant vigilance was called for."*

Her carefully planned route didn't survive long. Heavy rains had closed many of the roads through the Highlands, and Mavis got to explore any number of detours.

At the end of the first day, she gratefully accepted an offer of a real bed from the chairman of the Wick Council. By 5 am, the 'Mavis Hutchison road show' was on its way again. Philip Jones wrote that no matter what time she got to bed "after a punishing day through the Scottish highlands, she was always keen to get to grips with the challenge again."

Battling through the rain, she reached her goal of 80 km. "She did not complain. It's all part of the game. You just keep running, never mind the conditions."

Through driving rain, Mavis continued on to Fort William. Mornings as always began with *"everyone in the team was scurrying around to prepare for the day. Even Philip seemed energized to get the show on the road."* So far she'd maintained her planned average of 80 kilometers per day, and stayed healthy. By the end of the cold, bleak roads of day four her throbbing feet were minus a toenail, and Mavis *"attempted to maintain the high spirits within the team by not showing my discomfort and by producing a whole string of running anecdotes to keep my mind off the pain."*

Comfort came the next morning as she managed to phone her husband in South Africa. As he told her how things were back home, it brought back memories of how he had been with her on all her other long runs.

Along lochs and hills

Mavis might be in a bit of pain, but it was Philip who complained of aching feet and sore knees after six hours on the road with her. Meanwhile Mavis' *"hands and my face were beginning to swell due to the unrelenting wind, exacerbated by occasions of searing sunshine."*

It was a long way still to Land's End, and she worried about her 'novice' support team. Could they stand the strains sure to come? She felt a need to take charge. *"Foolishly I rebuked one of the members for not wearing shoes, informing him that catching a cold would be the last thing we wanted. 'That's all right, I'll put them on Ma'am', was the curt retort."* She looked at Philip and admitted she was just grateful he didn't call her granny.

There were fine days. One came as they passed Loch Ness 'with no monster in sight'. People recognized her along the way. In one small Scottish town, a woman rushed forward to announce that she was from Durban on the east coast of South Africa. Sometimes people found Mavis inspirational, as with the old age pensioner who ran up shouting that she would run the same distance next year.

There were encounters with others going the length of Britain. The wheelbarrow-pushing team had started ahead of Mavis, and she passed them on day six. *"It was like a reunion of long-lost mates and there was much celebrating by the support team."*

As on the America run, the 'graceful grandmother, slim and trim in her running togs', attracted offers from passing drivers. Shaking her head, she once commented, *"I can't understand these men. There I was, dressed in running shorts and vest, and they'd get out of their lorries and invite me to hop in."* What they thought of her standard reply, *"Sorry, I'm in a hurry!"* is hard to say. But along the road were finds as well as attempted pickups. Over the years she collected jewelry, watches, assorted tools, and enough hats for several families.

Mavis wanted to be able to prove where she'd been, so a team member signed the log book at the police station in each town as she passed. At one small village, this didn't work. The *"local constable locked the door and turned off the lights, refusing to sign the logbook because he was off duty."* Otherwise the local hospitality was *"generally overwhelming. Many hotel keepers offered me the luxury of a hot bath..."* She was a lot more likely to take them up on this if the bath wasn't at the end of numerous flights of stairs. British country inns had no elevators.

SCHOOL PROJECTS AND BUGS

Back in South Africa, people followed her progress. One enterprising teacher decided to use the run for a 7th grade geography project, and had her students write about the places Mavis passed, as well as writing her letters.

Some things don't show on maps, however. As Mavis kept moving south, the bugs began to bite, *"leaving the exposed parts of my body covered in itchy welts."* Through the clouds of insects, in driving rain and unrelenting traffic she approached what she called the 'Tangle of Glasgow'. For the first time, she fell 10 kilometers short of her daily goal. With the traffic bumper to bumper both ways on roads that *"twist and turn all the time"*, she dared not take her eyes off the danger.

KAMIKAZE BRIDGE AND THE LAMB'S WOOL CURE

It was time to face her fear of heights again. Mavis wasn't good at bridges, but the Erskine Bridge over the Clyde River was inescapable. Feeling like a *"kamikaze pilot, heading towards my doom in a blaze of glory"*, she gritted her teeth and plodded on. Philip Jones noted that her will power, determination and 'remarkable stamina' showed in her body language.

But this was only the beginning of the struggle. Sprays of cold, dirty water from passing trucks threw her off balance as often as ten times a minute as she struggled toward Gretna Green, and the wind from their passing often lifted her off her feet. Mavis was determined to reach the English border that day, and tried to ignore the headwinds as she pushed ahead. As Philip Jones ran with her for four hours, his ankles hurt but 'there was no sign of anything wrong from Mavis' as she 'plodded on silently'.

What was wrong with Mavis that day was anxiety. Knowing that she was now behind schedule, she tried to make up time by staying on the road after sunset. It was one thing to 'run in the headlights' when her support vehicle could crawl along behind her, but sometimes her team had to pull back, leaving her to run along an unfamiliar roadway in darkness.

"I tried to subdue my fear but I failed. I was expending a lot of energy for very little benefit." The team had planned to pop champagne corks after her crossing into England, but Mavis had spent 20 hours on her feet. The 'quaintness of the locality', famous for marrying eloping couples from England, was utterly lost on her. She just fell into bed after her shower, already in clean running gear for the earliest possible start.

She'd hoped for better condition as she approached England, but her farewell present from Scotland was a mist *"so heavy you could not see your hand in front of your face."* Philip Jones' company on the road for the first few hours eased her fears of getting lost, but her feet soon took most of her attention away from the dense fog. *"They felt as if they were on fire — almost as if I was running on hot coals. I had no idea what caused this problem. It was difficult to stay on my feet and I almost fell a few times. We decided to have a short rest sitting on the side of the road for about half-an-hour, with our backs resting against a refuse bin."*

Her support team first tried Zambuck ointment from South Africa, then soaking in alternating hot and cold water, but the burning did not let up. Medications from a local pharmacy were equally ineffective – the only cure seemed to be shortening her stride, which slowed her down and increased her anxieties about getting to Cornwall on time. Insect bites covered her, and continued to sap her energy.

She tried not to complain, or show her increasing depression. It wasn't easy. Finally they found a pharmacist who recommended wrapping her feet in lamb's wool – which helped. All the way to Land's End her feet remained wrapped in lamb's wool. Philip Jones used it too.

AH, TO BE IN ENGLAND

Raw relief at crossing the border was so strong that she threw her arms around an astonished Philip and kissed him.

But nothing changed in England. The traffic remained thick, the weather remained awful, and Mavis discovered that the true distance to Land's End had been underestimated by a hundred kilometers – which would somehow have to be made up in the schedule.

PAIN AND MURPHY

And the run nearly ended. A strained Achilles tendon reduced her to walking, and the pain was so excruciating that Philip Jones commented that 'she could hardly get her feet off the curb, grimacing with pain. Mavis could endure silently 'without a mummer', but the pain was too great to hide. She knew she was in serious trouble, and the team knew it too. It wasn't easy to hang on with 'sheer raw guts' when little else was left, but for Mavis it was also no longer easy to give up. But not even earlier starts were getting the job done.

"The team had alerted the hospital in Shrewsbury that I may need emergency attention. After much pondering and great hesitancy I eventually agreed to go to the hospital. I realized that the team members were very concerned and that I owed it to them to do what was necessary to alleviate their angst. Dr Thorne examined me and suggested that I pack it in. After brief consideration I disclosed that 'giving up' was never an option for me and that the only options I would consider were those that would keep me on the road. His response was that all he could do was to wish me good luck."

It was back to one step at a time. There was no more room for mistakes, but she *"felt that the record was still achievable, albeit not within the time I had hoped. The results of the coming weekend would be telling. Deep concentration and a steely willpower was needed."* The focus was now on getting to Bristol, but for her the choice between *"giving up because of the present physical pain or living a lifetime with regrets"* was obvious and clear.

Once more reduced to race walking, she stayed long hours on the road, passing the halfway mark with the wettest British summer in 300 years 'keeping us so damp we need web feet to stay the distance.'

By the end of day 10 over 800 kilometers were behind her, with 87 covered that day. Murphy kept up, although Mavis couldn't see why an Irishman was plaguing her in England. The extra hundred kilometers lost to poor route selection in Scotland also meant that the distance remaining at this stage was much longer than planned.

As she started on day eleven, her right ankle was so swollen that it was hard to sustain her *"fast fading hopes of breaking the record…Not wanting my negativity to influence the team, I encouraged them to spend a few hours visiting some of the historical sights we were passing. I gingerly took to the road as the team hesitantly went in search of the nearest castle."*

Only too clearly she could see her dreams fading into nothing. Alone for three hours with only Murphy for company, she walked onward – along the wrong road. That really was too much, and she *"was about to have a cadenza when someone recommended that we measure the exact distance I had traveled on the wrong road and measure it off on the correct road and drop me off there."* Although the idea made her a bit uneasy, it was the only way an emotionally and physically strained Mavis could cope. She carried miserably on for a time, but her sense of humor came to her rescue as she watched the workers of industrial Lancashire react to her appearance as this unusual apparition flitted by: *"fisherman's hat tied with the brim firmly over my ears, sleeveless padded jacket over a drenched tracksuit and a face full of blotches which were the remnants of the insect bites."*

LEAD KINDLY LIGHT

> *"It would not be because of any physical or emotional toughness that I would see this through, but ultimately it would depend on my spiritual strength."*

Mavis had reached her limits. She was more aware than ever that this run was *"being kept together by the most flimsy of threads."* And it was a thread balanced on a knife edge. She would later say that if someone had breathed on her she might have given up.

But in the same article she said, *"I have got to the stage where I don't know when to stop."* So to *"maintain the faint glimmer of hope of finishing within twenty days"* she hit the road at 2 am. *"Each step was agony as I pressed on by torchlight, bracing myself against the lashing rain"*, and wishing her feet were webbed rather than wrapped in lamb's wool. As she had done before under extreme stress, she recited parts of Newton's great hymn of hope in the darkness:

> *Lead kindly light*
> *The night is dark and I am far from home*
> *Lead thou me on*
> *Lead kindly light Light thou my feet*
> *I do not ask to see the distant scene*
> *One-step enough for me.*

By six she'd begun to 'stagger all over the road', and she and Philip Jones came off the road wet and bedraggled for half an hour's rest. In her tired mind, a realization that her original schedule was now impossible mingled with determination to break the record, hope that she could change to running within the next few days – and thoughts of how far way the tip of England still seemed. *"I remembered that the South African Embassy had promised us a cocktail party if I broke the record. Surely this was the least I could do to show my appreciation to the team?"*

And her sponsor still believed in her. Forced to communicate indirectly, he'd written:

> *"Please communicate with Mavis Hutchison and inform her of the continued faith and support of all South Africans and also that of her sponsors. Best wishes and thanks also to her support team.*
>
> Kind regards
> Ronnie Bass Sigma"

Buoyed by this encouragement and her own faith, she diverted herself by *"focusing on how I would go about getting my hair done at a hairdresser in preparation for the cocktail party.. The diversion helped."* She also attempted to brighten her hopes by buying *"a little Welsh doll, which I hoped was going to bring me some good luck even though I was well aware it was going to take much more than mere luck to get me through."*

Next day she got an encouraging cable from Dawie de Villiers, the South African ambassador, brought to her on the road by two South African boys living in England: "Good luck Mavis from us at the Embassy; we are holding thumbs for a successful run."

It helps to know people believe in you, and her 'grim determination' kept her going through the pain that followed her all the way.

THE WELSH DOLL DOES ITS JOB

Dense traffic followed her all the way as well, as she'd unwittingly chosen to make her attempt 'in the middle of a bumper holiday season'. It got so bad near Monmouth that Philip Jones called it 'almost suicidal being on the road'.

By the morning of day 13, Mavis was thinking of 'going through the night if she had to'. But first she had to cross another bridge. She gritted her teeth as she stepped out onto the viaduct that carried the roadway over the Aust Cliff, then over the mile-long suspension bridge, 445 feet above the River Severn. The view was probably magnificent, but every time a passing vehicle shook the Severn Bridge, she would grab hold of Philip Jones and 'not let go for a while'.

Nonetheless, what struck Philip was her bravery in facing her 'thing about bridges'. She kept going, and to her it seemed that her vertigo" was actually less extreme than in the past. *"Perhaps the physical pain I was experiencing numbed my fear of heights, or perhaps the Welsh doll was doing its job."*

That night they were in Hereford, and at 4 am the next morning she *"ventured out by torchlight onto the streets...to test my aching leg."* Philip Jones was the lone spectator. There was a slight improvement, but it was still too early to put too much stress on her leg by running – yet.

She knew she might need to gamble with the leg at a later stage to stand any chance of success. What happened after the race was less important: *"You can throw me on a bed at the end of the road, but I am going to make it."*

ALL THROUGH THE NIGHTS

She meant it. Next day came a knock on Philip's caravan door at 4:30 am. Mavis was letting him know she was ready to 'do battle with the road again'. The two groped their way out of the parking lot onto the southward road, with him 'acting as a sort of pathfinder' carrying a flashlight and leading the way. Since it was still too painful to run, she would simply spend *"more time on the road to maintain the mileage."* If this meant that *"fatigue would be an additional burden for the next few days...so what; there would be plenty of time to rest afterwards."*

Nearly twenty hours of effort later and 95 kilometers closer to Land's End, she came off the road for a very short 'night's rest'. But in her exhaustion- and pain-fogged mind, one question was paramount? How long could she keep it up? *"Few people will ever be able to test themselves to this extent and so not many will be able to fully understand what I was going through."*

Next day brought another twenty hours of punishing slog, battling through the rain against a strong headwind. Seven hours into the day, she came off the road for her lunch break in a 'deep depression', locked the door and 'fell completely apart'.

"I cried hysterically and felt everything was collapsing around me. At the height of the episode I thought 'this is it!'. But the experience was cathartic. In my attempts not to impact on the rest of the team I had been building pent-up emotions, which needed to be released. As with a flaming boil, once it is lanced the pain dissipates, and so I felt better." She reduced her planned hour's rest to half an hour, and kept on until 12:45 am the next morning, covering a hundred kilometers for the day.

That night in Devon, Mavis remembers thinking that if she made it, she'd certainly deserve her party at the embassy. She *"knew that over the next few days sleep would be foreign to me and fatigue would be my constant enemy."* Philip Jones could see her tension, and how she coped by withdrawing into herself, shutting out all that was happening around her.

With Philip Jones through the fog.

As she began day sixteen at Oakhampton, it must have surprised those around her that she could hardly stop smiling. She'd realized that despite all the setbacks she was actually going to break the record, even if not in the time she'd hoped. In her fog, she'd believed she had one less day to do it than she really had.

Still not able to run, still dead tired, she no longer worried. It was a good thing her anxiety decreased. Apart from that the fact that her 'more relaxed frame of mind' cheered her team, she probably would have caused permanent damage to the injured leg if the pressure of continued high anxiety had made her begin to run. All through that long day, she *"kept on singing (silently, of course) 'Keep right on to the end of the road. Keep right on to the end.' "*

But a more relaxed frame of mind didn't make the miles or the day shorter. It also didn't take away the fear as she walked deep into the night on the misty moors, wondering what would happen if she *"should bump into a stranger who was looking for trouble...What if she got lost in the mist and the team could not find her...What if she stumbled and fell and could not finish – so near and yet so far?"* By the time the 'team came to collect her' on this last night on the road, she was 'more than ready to come off', if slightly disappointed that she hadn't covered even more distance. *"I meekly agreed without any second thoughts of doing 'just a few more kilometers'. I was well satisfied with having covered over 100 kilometers but was left with the aching thought of 'What could have been.' "* Only forty kilometers remained, and there 'was growing jubilation in the caravan camp'.

A LAST MISTY LAP PAST THE RUBBISH BIN

> *"Across America I was tried and tested to the absolute limit. In*
> *England I was tried and tested beyond the absolute limit...*
> *That was when I realized that there are*
> *no limits – you limit yourself."*
> *(Mavis Hutchison)*

She arose very early on August 14 for that last lap, with her mind echoing the words of the poem she'd written toward the end of her run across America:

> *"A new horizon is what I seek..."*

But it didn't keep her awake. Philip found her that morning, ten kilometers down the road but 'curled up like a ball resting against a concrete rubbish bin'. Two hours sleep hadn't been quite enough. After a few more minutes rest, she started out from Red Ruth in the darkness and rain, engulfed by 'the swirling mist of the ghostly Bodmin moors', *"in familiar fashion with torch, pain, rain, traffic and trepidation for the final time."* Philip Jones went with her, anxious to be in at the finish, and she confided in him as they 'trudged through the dense gloom'. She had learned that there are no limits in life if you decide what price you are willing to pay, then go ahead and give it all you've got. She'd composed a song which she sang to him as they started out, and was profoundly grateful that her Heavenly Father had given her the strength of mind without which she could not have coped, grateful that she hadn't let herself, her country and her sponsors down, and her thoughts kept drifting homeward to husband and children.

The previous day had brought a new injury, a badly bruised left heel that Philip had drained with the aid of a needle, so that with a newly plastered heel she was able to get back on the road for the last time – at 2:20 in the morning.

Police stopped them on the way, and they stopped a motorist to ask the way through the fog. *"Silently we pushed through the last thirty or so kilometers to Land's End. Each of us was cocooned in our own world of thoughts, pondering what we had gone through and wondering how we could have done things differently. As we got closer to the end my weariness gave way to excitement at what I had achieved."* In her elation, she managed to run the last few hundred meters, 'ghosting out of the swirling mists' into Land's End – and beating the record by more than nine hours. Two women from South Africa were there to hug her at the finish, and the South African flag was flying.

"It was pouring with rain and the wind was blowing as I got to my destination at Land's End. When I saw the South African flag fluttering I burst into tears." It seemed almost as though her country itself were saluting her, and she felt deeply humble and grateful to have had the chance to achieve what she'd set out to do.

It was ten in the morning, 16 days 20 hours and 45 minutes after the start.

Her run had ended much as it had begun, *""in the company of others who were attempting to travel the same journey."* A fire brigade arrived on a fund raising run from Scotland *"with all the clanging that it could muster"*, and Mavis had herself photographed at the wheel of the fire truck.

And Mavis was ready for mundane life again. After that 'moment of finishing', she had only three things on her mind, a hot bath, a phone call to Ernest and a visit to the hairdresser.

She got all three, but first came the phone call. After an uncomplaining stay in a horribly 'grotty' trailer park, she was off next day to get her hair done at a top London salon, buy a new dress and shoes, and head for the reception at the embassy, where she 'finished her ordeal on the road still running around'.

Still hampered by her painful injured leg, she posed 'for many press pictures' and gave interviews – and remembered who'd helped her get there. She knew it was only a token, but for each of her support team she'd bought an crystal decanter set to remember the run by, and to Philip she presented the rubber tracksuit he'd worn as he'd run with her along the way, keeping her company about a third of the time.

"I became so attached to it I think she felt I deserved to keep it. I will value it more than the decanter. For when I look at it, it will remind of me of her great courage when she was crippled and the odds were stacked against her."

Mavis was still on a high, but what the woman the BBC called 'the toughest grandmother in the world' wanted most was home, where husband, family and rest would be with her again.

Of course the spotlight followed her home. This time it was Fair Lady magazine that named her Sports Woman of the Year, and agitation began immediately to give her Springbok national athletic colors.

But that would take another 11 years, and a major change in thinking from the athletics establishment. Meanwhile she was about to be kicked out of sport for nearly a decade.

At the start in Scotland: Mavis and the team

*Sandton traffic cop Wally Vermaak with Mavis on
her first public run after breaking the UK record.
Picture: Rand Daily Mail*

Chapter 21: GETTING THE BOOT
The Hypocrisy of 'Shamateurism'

◆◦●◦◆

"With athletes having to work hard and spend much money in reaching the top…the time is ripe for a rethink of the rules governing professionalism in sport."

THE 'OLD BOYS' AND THE COMMERCIAL

"Athletics must move with the times."

Being banned from amateur athletics after receiving money for appearing in a television ad, took its toll on Mavis, especially when she found herself completely ostracized from a world she was an intimate part of for years. And nonchalantly shrugging off the cold shoulders given her by former comrades in sport was particularly hard.

But she didn't wallow in self-pity. She squared up soon enough, faced the music and ran on – in events not organized by the South African Amateur Athletics Union (SAAAU), since the powerful Union barred her from all its races.

She freely admits that she knew she was taking a risk when she accepted the 1981 ad offer. But financial necessity following her husband's retirement that year forced the issue for her. Doing commercial endorsements was the only feasible way out of a real predicament, which was that her continued athletics career could not be funded with the Hutchisons' modest retirement income.

The banning debacle ensuing from the advertisement, in which she ran through a huge discount furniture store, and which was viewed on television and cinema screens across the nation, was all very painful and very public. In the end it played out as a nearly decade-long saga, causing quite a stir in its wake – one the media readily reported on.

The Sunday Times on October 11, 1981 headlined Mavis as landing 'feet first in hot water', reporting that the 'bosses of the popular sport', weren't 'charmed with Mavis' – or with other high profile athletes at the time, who were in trouble over their appearances at a professional Nike Marathon in America.

Mavis first got into trouble with the 'Lords of Amateurism' over this ad. She'd accepted sponsorship from Hall's Orange for her run from Pretoria to Cape Town in 1975.

WHO ARE YOU?

Mike Hewitt in another press piece that year fills in a good portion of the story:

"...athletics officials ...branded her an outcast and sent her into the runner's wilderness by stripping her of amateur status.

"The first blow... arrived by telegram at Mavis' Fish Hoek home the night before the Stellenbosch Isotonic Games marathon...

"It said that Mavis' licence had not been approved, but since she already had her licence issued by the Transvaal Amateur Athletics Association, Mavis pressed on to Stellenbosch.

"Though she is a member of the Fish Hoek Athletics Club, Mavis' Transvaal licence under Germiston Callies was valid until the end of the year."

Mavis was quoted in the article: "*When I arrived in Stellenbosch I was ignored and organizers pretended they did not know who I was.*

"They then said I could not run the race, but I got my money back and lined up with the field.

"When I finished, they said: 'Here comes another athlete.'

"They seemed to be embarrassed by my appearance."

"The hardest part", she said in the Hewitt interview, *"is that athletes treasure the spirit of camaraderie.*

"Now I find that barriers are being created and I'm hurt…"

'GENTLEMEN AMATEURS' VS. EARNING A LIVING

With athletes having to work hard and spend much money reaching the top, Mavis said the time was ripe for a rethink of the rules governing professionalism in the sport.

"One has to earn a living somewhere." (Mavis did not disclose how much she received for the advert, but it certainly was no fortune. She thought ads and other engagements might bring her $20000 or so per year. That didn't happen.)

Mavis continued: *"Athletics must move with the times, though I knew when I accepted the ad that there was a chance I would be kicked out. I am just disappointed at the way it was done. I have still not received any official notification of my expulsion."* Only after the Stellenbosch meet did a telegram finally arrive saying she was no longer allowed to compete.

Accustomed to running unofficially, she made it clear that she would continue going it alone if athletics officials *'didn't change their tune'*.

Her Fish Hoek club stood behind her, and secretary Mike Tiffin told the SAAAU that the club was not happy with the decision. Hewitt quoted him as saying:

"She should be allowed to run. Mavis appeared in the advert as Mavis the Personality and not as Mavis the Runner."

But Western Province Amateur Athletics Association chairman Jannie Momberg, who first told Mavis that the Transvaal association had suspended her, said: "The ruling on professionalism is strict. Runners should receive no direct payment from advertising. Things would have been different, however, if Mavis had handed over her advertising fees to her club or union."

That statement defies comment. Why accept doing an endorsement in the first place if you gain nothing from it?

Such absurdity was all part of the long fight over the meaning and importance of amateurism in athletics. The old rules had been formulated by the 'old boys' who for the most part didn't need to earn a living, and thus had little sympathy with the new athletic world where competitive performance required serious time, effort and money.

For many years the 'old boys club' tried to hold back the tide, creating endless problems in the process and becoming a catalyst for "under the counter, run-for-money payments to top athletes" - a state of affairs that clearly revealed the hypocrisy of 'shamateurism'. The line between amateurism and professionalism was indeed very thin, and it was hard to see how the purity of amateur sport was being served by relying on lies and deception.

WE'RE ALL CONTAMINATED NOW

"Under the old (amateur) system I could have made as much, if not more, under the table."
(Springbok athlete Johnny Halberstadt)

Mavis and other high profile athletes were only too well aware of how ludicrous the situation had become, but it would take many more years before the rule of the old establishment would be reigned in, in favor of new thinking. But at least the lid had been lifted off 'Pandora's box'.

Fellow athlete Johnny Halberstadt saw to that when he appeared before a committee of the SAAAU and admitted that he had accepted money for two top finishes in America. He also "made no secret of the fact that he accepted $25000 for winning the Jordache race in the United States." He saw no reason why there should not be honest sporting rewards for honest sporting toil.

That undoubtedly made him a professional, and Mavis now officially had company.

But the full extent of the problem was much bigger than the few athletes who openly admitted taking money. The real can of worms was accurately described in the media as coming from "one of the rules the world governing body, the International Amateur Athletics Federation, has long adhered to...Rule 53, the so-called 'contamination' rule."

If this was fully implemented, any amateur who knowingly competed against a professional automatically became a professional himself, despite having received no money. And this was by no means the end of the insanity.

If some amateurs became 'contaminated' by willingly competing against professionals, they in turn 'contaminated' those who knowingly ran against them. Then when still other athletes competed with the 'contaminated', the 'contamination' spread even wider. This meant, as Halberstadt indicated, that almost all so-called amateurs who ran in public races had already lost their amateur status if the rule were strictly followed.

But Mavis and Halberstadt along with other runners were basing their future hopes on the American interpretation of the rule, where according to Halberstadt the rigidity had been relaxed "so that so-called professionals can run against so-called amateurs as long as no non-resident foreign amateurs are involved."

But even that did not end double standards since he was free to run in the Nike Marathon and the Boston Freedom Trail Eight-Miler - two races he was paid for - but not in the New York Marathon.

OFFICIAL AGAIN

It was a happy day when the status quo finally changed and Mavis was reinstated, which happened as a result of the tireless efforts of the late and former South African MP Jannie Momberg. Despite his official support for the official rules, his heart was in the right place.

In June 1989 the newspaper Die Burger published a report announcing her reinstatement by the SAAAU. It was a bit late, but better late than never. Race officials would no longer have to pretend that they didn't know who she was.

Mavis and others had helped forge the freedom which modern athletes now have. Today amateurs *and* professionals compete in the Olympics, making it possible for the best in the world to compete with the best – and for those who are not 'gentlepersons of leisure' to devote themselves to sport.

There can be no more cases like Jim Thorpe, who had to return his Olympic medals because of a few dollars earned in a brief fling at minor league baseball, or 'ghost runner' John Tarrant, barred from competition because as a youth he'd earned 17 pounds for a few boxing matches.

At least in this area of life, sanity can prevail.

Chapter 22: BONE OF CONTENTION

———————•·◆·•———————

CATCH 22

More or less coinciding with the banning of Mavis from amateur sport, a second battle with the sports establishment raged over whether she should receive 'Springbok' status after her record-breaking run through the UK.

The struggle's final conclusion only came more than a decade later, around the time South Africa was making its way back into international sport.

Traditionally, the green and gold blazer with the graceful antelope emblem was awarded to South African athletes who were selected to compete internationally for their country. Mavis had unquestionably represented South Africa in running the length of the UK. After all, she did so with the full support of the Ministry of Sport, but in the eyes of the 'old boys' of the SAAAU that wasn't good enough. _They_ hadn't 'selected' her, so she couldn't be a Springbok athlete.

It was Catch 22. They were unwilling to approve anyone for competition abroad, so Mavis knew it was pointless to apply for any kind of 'official status' from them. Yet running without it, they wouldn't _recognize_ her as having represented her country because she hadn't received _their_ approval, no matter the official support from her government.

Besides this, ultrarunners like Mavis, Don Shepherd and John Ball were considered ineligible because their records were not set in a 'race', but only against the calendar and the clock. Purists considered even victories in ultra marathons like the Comrades or the London-to-Brighton race unacceptable as qualifications for Springbok status, because these races were not standard Olympic distances.

While the 'old boys' were clearly satisfied with their decisions and their timeworn rules, fans and other athletes were bucking. They loudly and publicly demanded that Mavis be made a Springbok. It took eleven years to beat the 'boys.'

At the end of the battle, a fellow runner and race walker summed up his view of the fray:

"The object of this letter is to let you know that I am thrilled to hear that you and other women have been recognized as wonderful athletes and have received your 'Colors' – **long overdue**." (T.I. Henderson, Pretoria)

MEANWHILE...GETTING ON WITH LIFE

The national print media published numerous articles about the controversy, but Mavis refused to allow the arguments to disrupt her life. Thinking about it now, she recalls that although the much coveted Springbok status was a big deal to her then, getting embroiled in the furor would have taken energy away from more important things.

"Whether I was thought sufficiently deserving or not, wasn't for me to decide anyway. When I was finally permitted to wear the green and gold, I remember I was very very proud."

CLIPPINGS FROM THE BATTLEFRONT

Mavis preserved some of the press to-and-fro on this issue, much of it from 1980. A few extracts highlight the passionate sentiments at the time.

"Mavis is Again Ignored in Colors Awards" (Sunday Times)

"Mrs. Hutchison, who broke the women's record for the 1400 km between John o' Groats and Land's End by nine hours, seems to have little chance of getting the coveted green and gold...

"Gert Le Roux, secretary of the South African Amateur Athletics Union...refused to comment...

"The president of the South African Amateur Athletics Union, Professor Charles Nieuwoudt, said no application had been received for the awarding of Springbok colors to Mavis Hutchison. But even if one had been received, the union could not consider it...

"She said: 'As much as I would cherish Springbok colors in recognition of my run, I cherish my self-respect more, and do not wish to become involved in any sort of controversy.

" 'I am not prepared to force the athletics union into making any award...which, in their opinion, is not deserved on the merit of my athletics performance.

"'I would rather be remembered as a true sportswoman than a Springbok under duress.'"

"She said the run was a wonderful opportunity to be an ambassador for her country —which was satisfaction enough for her."

"Bok Snub for Mavis" (Ray Smuts, Sunday Times)

"There is a goal beyond the reach of the courageous, all-conquering Mavis Hutchison - and it seems that no amount of running will bring it closer...

"Top athletes and administrators this week came up with a definite 'no' to Springbok colors for Mrs Hutchison, who brought the John O'Groats - Land's End record to South Africa after a 1400 km pain-racked run.

"Wearing the green and gold Springbok blazer would be the fulfillment of a dream for the veteran athlete.

"She said: 'It would really be the cherry on the top. I get absolutely cold thinking about it . .'

"...two prominent sporting personalities, former Springbok rugby star Wilf Rosenberg, and cricketing benefactor Wilf Isaacs, came out in strong support of the green and gold for Mrs. Hutchison.

"Dr. Rosenberg, who has two Comrades Marathons behind him, said: 'Whether the athletics administrators like it or not, Mavis was driven on by the fact that she was running for her country, even if she did not represent it officially.

'I don't know what excuse can be put forward for not granting her colors. If she does not get them the administrators concerned should have a good look at their consciences.'

"Referring to Mrs Hutchison's feat as 'incredible', Dr Rosenberg said:

'An Achilles injury is crippling and yet she ran halfway with it. Most guys would have landed up in hospital.'

"Mr Isaacs said: 'If anybody deserves Springbok colors Mavis does. Some have been awarded colors for lesser feats.

'Mavis' run is unique in our history. She showed tremendous courage and brought honor to South Africa. I would be bitterly disappointed if she did not receive her colors.'"

"Is This A Tour To Teach The Boks How To Samba?" (Sunday Express)

Wilf Rosenberg weighed in again on the subject in the Sunday Express. Sounding off about South Africa's "Mickey Mouse" tour of South America at the time (which he felt dragged the famous Springbok blazer through the mud, because it would mean that "the world rugby champions go skulking in back doors and playing against two-bit pick-up sides..."), he took the opportunity to campaign for Mavis.

In his disenchantment over the tour, he contrasted the "official blunder" of presenting Springbok colors to the rugby team doctor, with the refusal to award Springbok colors to Mavis.

"She was a wonderful ambassador for South Africa and her remarkable achievement made headline news. But no Springbok colors for her, and I feel she has done more than enough to warrant the green and gold blazer."

"World's Best...But Not Boks" (Daily Dispatch)

"Should ultra-distance runners Mavis Hutchison of Johannesburg and John Ball of East London be awarded Springbok colors?

"Since Mavis' record-breaking run...this bone of contention has once again become something to gnaw over...

"I know of many athletes in all types of sport who might have done enough to be awarded colors and never have. There is also the likes of Gary Player and the late Clarence Olander, who obviously deserved colors many years before the powers that be relented...

"On the other end of the stick there are some Springboks knocking around who have earned their colors by pure chance or for some endeavor that could be regarded more as a hobby than a sport.

"But one thing is certain: No athletes have gone through

more than Mavis and John to set a world record and boost the image of South Africa. If personal sacrifice, pain, suffering, agony, tears, determination and dedication earn Springbok colors then these two have qualified..."

"Mavis Deserves Colors"

Marika Sboros quoted the late Sunday Times writer, Phillip Jones, in her article: " 'Mavis Hutchinson deserves Springbok colors for her courage and relentless determination'. Jones spent 17 days on the road with her."

"'She went through a private hell to achieve her record run through Britain'", Mr Jones said in a telephone interview from Cardiff, Wales, yesterday.

"'It was the most unusual assignment I have ever been on and a tremendous experience - exciting, stimulating, sometimes depressing, but never dull,'" he said.

"He paid tribute to Mrs Hutchison's tenacity and determination to break the record despite harrowing conditions..."

"Determined Mavis Should Be Honored"

Rodney Hartman took his shot at the colors conflict on October 31, 1980.

"For sheer guts and determination they don't come much greater than Mavis Hutchinson...

"For more than half the journey she was hampered by an Achilles tendon injury which reduced her to a hobble and forced her to spend some 20 hours a day on the road.

"For her trouble she was refused Springbok colors - in spite of the fact that she had the official backing of the Department of Sport and had made no secret that she was 'doing it for South Africa.'

"Her hazardous slog from John O'Groats to Land's End captured the imagination of thousands of people not remotely interested in road running. Her courage to carry on long after the pain barrier had been shattered was the hallmark of a true champion, the sort that should wear the Springbok blazer..."

"Give her that Bok Blazer."

A letter written to the Sunday Times by Springbok hockey player, Shirley McCarthy, demonstrated where many sports folk stood.

"I am one of the lucky ones, having got Springbok colors for hockey. I get mad when these colors are given out for sport to people who really do not warrant them.

"But take Mavis Hutchison - here is one person who really deserves to be given the colors. What more can this woman do?

"She puts everything she has into it – makes a name for herself all over the world – is a great ambassador, and our athletics bodies just ignore her and her efforts, which are great.

"Yes – let her get the State President's award but GIVE HER A BOK BLAZER.

"Don't embarrass her again when she goes to the Big Do's in Pretoria and everybody has his blazer on and she wears her navy one. She is one of the greatest women athletes this country has. She would wear her blazer with great honor – not turn it down like Johnny Halberstadt!!! "

MORE PRESSURE FROM THE PUBLIC

Various other published letters from all over the country expressed similarly strong feelings:

"Our Mavis Hutchison deserves Springbok colors for her courage and achievements. All South Africa is proud of her."(Ria De Veer)

"Yes, yes, yes, yes, yes, to Springbok colors for Mavis Hutchison."(Van Niekerk Family)

"Mavis Hutchison deserves Springbok colors for her guts and determination. She has shown the world that despite boycotts and isolation in sport we can still provide competition with the best in the world." (Fighting Springbok)

"Yes, if any one deserves Springbok colors, it is Mavis Hutchison. What she did was just fantastic, and she is South African, so what more do they want?" (Mrs. J. White)

"IF anybody deserves Bok colors, galloping Granny Hutchison, at 55, does. Good gracious, running half of that distance with an Achilles injury.

She's really courageous." (M.G. Nkomo)

"Of course Mavis Hutchison deserves Springbok colors. Her run made me think of the long-ago days of the Greek heroes." (Elizabeth Rieker)

"What a pity it would be if Mavis Hutchison didn't receive her Springbok colors after such an achievement. Surely the fact that she was competing against a record (should) be enough to overcome objections."(Mrs. Mary Combe)

Chapter 23: CRUSADE FOR THE AGED
Running for Charity

———————•·◆·•———————

"When you are out running, you are on your own. It is
something you are doing for yourself, by yourself.
And there is that terrific feeling of personal
achievement at the end of the race."

"I don't recommend long runs such as this to anyone unless
they really want to do it…It is my way of growing and
developing, and becoming a better person."

After swallowing the bitter pill of expulsion from amateur athletics so soon after her record-breaking UK run, Mavis was ready for more of that 'terrific feeling' she got on the long road. After all, no rule prohibited her from taking on more of the ultraruns that were her forte. Being barred from amateur athletics may have been a blessing in disguise, forcing her to concentrate on what she did best.

Her first idea seems to have been running the length of the UK again. Her record had only lasted a year, and Mavis felt sure she could beat the new women's record of 14 days, especially if she didn't lose 100 km to a 'scenic detour' via Loch Ness and Loch Lomond, as she had in 1980. *"I've got the stamina and now I must quicken my stride to get within that 14 days."*

Sponsorship for that plan, however, never materialized, but she soon found other opportunities. The first was the monstrous 2000 mile (3200 km) fundraising run for the aged in 1982.

It was a charity run like the one she would undertake three years later for a different cause, organized as part of South Africa's Year of the Aged campaign on a route never attempted before.

This not only gave Mavis another opportunity to show what she still was capable of, but importantly, her endeavor stood outside of the jurisdiction of the SAAAU, which had barred her from all Union competition.

It was also her charity running during the years prior to reinstatement - together with Masters athletics and 'open' race walking, all of which functioned independently of the Union – that kept her moving on road and track.

RED CARPETS AND INSECTS

Fast approaching 60 at the time of the ultra marathon for the aged, but still as youthfully vigorous as ever, she planned a route that traversed the length and breadth of South Africa - an odyssey of close to two months, with the same old companions close at hand: rain, hail, heat, mist, injury and strong winds which could reach 75 miles per hour. Not everyone's cup of tea, and a brew even Mavis found a bit strong.

"Often when I'm in a bad way I ask myself why I am doing this and whether it is really necessary. But once the day is over, that sense of achievement overshadows all previous doubt", she told the Natal Witness.

In tiptop shape she set off from Kimberley on March 6, 1982. This time the modest mining town really rolled out the red carpet for the star who'd grown up there. Amid pomp and ceremony, complete with marching band and horse drawn cart, the woman of the moment made her way to City Hall where she was to be the guest of honor at a farewell function before taking to the road.

Recognizing her attempt to pay tribute to them, the town's seniors were also there to share in the fanfare of the occasion.

If she was a little nervous about the towering task ahead, which had captured the interest of young and old alike, she didn't let on, although she had previously admitted to feeling just that. At the time she was quick to add that once she started she knew she would settle down and just enjoy the adventure. And that's how it was, a series of testy moments notwithstanding.

She spent the major part of her trek, during which she was supported by the usual team of helpers (again with a journalist on board), running set daily distances. The rest of the time went to fulfilling an exhausting program planned by the South African National Council for the Welfare of the Aged, and the sponsors of the event.

But that did not rob her of a special treat associated with road running: getting close to nature. As she crisscrossed the landscape, she saw insects she said she never knew existed.

A 'Poster Granny'

She called on more than 30 towns en route, inquisitive bystanders and autograph seekers at times staring at her in admiring disbelief. Each stopover was accompanied by grand welcomes and mayoral receptions, delivery of mayoral messages, receipt of campaign contributions, adjudicating competitions, and talks focused on her extraordinary sports career, her achievements and personal goals - all to raise more awareness for the potential of the elderly to continue being productive, contributing citizens. Mavis of course got to be the 'poster granny' for that potential.

To add further impact to an already heavily media-backed campaign, a nationwide competition was launched with questions about the 'wonder woman'. *"All very flattering, but it didn't make the run any easier."*

Besides running, she remained very focused on what she had to achieve in terms of the campaign. *"It was important for me then to show older folks that they could still set targets and work toward reaching them. That message is still important to me now. Furthermore, I passionately believe that seniors need opportunities to be of service more than being recipients of welfare."*

She was also assigned to educate the public about the problems which accompany aging, to make both employers and employees aware of the important role played by retirement planning, and to persuade communities at large to accept responsibility for their elderly in appropriate ways.

'You Make Me Proud to Be a South African'

She might have been assigned to promote the cause of the aged, but to Mavis they were not simply an 'assignment'. She actually thoroughly enjoyed interacting with them, encouraging them and using the campaign opportunity to focus maximum attention on them.

During one of her stopovers she spent time just chatting to grannies and grandpas. Eager for a few life tips from a famous peer, they hung on her lips. She had learned how to draw an audience, but she had this particular audience in the bag not by virtue of her speaking skills, but because they saw her as a role model who could relate to them.

To further cement the main thrust behind her arduous run, she made it a habit to set off on each leg of the trail from a point close to an old folks center, presenting residents with quality gifts from the main campaign sponsor.

Wherever she went senior communities responded enthusiastically to their spokesperson. In Krugersdorp they welcomed her cheering, singing and waving posters that heralded her arrival: "She's Coming"! The acting mayor of the town shared their enthusiasm and later exclaimed, "You make me proud to be a South African."

In Bedfordview the great distance runner (and fellow banned athlete) Johnny Halberstadt ran with her into town, and the legendary Wally Hayward was also among the crowd to welcome her. That was awesome, but her single biggest thrill was the response she inspired in those who might have thought themselves over the hill.

As a newspaper in the area, the Eastern Express (March 25, 1982), put it: "She inspired hope and determination in the hearts of many old folks." Quite likely this was because she made age appear so irrelevant. *"I'm 57 now and I know that I am not over the hill. The hills are the hills on the road. They are my challenge until the race is won."*

Some time after the conclusion of the run she commented to journalist Anne Baron: *"Everyone is inclined to give up too soon with everything. In running I find if you just stay the distance, and sometimes a little longer, you eventually make the grade,"* a sentiment Mavis had learned to apply to life generally.

POLITICIANS REACHING INTO THEIR OWN POCKETS

When she reached Witbank, traffic police stood ready to salute her. The Witbank News (March 26) hailed her as "the greatest granny of them all." A prominent printed slogan, "The people of Witbank salute you! Welcome to our town," drove the point home.

Press coverage continued in glowing terms: "Your courage, determination and undeterred vitality are shining examples of individual achievement. Your devoting so much time and effort to the cause of the aged is viewed by all as evidence of personal sacrifice and generosity."

Inspired by her example, each Witbank Town Council member contributed to the town's own society for the aged.

'NO GENERATION GAP'

In another interview she said: *"If there's one thing I have learned from this run, it's that there is no generation gap"*, a statement born out by the fact that young people displayed a keen interest in what she was doing throughout - whether as excited spectators in a crowd, as athletes, as members of cadet bands or as drum majorettes escorting her into towns along the way. This was all very heartwarming to Mavis, who had a real grandmother's interest in the rising generation.

In Benoni drummies led a fire engine carrying the hero into town. In Newcastle a group of high schoolers, along with older and well known runners, received her in grand style by forming a guard of honor at the meeting point, from where they ran with her to the town center.

Schools generally made their athletes available to run with the traveling icon for designated distances, but also responded enthusiastically to an invitation to follow the monumental trek as a geography project.

Sponsored by parents and friends, young people found the running part of things particularly appealing, with individual groups joining the 'galloping granny' outside their towns and then escorting her in.

East London afforded another seaside stop and a similar hero's welcome of escorting runners, including the city's mayor. In his running shorts he ensured a distinct change from the normal robes and chains approach. He cheerfully ran along with Mavis for a few miles, after which she joined him in his official parlor to relive - on video - her great UK triumph two years previously.

YOUTH IS A STATE OF MIND

Later that day she assured her East London audience that *"youth isn't a time of life; it's a state of mind. And the way to meet any challenge and go beyond limits is to go one step at a time."* (East London Daily Dispatch, April 14, 1982.)

The marathon champion explained that while running had made her famous, it wasn't something she cared about that much. What really mattered was the way her sport had developed her as an individual. *"I used to be very shy. I didn't find it easy to talk to people and sometimes I used to feel like crying. Now I am able to hold my own.*

"You can't believe what I was like. I was too scared to do anything because I was worried I'd make a fool of myself, be a failure or say the wrong thing. I was always in a state of tension and worried sick about everything."

A Port Elizabeth Herald reporter captured the change in her, describing her as a "reserved but strong and confident person".

Passing the flame: Mavis jogging with granddaughter Tatiana

Gone was the woman who remembered herself as someone who had "let herself go physically and mentally", the "retiring little woman", the "self-effacing housewife and mother", which was how acclaimed sportswriter Sam Mirwis described the pre-athletics Mavis. He greatly admired what running had helped her become, and sometimes ran with her.

But a changed Mavis didn't develop overnight. Some of her self-defeating attitudes died hard.

"It took me three years to realize that it was my attitude that was preventing change. I'd blamed everything on my situation...it was always one excuse after the next."

But even after she managed to pull herself up by her bootstraps and became serious about changing her life, she didn't think her decision to do so would lead to quite so much running.

By 1982 she had probably covered a distance equal to running around the world a few times. But it gave her a lot of joy and she would give it up only when she *"found something to replace it that was as demanding"*, and that gave her "just *as much pleasure."*

Running through Klerksdorp, where she was again escorted by youth runners, gave the public another moment to remember how the grand dame of the ultrarun had acquired that kind of stature.

The Klerksdorp Record retold the story of how she started running as a temporary means of getting fit, adding this quote: *"My marathons have set for me mental and physical obstacles which have had to be overcome. I have been tried and tested, and after each obstacle I have successfully overcome, I have experienced a sense of achievement which I cannot describe."*

En route from East London to Port Elizabeth, which would be her ¾ mark, that feeling of achievement mingled with pleasure when she was whisked off to a beach front hotel for a brief moment of leisure at the end of a long slog.

No Funding

Although her schedule was a little more flexible this time and could include the pleasure of a little leisure - courtesy of her sponsors - as well as adjustments according to weather and other conditions, Mavis was very particular about covering the requisite distance to the last kilometer or mile. She insisted on being taken back the next day to the exact spot where she left off. No fudging for her.

Likewise, after being flattened by the flu in the Transkei on her way to East London, which necessitated car travel for a while, she made sure to make up any missed mileage by doing extra runs. She did that kind of thing whenever necessary.

Cruising into the university town of Grahamstown, once a frontier town in the days of Border wars, servicemen awaited her, joined by some of the town's best runners to ensure an exuberant welcome.

In George, on the lush Garden Route, her easy going manner, friendliness and natural charm, blended well with the picturesque surroundings of a town named after a man with a less than picture perfect background - being a suspected illegitimate son of British royalty.

Here she endeared herself to yet another community. Local reporter Ronel Venter depicted her as a lady "who radiates vitality and a love for life", and as one who "captivates" her audience. She had the full attention of her listeners in George when she talked about dreams. They took note that they should *"start now, for if you wait for the right time, you will never fulfill them."*

A River – Of Perseverance– Runs Through It

A personal highlight for Mavis on the road this time was being joined by a family friend, 25-year old Kapildeo Maharaj, an aspiring long distance runner whom she invited to run along with her from Newcastle to Durban. That was a good 200 miles, but also a dream come true for Kapildeo.

She was his idol, the undisputed marathon queen. His admiration, however, didn't make his undertaking (a first for him) any easier. But ongoing encouragement from his mentor helped him out when the going got rough.

The inexperienced young athlete found running for almost 10 hours a day - a lot of it uphill - tough enough that he almost persuaded himself to quit, and he realized he would need a lot more stamina and determination to achieve his dream: beating Mavis' time on the much tougher route between Durban and the Johannesburg metro area.

Sticking with Mavis paid dividends, though, as he shared in her rousing welcome by a banner-brandishing honor guard of 300 senior citizens, who cheered them into Durban's main street.

For Kapildeo this was the end of the road, but Mavis still had a long way to go before her eventual Cape Town finish on April 30 - 58 days and 2000 miles after her heroic send-off.

Pounding South Africa's roads in aid of the aged was a unique challenge that hasn't yet been repeated - certainly not by a 57-year old.

Sol Kreiner, Cape Town's deputy mayor at the time, recognized the uniqueness of it and ran with her for a distance during the final stage of the punishing marathon. Afterwards he said: "How very proud we all are of you."

THE USE OF PAIN

That pride was likely heightened when Mavis breezed across the finish line with an injured left arm in the sling she needed after falling and dislocating her collarbone about 13 miles outside Albertinia.

Not even when the injury occurred was she deterred. She picked herself up and finished the scheduled distance by running another 15 miles before seeking medical help, first in Albertinia and then in Mossel Bay where she was x-rayed.

Some physiotherapy was required, but she wasn't about to take too much time over that kind of thing. Next day she cheerily continued on her way in spite of a lot of pain. She chose not to take pain medication because she felt it could be dangerous to run with no pain signals to tell her if her body was in serious trouble. Avoiding the risk of permanent damage was worth enduring the pain.

As the Cape Town crowd cheered her in, pain seemed like a distant memory to this woman of steely determination who earlier on in the run was described as one "who has added so much glamor to the sporting scene."

It certainly was a moment of sporting glamor when she happily accepted the wreath put around her neck and the kiss placed on her lips by South African rugby hunk and team captain Morne du Plessis.

A BRONZED SHOE AND PERFUMED BUBBLES

He also presented her with a bronzed running shoe that had carried Mavis many miles, and with a compliment: "She can show even rugby players what guts is." It must have sparked memories of how veteran runner and beloved friend Fred Morrison had challenged rugby players to prove their toughness by running with her.

In the spirit of the moment, the gutsy lady decided to present the shoes she had just run in as a keepsake to the Year of the Aged campaign committee: *"I hope they bring them lots of good luck."*

She felt she had already experienced a good deal of luck herself while wearing those shoes. Reaching another finish line in reasonable shape, and with an injury that could have been so much worse, was proof.

Hitting that tarmac with such a vengeance could have stopped her run right there. She described the ordeal as the "most agonizing moment" of the run, agony undoubtedly aggravated by immediately continuing on after the brief x-ray stop.

There's nothing ambivalent about Mavis. She could always be counted on to carry on, no matter what. Her loyalty to the aim behind her run for the aged, and to her backers, was absolute.

And her most immediate need after a race was equally predictable: If not a nice soft bed, then a nice hot bath. This time it was a hot bubble bath up to her neck. And if it could have been richly perfumed, it would have been even better.

That her love of perfume stands right next to her love of running is a matter of record.

Interview on the run with Mark Botha of Die Burger newspaper
(22 Feb. 1982).

Chapter 24: 'DRUG RUNNERS'
The Last Long Run

———◆•◆•◆———

"Drug abuse is a universal problem. Dependency is like flu;
it can attack anyone anywhere at any time."

Mavis displayed strong feelings about drug abuse and thus it came as no surprise that fund raising for the fight against drugs became her pet cause in 1985. She did this with another stoic performance, running from Pretoria to Cape Town a second time. But this time round it wasn't a solo affair.

DYNAMIC DUO

She joined forces with an up and coming ultrarunner from the South African Navy, Dave O'Kill, under a scheme best described as "running together separately" since partway through the run they parted company.

Under the auspices of the South African National Council on Alcoholism and Drug Dependence, 'D-day Marathon' was organized with the goal of providing much needed educational aids and rehab centers for drug addicts. Soroptimists (a worldwide society of professional women concerned with the 'welfare of all humanity') led the way.

The fund raising run placed special emphasis on youth. To increase awareness of the dangers of drug abuse among this segment of society, the sponsor of the event (a major insurance group) hosted multiple youth forums at schools all over Johannesburg and Cape Town.

Mavis identified very strongly with the drive to educate youth, and Press interviews along the way provided her with ample opportunity to speak her piece. *"Every person has a marathon to run, also people with drug abuse problems, and one has to take every step (toward recovery) oneself."*

She emphasized the necessity of having a purpose to accomplish anything of worth. Without a purpose, she herself would not be able to complete the marathon at hand. She drove the point home with a proverb:

"Where there is no vision, the people perish."

Both she and her co-runner understood this age old principle and used it extensively as they beat their paths to the winning post, running together for the first leg and parting company later at Potchefstroom to follow separate routes toward Cape Town.

They were to join up again at Bellville on the final day of the run, after a brief rendezvous in Bloemfontein, giving fans in the 'City of Roses' an opportunity to rally around the 'D-Day' flag.

Sixty one-year old Mavis (she celebrated her birthday along the way) was assigned a fairly straight course to the finish along the national road, covering about 930 miles, and Dave a more winding and slightly longer coastal route.

Neither of the routes were for the faint of heart and at completion of the distance, 'prodigious feat' would accurately describe the runners' achievement. It was a six days a week slog at a brutal 40 miles a day. Newspapers pointed out that this was more than the equivalent of a 35-mile Two Oceans ultra marathon every day for a month.

A rousing send-off from Pretoria's historic Church Square launched 'D-day', with various dignitaries ensuring the required amount of ceremony. Among them was the Minister of Health Services and Welfare at the time, Dr George Morrison, who gave the farewell address.

To add a little extra luster to the event, Springbok trampolinists strutted their stuff and the South African Police Band provided a rousing 'sound track' before the fanfare had to make way for the most exciting moment: the gunshot that signaled to the duo that it was time to be on their way. A group of provincial rugby players and track athletes ran along for the first few kilometers.

The show of solidarity was appreciated, but they all knew that when the crunch came and the marathon developed into what long distance running is all about – true grit, and physical and mental stamina beyond the layman's imagination – the twosome would be on their own. But their backers knew what they were capable of; their track records put them in a class of their own.

Mavis and O'Kill in a publicity shot before the D-day marathon.

For 'A Better Day'

The hype around the widely promoted 'drug run' was not just the standard promotional buzz. It put into play, quite literally, creative efforts from the world of music. Well-known singer Mynie Grove wrote a song for the occasion, and her recording of 'A Better Day' was aired on television during a youth program on the day of the marathon's launch and throughout the race.

Another prominent entertainer and Soroptimist, Dawn Lindberg, also did her bit to promote the anti-drug drive. She teamed up with her singing partner and husband, Des, to release another specially composed song to celebrate the event. For a while it became a chart topper.

At the outset Mavis made it clear that she was not out to break any records, but just to make the specified mileage of at least 60km per day. She confidently added: "I've done all my preparation – I feel physically and mentally geared up to all possibilities."

Her age, she believed, would be no obstacle, in spite of those who felt it would. "I'm very healthy and fit and I don't know why people keep harping on about age."

She pointed out that politicians were often in their 60s and 70s, and that didn't seem to matter. *"The reason why people give up pursuits at a certain age is because they lose interest, not because they can't do it anymore. We impose limitations upon ourselves."*

Black and Blue

But age aside, the weather is always an unpredictable factor and always a potential hazard for the runner. She knew it was a bad time of the year and that she would have to run every day regardless of blistering heat or torrential rain. Besides, no Mavis race would be complete without a few weather challenges dropped into the mix.

And they dropped in all right - not so long after the start. While they were still near Pretoria the weather turned mean, with rain and hail hitting the runners hard. Black and blue and thoroughly drenched the pair arrived in a wet and windy Johannesburg where they were received by the city's Mayor, Ernie Fabel, a little worse for wear.

If perseverance was going to be tested, the test was off to a good start. On day two the Hutchison team took a few wrong roads, losing precious time. But time loss and getting soaked was probably not the worst case scenario anticipated by the seasoned runner. Before the race she said:

"Many times...I'm going to feel as if I've had enough. I'm going to want to sit down at the side of the road and cry. But with the support of my team I'm going to pick myself up, take another step and succeed, because I have a goal, and I know I'm going to get to the end of that road."

Ernie, her most dedicated supporter, unfortunately had to sit this one out, but her daughter Gayle – 23 at the time – and fellow Soroptimist Cleoni Bond-Smith happily stood in and did their part to help Mavis reach one more finish line on time.

O'Kill had a different kind of support. His help came from Navy man Moses Mathews - on a bicycle "to encourage him to keep running...when the going got really tough." Another Navy helper, Springbok weightlifter Harry Webber, filled out the team. They were equally dedicated to getting their buddy to the goal post.

But for both O'Kill and Mavis it was about much more than just getting to the finish. Mavis especially was known by this time for being very eager to make a difference in people's lives.

'YOU DON'T FAIL UNLESS YOU GIVE UP'

"I hope that those with a drug problem will identify with me, know that there are plenty of people to support them and that they've got to take those (recovery) steps. There are many marathons in life, but you don't fail at them unless you give up. Every drug user must view his battle against enslavement as a personal marathon. Mine will also not be easy, and there will certainly be many times when I will want to give up."

On this run she again had ample opportunity to speak to audiences, on occasion honing in on the young. She reminded them there were many starters, but few finishers. She urged them not to start something and then to simply lose interest, but to persist with determination. *"The eventual victory is...very sweet."*

Once more she delivered her 'one step at a time' line to make eventual victory a reachable goal for all. According to The Courier of November 29, 1985, "the audience claimed her message by spontaneous response."

In spite of the usual rigors of a long run, which were never fun, Mavis really liked to be out on the road on her own, and this time round it was no different. As always, running gave her time to think more clearly, to come to know herself better, and to feel God closer to her.

As was the case with her crusade for the aged, scores of escorting runners along the route were at their posts to spur her on - some from schools and athletic clubs, and others from the ranks of Springbok athletes and rugby players, who often could not keep up with her.

Some groups put in upwards of 20 kilometers with the 'running machine'. And in one town an enthusiastic group of bikers pushed the spirit of things up a notch, encouraging Mavis to stay the course.

Approaching Worcester, with the final destination almost in sight, she was joined by over 270 local school children who ran the last five miles to the town with her, much to Mavis' delight. And much to their delight, she took a moment to express her gratitude for the friendly reception and for the sacrifice they made to be there.

At that point 'over 30000' kids had joined her at different stages of the race, a fact she found extremely gratifying. To the Worcester Standard she said: *"The children are very intrigued by the distance I run. I usually have to explain to them that I run the equivalent of a 60km marathon each day before they can grasp the distance involved."*

She again expressed the hope that her run would help to inspire young drug addicts to fight their problem. She saw the marathon as a symbol of all the hardship they would have to endure if they did decide to fight. And it would be a lonely battle, but if there was anyone who could understand what that was really like, it was the long distance runner who had to persist, whatever the odds.

Both 'D-Day' participants, as seasoned members of the long distance fraternity, could fully empathize with the agony of the addict, and thus all the royal welcomes and center stage treatment at events arranged by mayors, mayoresses and school principals (Kimberley again outdid itself for its 'protege'), could not detract them from the real purpose behind their undertaking.

TO THE FINISH

"I must go the distance with my head held high."

Being bombarded by masses of mosquitoes made that a real challenge, the annoying little creatures turning running into a new kind of battle field with a rather itchy aftermath. Then a dust storm (at Strydenburg) and a nasty wind that had her virtually "running on the spot" for a considerable time, were thrown in for good measure. She had to push hard to measure up.

She remembered again what she had said on a previous occasion: *"When you're on the road for 12 hours a day you find out WHO you are, not who you THINK you are. "*

Schoolchildren on the road with Mavis find out who they are, not who they thought they were.
(Worcester Standard & Advertiser, Dec. 6, 1985)

Her partner experienced his share of woes too, which included heat exhaustion and debilitating muscle spasms. But, like Mavis, he kept going, seeing *that* course of action as the only cure. Later, just outside the coastal town of Mossel Bay, he developed the dreaded shin splints that would put the best to the test. Through intense pain he just ran on.

Mavis' route took her through 47 cities and towns, landing her, along with her running companion, in Cape Town on November 30. By that time she had accumulated a total running distance equivalent to nearly three times around the world – calculated from her entry into athletics at age 37.

THOSE TRUSTY LEGS

Extraordinary legs are required for that kind of statistic and Mavis was blessed with a pair reporters wrote about. Jacky Salton said at the time: "The seven years since Mavis completed her trans-America run…have not perceptibly changed her. She's no Joan Collins, nor would she want to be, but those trusty legs would be the envy of many a 16-year old."

For the umpteenth time those very legs carried her to the very end, where in company of her co-runner she met with a hearty welcome afforded by a cheering crowd of thousands, all gathered at the Newlands cricket grounds.

Playing to the crowd, the victorious athletes ran a lap of honor around the field, after which the then Administrator of the Cape, Gene Louw, took care of the official side of the welcome.

It was clear that the Sunday Times 'fun' poll of April 1983, listing Mavis among the most popular women in South Africa, still held true, and even the young and dashing O'Kill's presence couldn't diminish that.

But for her it was not about popularity and she happily shared the spotlight with a great runner who deserved his day in the sun. Above all, it was mission accomplished for both sore footed, but satisfied marathoners. Another torture trail lay behind them – for Mavis the very last one.

Chapter 25: AMONG MASTERS
Back on Track

———•·◆·•———

"When I compete, I am always an athlete and not just an inconvenient old lady."

"I will run as long as my legs will hold up. I'm very blessed that I can still do this."

In between establishing herself as the sine qua non of endurance, Mavis got involved with Masters[1] or veteran athletics, testing herself on the track and field. A unique feature of this type of competition is the emphasis on competing according to age. In fact, age-graded tables are employed for realistic comparisons between athletes.

Her first exposure to international Masters games came in 1977 when she competed in Sweden, a part of the world she found fascinating, just as she did Japan when she ran there in 1993.

She did particularly well in her maiden Masters in Gothenburg, winning several medals including gold. But whether she shone or not, Masters meets always brought her enjoyment.

"I loved Spain, I loved Italy and Australia when I competed in those countries and was fortunate to take home gold and silver medals there too. In Germany I didn't do so well, although I thoroughly enjoyed the country.

"At the 1979 German Masters I didn't place at all and was rather disappointed, but that experience couldn't compare with what happened seven years earlier when I attended the 1972 Olympic Games in Munich. The massacre of Jewish athletes will remain imprinted on my mind forever. I can vividly remember the day of mourning and how traumatic it all was."

'AMERICANS' ON THE STEALTH TEAM
Officially, the 30 or so South Africans competing in the 1977 Swedish Masters had to pose as Americans in order to participate. This was due to South

Africa's Apartheid policies at the time, which made South African sportsmen exceedingly unwelcome in Sweden. To circumvent the problem they joined the US Masters organization with the aid of friendly American athletes who entered them in the Games.

"We had to compete as Americans and with the necessary assistance this was made possible. I remember an American athlete named Ozzie Dawkins, who went to bat for me at the US Consulate in LA."

This 'secret tour' included such luminaries as the great Wally Hayward, and according to sportswriter Sam Mirwis, was planned "like a military operation".

Quite naturally there was considerable strain in the 'stealth camp' as they arrived in Gothenburg by train from Amsterdam. They had trained hard, hoping to peak at the right time, but would they be accepted?

There was great relief when they got the envelopes with their numbers, programs and instructions. They were in! The secret only leaked later; the feared demonstrations and banning never materializing.

Now they could concentrate on what they really cared about and wanted to get the first event behind them. For Mavis that was the 100 meters. As always she was slow out of the blocks, so slow that at first she was running seventh. But she felt strong and started gaining ground. If the race had been a few meters longer she probably would have been first across the line, but as it was she took silver.

Surprisingly, her second event was a disappointment. The 10000m (6.2 miles) cross-country race was more Mavis' sort of distance, but it began with a mass start in the rain and she couldn't see who her opponents were. That meant she couldn't pace herself against runners in her age bracket.

Running as she had never run before, she still came in fourth. The competition was stiff, and the distance may still have been too short for an ultrarunner to get into her stride. As a South African newspaper article said of another race over the same distance, it took that long for Mavis to warm up.

In Sweden she was among over 3000 veterans from 46 countries. While language was a barrier, *"armed with the necessary sports vocab so as to be able to respond to instructions on the track and field, I coped OK. The gun went off the same in Swedish as in English."*

STRANGER IN A STRANGE LAND

Mavis was definitely not in Moffat View any more. In this land of the midnight sun there were a few real oddities. *"What I found rather strange about Sweden was the absence of children. I remember asking where they all were.*

"It being still light at midnight was another strange phenomenon for me. The SA group took advantage of that and rather than sleep we trained. Somehow the lack of sleeping didn't bother me or my performance."

It probably affected her more than she thought. Before the 5000m walk she was feeling very tired and all she wanted to do was have a good sleep. She walked hard, but could do no better than fourth. After that she went to bed earlier.

She did better in field events she'd never tried before.

"There I was introduced to discus, javelin and shot put, encouraged by fellow athletes to take part...Lenie Grobbelaar, SA's javelin, discus, hammer and shot put champion at the time, with whom I roomed while at the Masters, made sure I took my shot at it."

Mavis' 'best shots' in field events were in the javelin and shotput. Although *"some of the girls were masculine"*, at least this time she could see who she was competing against. She was thrilled to take silver in both, an amazing result for a novice.

'BY BRUTE FORCE AND IGNORANCE'

One thing that was to plague Mavis in later Masters Games caught her in Sweden as well. After a strenuous warmup she reported to the starter, expecting to have 10 minutes rest before the gun went off 'in English and Swedish'.

No sooner did she arrive than she and the other athletes were told to line up. Not surprisingly her miscalculation cost her. *"Later I was told by my team mates that for the first 300m I looked like a real champ, but for the last 100m I looked as if I were in real trouble."*

Actually they thought she looked more like she needed a stretcher, and might not even make it across the line. She was in a disappointing fifth place up the home straight, but refused to accept that as the best she could do.

"I pulled out all the stops. My legs felt like jelly and I felt my lungs were going to burst, but I knew I had to push for all I was worth..." That push, *"by brute force and ignorance"*, got her the bronze.

MASTER AMONG MASTERS

But long runs were her game. That's where she made her name. Her last event was the standard marathon and she knew that if she broke four hours she had a chance.

There were 1500 athletes at the starting line and this time she could see who the opposition was. When the gun went off she charged to the front, but was still relaxed enough to take in the 'rather lovely scenery' as she strode along. She knew she could catch up with her opponents if they passed her. But they didn't.

She took gold, setting a new course record for her age group – 3 hours 59 minutes. Not as fast as when she was 38, but surprisingly close. All that was missing were helpful seconds: "*I would have enjoyed…sponging, especially in the midday heat.*"

APPEARANCES

Also still vivid in her memories of Sweden is a 60-year old Asian athlete with severe war scars after his plane was shot down. He was blinded and his face was burned, but he courageously took his place at the start.

"*After being led onto the track by his son-in-law and coach, he positioned himself for a standing start as opposed to the usual starting block start.*" How he did in the race she doesn't remember. What impressed her was the story behind his appearing in the race at all.

"*After his injuries forced him into a very dependent life, his coach helped him start over. His new life fascinated me. I learned more about it through the broken English of his wife. It made me realize nothing is what it seems. There is a story behind every face, so it's better not to judge on appearances.*"

Mavis' performance at her first international Masters brought her five medals: One gold, three silvers and a bronze, and high honor in her own country when in 1978 she received the State President's Award. That wasn't just a matter of appearances.

THE GERMAN COBBLESTONES

Mavis had great hopes for the 1979 Masters Games in Germany, and great hopes that a new 'running machine' she'd been given would get her fighting fit, enough to break the world record for the marathon in her age group. But the German cobblestones defeated her, and she took home only a bronze for the javelin.

"I think my problematic right leg, which has always slowed me down, played a part in my poor performance. I remember it was a problem from my arrival. I managed to make the finals for the 100m, 200m, and 400m, but that was about it.

"The marathon was a total disaster when I twisted an ankle on the cobblestone road I had to run on. I came in fourth. In the javelin I was third. In the shot put and discus I was completely intimidated by the huge German ladies. Apart from my mediocre performance, the SA team as a whole didn't fare too badly, as far as I remember."

FEVERISHLY FESTIVE

It's not her athletic performances that stand out in what she remembers about Japan in 1993. What does, is the memory of the giant sports complex that had the most amazing buzz about it. It was almost feverishly festive and the friendliness was second to none. *"Everybody was so polite and full of smiles and bowing,"* Mavis recalls.

She was also extremely impressed with the overall organization of things. *"It was really exceptional, complete with an excellent bus service for the athletes, as well as a post office, a bank, a gym, a pool and training venues on site - and food on tap."*

A particular plus were the staff badges indicating language proficiency, so all the foreign athletes could easily find their way around. *"It is the best run sports event I've ever attended."*

The competition was good too, maybe too good. Mavis entered for the 5km and 10km walks, the 100m, 400m and 800m sprints, and the shot put and javelin. She only made it to the finals for the 100m. *"I don't know what happened. I trained hard – maybe I over trained. Or maybe the competition was just too good for me."*

NEVER ON A SUNDAY

2005 was a much better Masters year for Mavis, then 80 years old, but still sprightly and young in spirit. She won medals in both the South African Masters (setting records for women 80 and over for the 100m, 200m, 400m and 800m), and the International Masters in Spain. But success didn't come easy in Spain.

Shortly after arrival she made an awful discovery: she had cellulitis (swollen legs from knee to foot). A fellow athlete, a medical doctor from Durban, made the diagnosis.

"My legs were the size of balloons, very red and on fire. I was very grateful for Dr Jan Roodt who gave me antibiotics and valuable advice so I doctored myself with ice packs from the nearest pub. I did the ice pack treatment for a couple of hours during the official opening, after which I took a train back to my accommodation." Needless to say, she didn't march in the opening ceremony.

Dr. Roodt's advice was to withdraw from her first event. Being Mavis, she decided to give it a go anyway and took second.

Mavis also owed a debt of gratitude to an athlete from Puerto Rico who gave her much-needed antibiotics. *"Since then I also travel with antibiotics on hand – when I go overseas. The fourth day into the seven day course I felt well enough to do two events a day. I knew my prayers to recover were answered."*

Ultimately, she came away with a gold medal in the 400m, silver medals in the 800m, 1500m and 5000m, as well as silver in the 10km walk. Two days before the walk there was another test to face: she developed bronchitis.

She walked nevertheless, hating every minute on the rough, uneven road in 100-degree heat – but she got her silver before returning to her hotel and collapsing in bed. By the end of the Games, she also held three new South African records.

There were some medals she didn't try for. *"I never participated in any of the field events since they were held on Sundays."* She also didn't try to see any of the sights – when she wasn't at the stadium she was resting in her room to have strength for the next race.

Heartwarming memories had helped sustain her through the Games.

"Back in South Africa, while on the track training for the Spanish Masters…a young girl of about 12 gave me all her savings as a contribution to my sponsorship for the Games…How can incidents like these leave anyone cold?"

TEARS AND CHEERS

Besides medals, Italy brought another learning curve. It came shortly after arrival in the host city when everything seemed pretty laid back and Mavis was enjoying the chatting among a group of athletes. But her tranquil mood was soon to be rudely disturbed when a member of the group, a fellow South African, said: 'You missed the 100m.'

"It was like someone poured cold water over me. To my horror I discovered I hadn't read the program properly. I thought my events were the next day and I burst into tears. To make things worse, I did not receive any sympathy from the person who broke the news to me. She said in Afrikaans: 'It's your own fault. Go cry'. Others in the group teased me and had a good laugh."

The whole thing could have turned out really badly for Mavis since missing an event is taken seriously, and can lead to disqualification from the remainder of a Masters tournament. Fortunately, she was permitted to stay on and participate. She came second in the javelin and the 400m, third in the 200m, and fourth in the 1500m.

It wasn't a startling performance by her standards, but going home with two silver medals and a bronze was much better than being disqualified. So was setting a new South African record for the 400m.

But although she only took bronze in the 200m, this shorter race remains a highlight in her memories of Italy. Just as in the 400m in Sweden, she had to come from behind after a slow start from the blocks.

Her immediate competition was 20m ahead of her at one point. But once again, with a tremendous effort, she surged ahead, making up distance on the bend and beat her opponent to the finish line. Spectators rose from their seats spontaneously and cheered.

"That almost made up for the lost 100m."

ON TOP OF DOWN UNDER

Sydney, Australia brought more victories for our plucky lady in 2009, and in a magnificent setting. She enjoyed the Aussies' gorgeous parks, their impressive opera house, the Olympic stadium with its history inscribed on beautiful columns, and the awe-inspiring suspension bridge over the bay. Of course, she could only admire the bridge from the ground because of her persistent fear of heights.

She also enjoyed the fact she would not return to South Africa empty handed. Two gold medals were among the spoils - for the 800m and the javelin. To that she added three silvers - for the 100m, the 200m and the 400m.

Her time over the 800m (5min 6.27sec) and her distance for the javelin (9.48m) were not exactly earth shattering but not half bad for an 85-year old, especially considering that many of her contemporaries move about rather slowly - with a shuffle or a walker.

Mavis was one of 12384 masters athletes at these games.

African Gold

Mavis also participated in the 7th All Africa Masters Games in Mauritius in 2008, and won four gold medals: for the 100m, 200m, 400m and the javelin. Aside from her outstanding performances, she received a special award for being the oldest competitor at the Games, and for being an active participant in athletics for 46 years. Persistence 'hath its privileges.'

Local Gold

In between opportunities to compete internationally, the master athlete certainly didn't remain idle. In 2005 alone, she competed in at least four local Masters meetings in three South African provinces, as well as in the South African Championships – besides competing in Spain. There were many first place finishes and many seconds.

She remains a regular fixture at Masters competitions, competing at the 2011 South African Masters in Durban and the 2012 SA Masters in Pretoria. From Pretoria she brought back gold for the 100m and 200m sprints, as well as for javelin and shotput.

Colors and Service

During the years when Masters competitions and sprinting replaced ultramarathons in Mavis' life, national recognition for her achievements flowed in. In 1990 it was the Masters Award for service to sport. In 1991 she could finally wear the coveted green and gold as a Springbok athlete, and in 1994 she was awarded South Africa's New National Colors.

It was a long time since the mouse had learned to roar.

[1]*Separately organized track and field meetings for veteran athletes began in the 1960s, spreading first among enthusiasts in the US Touring groups of mostly North American veteran athletes, and then sparking enthusiasm in Europe and elsewhere as they took their age-grouped competitions to a wider world in the early seventies. The first World Masters Championships was held in Toronto in 1975. South Africa's local Masters athletics organization, catering for male and female athletes 30 years of age and older, dates from 1974.*

Mavis in track and field at the Vaal Triangle Masters

Chapter 26: PLOWING BACK

"I have learned so much from running. I have gained knowledge that one can't buy over a shop counter. I would like to share this knowledge with other people."

Plowing back into the community some of what she had gained was always a Mavis refrain. And her gains total a wealth of valuable experience, which never did bring her much of fortune. But it did increase her opportunity to use her skills for the benefit of others – both in sport and in life.

AND THEN THERE WERE EIGHT

One high point in her later career came in Natal during the 90s, when she worked to encourage race walking, which took her right back to her beginnings in athletics. She also took the opportunity to duplicate herself, training more 'galloping grannies'.

By then she was comfortable enough with the 'galloping granny' suffix and well over her initial concern that it might turn her running *"into more of a circus act than a straight race run by a serious athlete."*

Her 'grannies', who all started out with her race walking group and then graduated to running, were members of the Pinetown Highway Athletics Club - the oldest 65 and the youngest 46. They proved to be a lot of fun. *'A lovely bunch of women'*, was Mavis' description, and they gave credence to her belief that the time to start is 'now':

"People say they will start training when they are ready. If you wait until then, you'll wait forever. Start from where you are at and work up from there."

Mavis, then 76, coached her grannies rigorously for six months, and for none other than the strenuous Comrades Marathon. The assignment was to run at least a third of the 54-mile distance and race walk the rest.

This approach to the Comrades paid off fairly handsomely. Although one dropped out three quarters of the way, one close to Pietermaritzburg, and one about 19 miles into race, five finished - a major achievement for the Comrades - three of them inside the cutoff time.

Hats off to the coach!

"I've got so much to give as a coach" she once said to an interviewing journalist. *"I know what self-discipline and self-sacrifice mean; I know what pain and suffering are. I know that you must go on however you feel."*

So she rightly felt she could give both of her knowledge of athletics per se, and of her personal understanding of what it costs to succeed. But she didn't just reach out to athletes or would-be athletes. She sought to influence people generally, especially women. She believed that her success, in spite of starting her career so late, could convince them that it's possible to do anything if you really want to badly enough.

The 'Nursery'

Her 'galloping grannies' project was all part of a larger undertaking that could be referred to as a 'nursery for race walkers', when she developed a new health and fitness program for walkers in 1994.

As always, she was very thorough and program participants got to understand exactly what achieving health and fitness entailed, and that exercise and walking programs had to be individually tailored. Her program combined stretching, aerobic endurance and strengthening exercises, as well as coaching on proper posture, correct technique and rhythmic breathing.

She also encouraged her walkers to take it easy at first: *"It's tempting to go off at a pace, but very dangerous. Walk a bit slower for the first kilometer, then tuck in behind someone experienced and let them pull you through."*

Although newcomers weren't pressured to perform and were allowed to progress at their own pace, they were always taught the correct way to train.

As with everything she did, she made sure she did it right, right down to keeping training logs and progress reports on all her race walkers in the making.

"Walking, what can be more natural? Walking is the ultimate exercise, virtually injury free and works all the major muscle groups. Fitness walking burns the same number of calories as running or jogging a comparable distance. While running decalcifies bones, walking strengthens those bones. Walk, it will change your life." Those were the messages her trainees received.

Her walking enthusiasm was supported by a 1993 article published in the Woman's Weekly section of the Natal Mercury. It quoted US-based research that showed that by "adopting a simple walking program, not only were the heart and lungs exercised, but walking actually changed the body shape."

This was the case with a group of women in an experiment who lost four inches from their waists, hips and thighs in two months after increasing walking sessions to two hours per week with no dieting, and at an average speed. Their weight and proportion of body fat, however, remained the same.

Being able to add such findings to her bag of tricks only added fuel to Mavis' fire.

THE JOYS OF THE GYM

Preceding the 'nursery', just after Ernie retired and relocated to Cape Town, the big enterprise for Mavis was her gymnasium and health center, which also helped to keep her going during the eight-year banning from amateur athletics. She coupled that with a jogging club.

And to make sure she would do her new job justice, realizing that all those solitary hours of road running didn't automatically equip her as a gym instructor, Mavis enrolled in a course to give her extra credibility.

Mavis in her gym

She had just turned 60, was still a bundle of energy, and her enthusiasm was catching. She was remarkably fit and trim, had no trouble keeping up with the younger set, and still went splashing through the shallow surf near her home on training runs.

When asked by a reporter if she had any difficulty keeping up with the younger crowd on the gym circuit, her look indicated it was the first time such a thought had crossed her mind. *"Oh no!"* she exclaimed, *"not at all."*

It was only too evident that Mrs Hutchison was not ready for retirement and the old folks home. That, of course, didn't mean that she didn't thoroughly enjoy all the granny things and loved to be with her children and grandchildren. But she was 'looking for further fields to conquer', putting her motto, 'idleness is a destroyer' into practice.

In another interview (the press was always hot on her heels and she had lost count of the number of interviews over the years), she commented: *"Somebody said to me yesterday on hearing about my gym, 'you're too old'. But age is completely irrelevant! Nobody ever says, 'Look at Gary Player, father of six', or 'Gary Player, the Golfing Grandfather'.*

"You know, attitudes influence your whole life...A lady asked me the other day: 'Do you think I am too old to run?' I asked her if she thought she was too old. When she said yes, I answered: 'Well, then you are too old.' "

Her total defiance of age truly became her trademark and fueled her feelings about retirement villages. She still holds to her press statement of December 21, 1988.

*"...*She is against the village idea on principle - unless they build them next to orphanages...*'The old have such a lot of wisdom, experience and above all, time, to offer children. It's such a waste to remove them from the mainstream of society.*

"'When I started my gym a couple of years ago, people said: 'But you're too old!' I said, do me a favor - come to one of my classes and see for yourself!

"'One gentleman used to come regularly until he moved to a village; then his image of himself changed and he thought he was past it. It's easy to fix a label like 'old' to yourself and start believing it.'"

Operating her own gym was just one more adventure that gave her one more opportunity to coach so she could help others on their way. She made sure she gave her patrons all the health advice she was capable of.

One thing she always got straight in their minds was that people should walk or run at least two to three kilometers daily if they wished to remain healthy. And with exercise admonitions came diet suggestions, emphasis on healthy interactions with people, and good sleep and rest.

"*But whatever you neglect, DO NOT NEGLECT exercise*", was the never failing bottom line. "*Select one you enjoy, don't do too much too quickly and listen to your body. And don't neglect stretching after muscles are sufficiently warmed up.*" Never never stretching a cold muscle was a Mavis absolute.

So was 'stopping when it hurts'. "*I'll never be a fan of Jane Fonda's advice who was fond of the 'make it burn' routine.*"

But that, notwithstanding, she was a fervent believer that her gym goers should push on when they simply didn't want to anymore. "*Pushing is a bit easier, though, when you've chosen the right kind of activity. Having an exercise buddy will help too.*"

Backed up by her experience, she also advocated the necessity of developing core muscle strength. She personally found that to be a great asset and still does. "*I started that kind of strengthening when I was younger and continue to work at it at least three times a week.*

"*If we take exercise seriously, we can reach the levels we want. But whatever level is reached, being at some level is better than no level. I'm not on the level I used to be, but that's okay as long as I keep working with myself. If you work at it in a dedicated way you will be reasonably okay in six months and pretty fit in two years.*"

Even without the benefits of a gym, she feels. When Mavis no longer had her business, after moving to Durban to join her son Allan after Ernie's death, she improvised some of her own circuit items that fit into the trunk of her car. Commercially purchased light weights rounded out her 'home gym.'

But as good as exercise is, "*by itself it won't cure all ills. Good nutrition always played an important part in my running life too – not that my passion for ice cream ever left me.*" Intelligent supplementation is another emphasis, which she maintains enhanced her athletic performance. "*At one point I took quite a lot of supplemental extras – so much so that my husband reckoned I rattled like a pill-box.*"

But back to the gym. It was another dream come true. It was like catching her second wind in a way, when her sponsorship for one more America run (the first one in reverse), failed. She needed an outlet for that frustration.

Her establishment had the Mavis touch all over it, right down to the fragrance of the interior with its smell of dried tangerine peels, and the 'welcome, it's warmer inside' sign on the door.

Those who came in didn't just go through various routines under her personal guidance. They also learned that although physical health is vital, there is more to it than just the physical. Talks and workshops, conducted either by herself or by others, ensured that patrons had some life skills thrown into the bargain.

She wanted them to benefit from all those 'hellish moments' on her ultraruns when she was tutored in human limitations. She wanted them to gain from the skills that were developed within her as a result. She wanted them to learn that feeling pushed to the absolute limit is part of the human experience, as is feeling pushed beyond your limits. She wanted them to be able to echo her statement: *"There are no limits; you are capable of what you desire."*

And she also wanted them to be aware that *"whatever they are is their own responsibility"*. *"We cannot blame others for our state,"* she told them.

She was equally strong on the idea that nobody has automatic rights. *"So many people are so busy fighting for their rights, instead of just quietly earning them."*

The gym and health center was indeed a new challenge, but not one that ever excluded her first passion: running, and planning a few more long ones, which came to pass in 1982 and 1985.

It was another memorable phase of her life, of which she said: *"I find it very rewarding to see people shape up and improve physically."*

INSPIRING LIVES

In and out of the gym setting Mavis impacted many fitness enthusiasts, athletes and others over the years.

"They came to me quite often – younger and older, male and female, and also at times non-athletes - to thank me for inspiring them to take up running, or motivating them not to quit, whether runners or not. I was especially pleased when they said my example motivated them to go after personal goals."

The hordes of letters Mavis received from grateful and admiring folks attest to that, and will always be part of her treasured memorabilia. She was particularly gratified when she felt her athletic successes positively influenced the lives of non-athletes. An extract from a letter written to her by a C. Richards on June 24, 1982, speaks to the point.

"I feel quite inspired by the article about you in the Cape Times.....

I emigrated from Rhodesia (Zimbabwe) in 1980 and bought a small typing and duplicating business...there have been many days without a single customer...This lack of clients has made me really depressed...and I have felt like giving up on many occasions, but after reading your article I realize I have not tried as hard as I could..., and I have now decided to make a much greater effort."

A letter from a United Building Society manager on August 5, 1982, was kept because it underlined her own belief that success need not be accompanied by aggressiveness.

"Looking back on the activities of our sports club during the past year, the members and Committee are unanimous that your visit was undoubtedly one of the highlights...thank you for...bringing into our rushed life that quiet and restful personality. It proved beyond a doubt that ambitions can be attained without destructive aggressiveness."

Always eager to assist the rising generation, she appreciated the response from Mr. J. F. Pauw, then principal of the Regent's Park Primary School. On November 1, 1975, he wrote:

"Dear Mavis,

We want you to know just how much we appreciated your interest in our "Mini-Walk".

Your willingness to participate certainly acted as an incentive to the children.

Watching your attack and spirit was a lesson to all of us..."

Then there was 73-year old Lily Krugel. She undertook a 4-day, 63 mile fund raising walk from Potchefstroom to Pretoria for a childcare center as a direct result of being inspired by Mavis, whom she designated as her role model.

Though this sentiment wasn't expressed in a letter to Mavis personally, it was a memorable part of a July 2005 Beeld article, which she kept on record. The article added that Krugel always wanted to be a 'galloping granny' like Mavis. Thus, when her daughter told her she was to become a grand-mother, she figured the time was right and she started to jog at age 54 – albeit just around the block.

'THERE'S A LIFE AFTER 50'

Inspiring people has always been of primary importance to Mavis, whether it happened through her running, coaching or speaking. Of the latter it has been said that her talks could make an audience really think about life, and could turn lives around.

"Feeling that you made a difference in people's lives is a very gratifying emotion – I think more gratifying than the obviously very special moments when you are rewarded for your achievements."

One such reward that will always stand out in her memory came when she was chosen Fair Lady's sportswoman of the Year in 1980, and singled out at the awards ceremony as "an inspiration to all women."

At that auspicious occasion in Johannesburg, in view of a very emo-tionally charged audience, a teary-eyed Mavis not only became the recipi-ent of a stunning diamond/emerald/platinum necklace, but heard the awards judge Chris Greyvenstein say: "Mavis is not just a magnificent long-distance runner. She's telling all of us out there that there's a life after 50."

If there were any doubts in her mind about the impact she had made with the endurance and determination she displayed as an ultrarunner, and that she had captured many hearts as a result, they surely were swept away that night.

Chapter 27: REFLECTIONS

"I think with age comes reflection. It's natural. Sometimes it's rewarding, sometimes less so. I wish every memory was joyful."

WHAT IS SUCCESS?

Even though people would likely think of her as an example of success, she wonders about that. These days when she reflects on her life, she thinks more about whether or not she has made the best of her life as a whole.

"Thinking about success reminds me that I have broadened my definition of success. What it is at age 87 is not what it was at 37 when I started in athletics. Now I ask myself whether or not I have lived up to all of my potential, and how significantly I have helped others to live up to theirs. I also

wonder how I measured up on the home front."

She is often reminded of the words of the late David O. McKay that 'no success can compensate for failure in the home'.

"I think the world more often than not sees success mostly in terms of fame and fortune. Though I had my share of fame - fortune definitely never came - there is so much more to it than that!

What she also realized over time was that such achievements as she had managed, were primarily the result of following the standard principles that govern success in every endeavor – whether consciously or sub-consciously.

"In retrospect it is especially clear to see. Furthermore, these principles are really just the accumulative wisdom gained by men and women over the ages. And a lot of them are even found in the scriptures."

Other inspiring literature that added to her personal store of wisdom and that taught her valuable success principles, included biographies, auto-biographies and artists' histories. The latter she got interested in while working at an art gallery.

"I could relate especially to the strugglers – Van Gogh, the dwarfish Tou-louse-Lautrec, Douglas Bader (who became an ace pilot in WW2 after losing both legs), and concentration camp survivor Corrie Ten Boom. Ten Boom's story touched me particularly deeply.

"What I learned from these people centered around enduring, that you cannot just sink with your struggles, and that you needed to prepare properly for a task – doing your homework.

"I became a very keen reader and that deepened my regret over leaving school early. I understood more clearly why my parents were totally unimpressed with Doreen's and my decision to quit. What an unbelievably dumb idea that was.

"But at least I started to read and got the kind of exposure that began to bridge some of my educational gaps, and began to lay a foundation for my later success. I'm still hopeless at math, but I can balance my budget!"

CHISELING A STRONGER SELF

But back to those age old, sage-taught principles that Mavis agrees are really life laws, repeatedly used by motivational speakers in one form or another.

Those with particular appeal, that helped to chisel the Mavis she developed into, she enthusiastically endorses. "When you have successfully used a principle yourself, you're happy to sell the idea to others". Her 'sales list' is pretty comprehensive:

- Understand yourself and the overall purpose of your life, because success is ultimately about personal growth within the framework of that purpose and the core values that develop from it.

- Figure out your talents, passions and strongest motivators.

- Set goals that are meaningful and are aligned with the above, that are clear and precise, and that you can be enthusiastic about.

- Break them down into achievable chunks and visualize achieving them. (Mavis repeatedly *saw* herself crossing that finish line.)

- Put a time frame on your goals.

- Have practical, workable, yet flexible plans and supporting activities to help you fulfill your goals. But never confuse flexibility with compromising principles and values and commitments.

- Don't scatter your energy in a million directions – focus. Think constantly of your goals and prioritize them.

- Believe in yourself and what you want to achieve. If you don't, why should others.

- Accept opposition and show courage. *And* have stand-by plans ready.

- Self doubt and fear is natural, but don't let them take over.

- Figure out your fears and learn how to best deal with them.

- Never worry about things you don't have control over, but do take time to prepare for those things you need to do and can control; preparation is half the battle.

- Try hard to see the positive. (Beginning the day with laughter is a good idea, though Mavis admits she didn't get that one down. The rationale? It will change your brain chemistry.)

- Don't do too much too soon. Pace yourself.

- Develop self-discipline (over appetites, attitudes, etc). When you make up your mind to do something, do it. Just talking about it won't make it happen.

- See criticism as an opportunity to get it right.

- Always grow in understanding – of yourself, of others, of things around you, *and* of things which pertain specifically to your goals.

- Be aware of negative habits and work to overcome them a step at a time. Procrastination is an especially negative habit and a real achievement killer.

- Beware of 'flap' mode - being over reactive. If you're a 'flapper', find ways to 'de-flap'. Then you can see reality for what it is and make good decisions.

- Move the goal posts periodically so you can continue to stretch.

- Don't expect instant success, but do remember that success breeds success.

- Failing along the way is okay, but learn from it and try again.

- Don't settle for second best.

And she agrees wholeheartedly with those in the 'success trade' who are strong on:

- Taking complete responsibility for your own life and accepting that it's more about attitude than circumstance. (Understanding that blaming failure on things and people get you nowhere, is a principle that presented a major learning curve for Mavis.)

- Practicing visualization at *night*, just before going to sleep – not an idea she's worked with, but one she'd like to try. (According to the experts this kind of visualization of the accomplishment of dreams/goals puts very firmly into the subconscious the idea of actual achievement.)

- Passing on the blessings of achievement to others.

- Allowing others' successful efforts to feed into your own so yours are ultimately magnified. Success is seldom a purely solo effort.

"In my area of success many principles combined to get me where I went. But for me there are three that stand out: effective preparation, enduring to the end and getting the right support team to help you to the finish."

And she echoes Napoleon Hill of 'Think and Grow Rich' fame: If you want success, you'll have to get up and go after it. It won't come to you.

Like Michelangelo, who said the statues he sculpted were already inside the marble, she believes that the individual who is striving for accomplishment already has within him or her the person he or she wants to be. You simply – or maybe not always so simply – have to chisel at the stuff that's in the way.

"I've done a lot of chiseling on myself and it wasn't always comfortable."

But chiseling happens one chip at a time. And just as Michelangelo refused to accept limits to what he could find deep in a marble block, Mavis refused to accept limits to what she could find within herself – in those 'deeper recesses of the mind' where few care to go.

MIND POWER AND THE MATERIAL

She began to know these 'deeper recesses' in her first Comrades race and her understanding broadened and deepened with each subsequent test of endurance. In our interviews she tried to explain the process:

"It wasn't that the physical distress of that race, or other long runs, magically disappeared because I was fit and willed it so. It was more like learning to 'float' over the pain. In some way or another, which is very difficult to explain, sufficient strength to endure just kicked in - right after the moment when I felt I had not an ounce of strength left. It was like tapping into power from somewhere outside myself – like the power that can come when you pray for help.

"As an athlete, pressured to perform by my own expectations as well as those of sponsors and fans, I felt very strongly motivated not to give up. That often meant sourcing strength beyond my own. That never did away with the necessity to be super fit, of course. I strongly believe we need to fully do our part before we can expect miracles."

As she learned more about 'mind power', she also learned that she could make do with very little – that her mind was happy enough with the compactness of life in a trailer, her home during ultraruns. *"It was a rather liberating discovery that stood me in good stead.*

"Material things became far less important to me. I personally think we have way to many 'things' in our lives that just cause clutter, as nice as these things are. Decluttering, I believe, is a very good idea on all levels - not just materially but also mentally and emotionally."

SPORT AND THE FUN FACTOR

As she reminisced about this, that and the other, the topic of sport as currently practiced in South Africa and the world, was inevitable. Mavis has but one question: *"Where's the fun? It seems to me it's win at all costs - a trend that seems to be present everywhere and in everything.*

"Already at school level, athletics and other sport become fiercely competitive and is often reserved for the gifted only - like in American public schools. The fun factor is largely removed as is the physical value for the bodies of all kids, not just the gifted ones. Those without great talent are basically driven from school sport, I think.

"And when big money is added to the picture in the case of professionals, winning is even more consuming. I'm not saying it's wrong for sportsmen and women to earn, but money seems to overshadow everything else. And along with the money fever come the demands on athletes, who I believe are often brought to breaking point stress levels. And as for the size of earnings, they strike me as maybe a little over the top - especially in some sports."

THE TREASURE OF FRIENDS

"My involvement with sport brought me a treasure trove of friends. The great Springbok issue was proof of that. But it was in participation that the greatest camaraderie was built. A bond developed that did not rely on social position. Distance running, especially, I found to be a great equalizer.

"Whoever you are...you understand without a word being said what it means to run for the highs and to slog through the lows, whether you're a plumber or a lawyer. You share the pain and the fatigue, but also the satisfaction of the finish, whether you're a meter reader or a university professor.

"And then there's the glow of the aftermath, which, it seems veterans still like to bask in a little longer as they reminisce."

Some of the special people Mavis recalls with fondness include Bernard Gomersall, the British marathon champion who won the Comrades when Mavis first ran this punishing race, and who later was very helpful with her memorable 1969 UK cross country expedition.

Then there's the late Fred Morrison she can't talk enough about. *"He was such a wonderful mentor to me. I don't think I would have reached the heights I did if it wasn't for Fred.*

"Ozzie Dawkins, a great American athlete, likewise made a lasting im-

pression on me and it was a comfort when he showed up at the start of my US run. He was extremely helpful and organized everything for me in Los Angeles. I first met him as a Masters athlete in Sweden during my first Masters participation.

"Allan Ferguson, now in his nineties, formerly chairman and currently president of Johannesburg Harriers Athletics Club, stands out in my memory as another stalwart and as someone who helped to start race walking in South Africa, a sport I was very active in."

Allan remembers Mavis well and was enthusiastic about her biography. He expressed some of his feelings in a short note: "Mavis, the Galloping Granny from the South. What a girl! No race too long for her. Always ready to run every race going on the calendar. A book about her is a must for the road runner."

She treasured the friendship of the legendary Wally Hayward, the only man ever to finish the Comrades at ages 79 and 80. And he was an avid Mavis admirer, proclaiming her as one of the world's best.

"I remember him particularly for the support he gave me during my first, and crucial, Comrades, and in both my 100-milers. He ran part of the way with me during the Comrades and was very actively involved with both the 100-mile walk and the 100-mile run."

Another athlete who left a permanent imprint on her life was the Golden Boy of the Comrades, Bruce Fordyce, who won the race a record nine times, eight of them consecutively.

He remembers Mavis as a household name, a woman who ran 'double monster hilly marathons like the Comrades' as a mere training run for long-distance feats of endurance – at a time when women her age were supposed to be 'quiet retiring grannies'.

"Everyone knew who you were talking about if you simply said 'Mavis', or the 'Galloping Granny'. It was because she did the most extraordinary things." He believes she tackled enterprises like her trans-America run for the same reason George Mallory climbed Everest:

"Because it's there," and "because of a great love for running. This passion for running can't be better illustrated than by the fact that Mavis Hutchinson has excelled in every distance from 100 metres to a 1000 kilometres.

"And she still continues to run. A few months ago I chatted to Mavis at the finish of the Sasolburg marathon. She looked fit and well and was as bright as a button. I realized then that she had inspired me to be a lifetime runner. I may never run across the USA but I want to be a lifetime galloping Grandpa."

Mavis' inspiring influence seems to have worked. At age 56 he's now completed the Comrades a staggering 29 times and the Two Oceans Marathon 27 times. In the 2011 New York Marathon he once again demonstrated his rare caliber, completing the race in 2 hours 58 min - his fastest time in 15 years.

IN RETROSPECT

"If I could have my life over again, I would say, 'cut, take two'. But I'm not a movie director and cannot re-run the scene. But if I could, I possibly wouldn't have been quite so involved athletically when my youngest girls were small and needed more of my time and energy.

"I also worked for part of their younger years to help make ends meet, and I guess it just all added to the amount of time they didn't get from me.

"During the US race, when I was away for a considerable time, my girls were older teenagers. But even then I felt guilty that I wasn't there for Beverley's birthday who was 17 at the time.

"Having a couple stay in our home (to give my live-in mother-in-law a break), and having family close by, may well not have completely met her needs – at least as I look at it now.

"I think I would also have had less stress by not being so worried about the kids when I was gone, especially during my first longer races when Ernie was away as well. Fortunately, they seemed to have survived well enough – at least as far as I can tell.

"When I recently apologized to them, they didn't say much. The only response was that I shouldn't worry about it. I guess being a Latter-day Saint heightens my feelings of parental responsibility."

She remembers answering a question once put to her by a member of the press at the time of her 1976 Fair Lady run, who wanted to know whether she put her running before everything else in her life, including her family. Her reply then was that she didn't really know, but that she supposed she did since she'd left two teenagers at home. The journalist was skeptical because she knew they had their two grandmothers looking after them.

"I know I've not been perfect, but I've tried to be the best I can be, especially since coming to an increased understanding of the purpose of life, and the purpose of my own life."

Best wishes from Bruce Fordyce on her last long run in 1985.

AN INEXPENSIVE LESSON

"Having learned more about my life's purpose did, however, not shield me from unpleasant experiences, like the one in 1994 in Durban, when I was taught a very expensive lesson. I think the lesson was not to be so gullible."

Besides feeling embarrassed about it now, she's convinced she would not easily fall into the same kind of trap again.

"One day at a shopping mall I was approached by two white men, possibly in their forties – first by one, who offered participation in a 'really good investment opportunity'. Shortly afterward he was joined by man number two, who pretended to have unexpectedly bumped into a long lost buddy. It was a jovial 'reunion' and man number two promptly started to praise the abilities of his long lost friend as an investment expert and as a good, honest Christian.

"I remember feeling a little hesitant and wanting to move off, but they were very persistent. They said R10 000 (then about $3000) would get me into the investment scheme. Man number two was a particularly slick operator and before I knew where I was, I was off with them to my bank some distance away.

"There man number two went into the bank with me, and managed to get me to draw the money in cash, in spite of the fact that I was not comfortable with the whole thing. And all this in spite of a warning from a bank official, who told me there was a scam going around.

"When I think back it all seems unreal. How could I have allowed this to happen, no matter how persuasive those men were? Why didn't I listen to the warnings? They were loud and clear! I even noticed that the vehicle the men drove me in was past its prime – not exactly the sort of car a great investor would drive, I thought."

After the transaction at her bank, her escorts drove her back to the mall, at which point man number one said she should give him the money to take to his office, somewhere in the same shopping center she presumed. He needed to 'start the deal'. Now all Mavis' alarm buttons were flashing and she declined to hand over the cash. She held on to it tightly.

"I was scared by now and just followed them to the so-called 'office'. As we went up some stairs to an area of the mall I didn't know, man number one suddenly grabbed the money and made a run for it.

"He was faster than I over the short haul and got out of sight quickly. His partner ran in the opposite direction and also disappeared out of sight.

As far as I know they were never caught.

"*It was a miserable day and one I will never forget. It was money I couldn't afford to lose. But so we live and learn.*"

In Black and White

Ten years later there was another life lesson to learn, bit this time the culprits were dressed in an even more convincing style of 'sheep's clothing.' "*I guess I was still a bit too trusting. That was the lesson, it seemed.*"

The 2004 tutorial involved a public education institution. Who would suspect a respectable college a few hundred miles upcountry to be less than upright and honorable?

" *A friend did some ground work for me at the sports department of a technical college. The idea was that I would coach both college and private athletes, having at my disposal an office as well as the college infrastructure. I was to concentrate my efforts on younger athletes and also conduct health and fitness programs for both local and other top athletes.*

"*The college even committed itself to paying for advertising my coaching services. It appeared that they really wanted what I could offer. I spent a week there, checking things out with the help of my friend. Unfortunately, there was no written contract, and after all the expense of moving to the new location the college pulled out of the deal. My take home line? I want everything in black and white.*"

Ernie's Pension Dies with Him

Just to round things out on the financial front, she had also lost Ernie's retirement some years earlier. After his death in 1991 at the age of 79 she received only a one time token payment.

"*What I was given by the mining company was a slap in the face if ever there was one. Without help from my children life would have become very difficult.*"

Memories of 'Mr. Mavis' Live On

Mavis wouldn't want her story to end without some final words about the one person that made it all happen for her. Sue Fox said it well in her 1980 Sunday Times article, headlined: 'It's Mr Mavis who keeps her going'.

Sue wrote: "Behind every successful man there's usually a stalwart woman. Once in a blue moon, the situation is reversed.

"Marathon miracle Mavis Hutchison wouldn't have reached her pinnacle of long-distance running acclaim without husband Ernie.

"Who would be there to second her, to rub wintergreen on her legs, to massage her aching muscles and to mend her running shoes?

"Who would lift her spirits when blistered feet, shredded shins and foul weather put her in the doldrums?

"Who would understand her need for isolation? For Mavis, the loneliness of the long-distance runner is no myth."

Mavis herself remembers other things, equally vital, including how Ernie's housekeeping skills helped assure her success. He was the one who owned cookbooks.

"He took charge of the home for many years to make time available for my running, taking over from his mother who had lived with us previously. Even when she was still alive his sense for the practical was evident. He rightly figured, as I did when I married him, that two women couldn't run the house.

"Ern was terrific in the kitchen and his success rate there beat mine hands down. He was also a great shopper, which I never was. Maybe I'm still bad at it. I was a bit extravagant. I'd take the first thing I saw. Ernie was always the one who compared prices.

"I remember giving him a cook book for Christmas, which he used a lot. He loved entertaining.

"He also made sure I ate the right food. In training, for instance, it was important for me to eat plenty of carbs, which I needed for fuel, and a lot of protein and fruit – and Ernie made sure it was on hand.

"Although he wasn't so enthusiastic at the very beginning of my running career, it took him only a year or so to give me his full support. To him I will be ever grateful."

Chapter 28: PAST IS PROLOGUE

Toward the next hill.

For Mavis the end of one thing is always the beginning of another. As she has said so many times, age is irrelevant and you only grow old when you stop growing, especially in character. So she's always ready for another challenge and for a new idea.

So no, at 87 she's just not ready to sit around idly on the porch in her rocking chair, waiting for the undertaker to come by. She'd rather **be** the 'undertaker,' undertaking many more interesting things .

DON'T PLANT ME YET

"I don't want to 'go to seed' and be 'planted in a box' just yet, if it's all the same with everyone. I want to continue running for a start. If I'm still alive and well in 2013, I think I'd like to compete in the next World Masters games in Brazil – if I can get sponsorship. Whether I win or lose wouldn't matter as much as just being part of it all and giving my best.

"Competing allows me to go places, meet people, do things. And it opens doors for me like in the past. Running taught me so much, including how dependent we are on structures and events to keep us motivated and moving.

"That's why I made plans to go to the 2011 World Masters in Sacramento. Too bad I didn't make it. A lack of enough sponsorship saw to that. I've never been back in the US since I ran across it 33 years ago. I would have loved the opportunity to compete there."

Although missing the US Masters was disappointing, she was able to participate in the South African Masters in Durban, although she wasn't altogether satisfied with her times. That's Mavis for you. She knows her pace has slowed down, both in the training and in the race, but she still wants the best possible performance.

That's why she jumped at the opportunity to work with a young coach in preparation for the Durban meet, who didn't just succeed in making her feel like she was 20 again, but facilitated a recapturing of an extraordinary moment at a Pretoria event in 2005 when she was 80.

"It was kind of freaky. I ran like a young athlete. I don't know what I did differently. If I knew I'd try to duplicate it. I felt so good and my times were excellent. Even the people watching commented on how good I looked. I felt as though I was floating along the 100, 200 and 400 meters, and that I could take on anybody that day. I'm always trying to get that moment back."

But whether she floats along the track or not, she always gets a special lift when she's among other athletes, older or younger, as was the case in her very latest SA Masters meet in Pretoria where she won four gold medals.

"There's such a wonderful rapport between athletes. It's like I'm part of the action and that feeds the desire for continued achievement. I still feel like an athlete, not just a hanger on.

"It's not fun getting older and over the last ten years I've really felt the difference. I have to train much harder for far fewer results. That's brutal. Yet when people talk of old folks, I think they're talking of someone else – as long as I don't spend too much time in front of the mirror!

"I remember a rather uncomfortable moment in my mid 70s when a little boy (four or five years old) said to me, referring to my elbow, 'You're old', to which I replied, 'Yes'. But then came the line that bowled me over: 'I'm brand new!'

"As an athlete I still feel good as I run. But I know I don't look so good. I lean too far forward and I'm too tense around the shoulders. And my knees aren't coming up high enough. When I see my shadow running it's really not good. The poor action is clearly reflected, but I still visualize myself as a powerful runner, belting it down the track."

LEGACY

With a lifetime to look back on, she hopes she will be able to leave behind a legacy that depicts her at the very least as someone who worked with her talents and in the process influenced the lives of others for good; someone who didn't give up and who refused to limit herself.

She still keenly remembers a man in his eighties who decided to become a medical doctor. He only practiced a few years, but he did practice. He was not going to limit his personal growth. For Mavis he became an unforgettable example of success that continues to inspire her to compete and to train even when it hurts.

"It's so easy to give up or stop just short of what you desire." No wonder Kipling's 'If' became and remained such a favorite with her, with its emphasis on forcing the 'heart and nerve and sinew' to hold on when there is 'nothing in you except the Will that says to them: Hold on!'

The last word goes to Mavis: *"I don't want to be a spectator, but a participant. I want to continue to work with those same principles that helped me when I was younger, and go out with a bang.*

Postscript 2014

The Great Brazilian Saga

Mavis made good on her closing wish to compete in the 2013 World Masters Games, should she still be alive and well, coming away with 5 medals, among them one gold.

Sadly, 'alive and well' separated company shortly after arriving in Porto Alegre, when a devastating flu set in.

'On fire' with fever, she participated in her first event and somehow still earned a silver medal in the shotput. By the time she tackled the 200m race, her last event, she 'ran her legs off' for first place, but in a time that left her very disappointed – just over a minute. Still struggling with a high temperature, she collapsed into bed immediately afterwards. But at least she was in possession of two silver medals (shotput and discus), two bronze (100m and javelin), and one gold.

But medals were not all she brought home. On arrival in Cape Town, she was diagnosed with full blown bronchitis. Adding to the great Brazilian saga were some earlier glitches. Her baggage went missing right at the outset, stranding her in Porto Alegre in the same clothes for four days, and unable to find spikes to run in.

She also completely missed her connection to Brazil due to a 7-hour airport delay in Cape Town, and almost missed the next connection to the Games because of incorrectly issued boarding passes. And to crown it all, when she did arrive – late – she had great difficulty finding anyone who could help her register in a language she could understand.

In November Mavis turns 90. Will she run in Lyon, France at the next World Masters in 2015? Health and sponsorship will likely dictate the answer – grit and determination will surely be a given.

A Few Months Later – the Surprise of Her Life

In recognition of her major contribution to world athletics over the past 53 years, Mavis Hutchison was uniquely honored by the South African government, when the Minister of Sport and Culture appointed her his special ambassador.

Dr. Ivan Meyer officially announced her new position during his Budget Speech to Parliament on March 20, 2014, at which time Mavis was his special guest. He added that she should now be designated a "Sports

Legend". Visibly overcome, her response to this surprise came softly after a long silence: "Thank you, sir."

RACES

1963 Rand Daily Mail Big walk - 50 miles - 1st (9 hrs. 35 min., new women's record)

1963 Jeppestown Marathon - standard marathon distance (3 hrs. 50 min.)

1965 Comrades Marathon - 56 miles (10 hrs. 7 min.)

1965 Harrismith Mountain Race (95 min.)

1965 Pieter Korkie Marathon

1966 Comrades Marathon (10 hrs. 45 min.)

1966 Rand Daily Mail Big Walk - 50 km - 1st (6 hrs. 0 min.)

1966 Pieter Korkie Marathon

1966 Harrismith Mountain Race

1967 Rand Daily Mail Big Walk - 50 km - 1st (6 hrs. 12 min.)

1968 Rand Daily Mail Big Walk - 50 km - 1st (6 hrs. 14 min.)

1969 Manager - South African Ladies Cross Country tour to UK

1970 Cross Country Secretary - Transvaal (5 years)

1970 Pieter Korkie Marathon

1971 Comrades Marathon (10 hrs. 35 min.)

1971 100 mile/24-hour race (world records for 25, 50, 75 and 100 miles)

1972 Rand Daily Mail Big Walk - 50 km - 1st (6 hrs. 19 min.)

1972 Swaziland Marathon (4 hrs. 21 min.)

1972 Pieter Korkie Marathon

1973 Comrades Marathon (9 hrs. 7 min. – personal best)

1973 Germiston to Durban - 602 km (6 days 13 hrs.)

1973 100 mile/24-hour walk - Germiston

1973 Rand Daily Mail Big Walk - 50 km (5hrs. 48 min.)

1974 Durban to Germiston - 602 km (7 days 7 hrs.)

1974 Karoo Marathon.

1974 Rand Daily Mail Big Walk - 50 km (5 hrs. 59 min. – personal best)

1975 Pretoria to Cape Town - 1562 km (22 days 4 hrs.)

1976 Comrades Marathon (10 hrs. 6 min.)

1976 Germiston to Cape Town - 1471 km (19 days 50 min.)

1977 World Masters Games, Gothenburg, Sweden

1977 Comrades Marathon (10 hrs. 36 min.)

1977 Messina to Johannesburg - 548 km (7 days 6 hrs. 15 min.)
1978 Los Angeles to New York - 2871 miles (69 days 2hrs. 40 min.)
1978 Masters Marathon, Cape Town
1979 World Masters Games, Hanover, Germany
1980 Masters Marathon, Cape Town (3 hrs. 49 min. – S.A. age group record)
1980 John O'Groats to Lands End - 1400 km (16 days 21 hrs.)
1980 Comrades Marathon (10 hrs. 18 min.)
1981 Comrades Marathon (10 hrs. 39 min.)
1981 Two Oceans Marathon.
1982 Kimberley to Cape Town - 3200 km (57 days)
1985 Cape Times Big Walk - 32 km (4 hrs. 39 min.)
1985 Pretoria to Cape Town - 1491 km (30 days)
1989 Cape Times Big Walk - 32 km (5 hrs. 30 min.)
1990 Cape Times Big Walk - 32 km (4 hrs. 43 min.)
1992 Cape Times Big Walk - 32 km (4 hrs. 53 min.)
1993 World Masters Games, Miazaki, Japan
2005 World Masters Games, San Sebastian, Spain
2007 World Masters Games, Riccione, Italy
2009 World Masters Games, Sydney, Australia
2011 South African Masters Championships, Durban
2012 South African Masters Championships, Pretoria
2013 World Masters Games, Porto Alegre, Brazil

AWARDS
1965 Arthur Newton Certificate
1971 Fair Lady Magazine Honours List
1978 Johannesburg Mini-council Award for outstanding achievements
1978 Star Sports Woman of the Year
1978 State President's Award
1978 Pro-Nutro Sporting Great
1980 Sports Woman of the Year
1984 Dewars Achievement Award
1990 Masters Award for service to sport
1992 Golden Achiever Award
1997 Natal Athletics Service Award
2002 Premier's Golden Sports Award for lifetime achievement

PROVINCIAL COLORS
Southern Transvaal
Western Province
Natal

NATIONAL COLORS
1969 National Cross Country
1991 Springbok Colors
1994 New National Colors

Made in the USA
Lexington, KY
02 April 2015